The Guggenheims and The American Dream

☆ Books by Edwin P. Hoyt, Jr.
The Vanderbilts and Their Fortunes
The House of Morgan

[EDWIN P. HOYT, JR.] [THE GUGGENHEIMS ☆ ☆ ☆ ☆ ☆ ☆ ☆ ☆ ☆ ☆ AND THE AMERICAN [FUNK & WAGNALLS] DREAM]

1]

IMAGINE, IF you will, the plight of the intelligent Jew in nineteenth-century Europe, and particularly in the nation that is now known as Switzerland. Since the Middle Ages the European Jew had been made the object of contumely by his Christian neighbors. "I had rather be a Jew than enter a plague-ridden house" was a common expression—any repugnant act was so characterized by many Christians who would prefer to die and be reincarnated as dogs rather than Jews. In most places, even by the beginning of the nineteenth century, the Jew's lot was scarcely better than that of a dog.

By then, of course, rich Jews were tolerated. They were necessary to the conduct of European business. Still, they were little more than tolerated. In the Middle Ages and in the Renaissance, churchmen spoke comprehensively of Jews, witches, and heretics. The Jew was no longer, by 1800, burned alive or stoned to death in the streets by legal authority. Yet, Jews were still burned and stoned in pogroms, while the duly constituted authorities looked the other way. Among all Europeans, the French, and particularly the people of the south of France, were most sympathetic to the Jews. The people of the cold northern countries were most antipathetic.

In medieval times no one but a Jew was permitted to lend money, and the Jew was permitted to do little else. Certainly he could not be educated in the universities or schools, even though he, the Jew, had been largely responsible for carrying the knowledge of Greece that was preserved by the Arab world to a Europe in rebirth. The Jew was the whipping boy of all the community, the object of sport or hatred or avarice, depending on the whim of the Christians. He was blamed for any community misfortune. The rulers of Europe often valued the Jews as an engineer values the exhaust valve on a pressure tank; when tensions became unbearable the Jew was a prime target for action.

The hysterical treatment of Europe's Jews began with the emergence of a proselyting Christian church in Rome. When the First Crusade was organized at the end of the eleventh century, ignorant knights and nobles could not tell Jew from Saracen in the Holy Land—where Jews were tolerated. The Christians returned from their Crusade filled with zeal against the Jews who had killed Christ. In this wave of religious fervor the accomplishments of the Jews were forgotten, and in the middle of the twelfth century, when Pope Eugene set out to establish a Second Crusade, thousands of Jews were slaughtered or they killed their families and themselves rather than be tortured to death by the Christians.

The Jews in Christian Europe were forced to wear the Star of David or special hats or cloaks, in order that they might be distinguished from Christian peoples. On every official document a Jew's *Jewishness* was proclaimed, lest he be mistaken for a Christian.

During the fourteenth and fifteenth centuries, when the witch mania swept across Europe, hundreds of Jews were sent to the rack and broken on the wheel after denunciation, perhaps by one who owed money to the Jews. The fining of Jews by the governing powers brought income to the state; kings sometimes sold their Jews. Late in the sixteenth century, Louis, princeling of Bavaria, pawned the Jews of Ribeauville to a lesser noble for 400 silver marks.

In the sixteenth century the Jews of Europe were concentrated in ghettos within the towns. Usually the Jews were walled into these cities-within-cities. The walls might be sealed up and the entire Jewish population starved to death if the community displeased the rulers. Nearly everywhere in Europe the Jew was forbidden to farm—no Christian would eat a vegetable or a piece of meat that had been contaminated by a Jew. In the part of the Holy Roman Empire that would later become the Swiss Confederation, the Jews were confined to a few towns. In the principality of Baden, two of the towns were Lengnau and Endingen, although all Baden was more or less open to Jews in the beginning of the sixteenth century.

Times were to change rapidly.

Throughout the Renaissance and into the Reformation the church had forbidden Christians to lend money at interest. The Jews were the money-lenders until the beginning of the sixteenth century, when the church removed its prohibitions against lending. Naturally, as Christians took up money-lending it was in their interest to suppress their Jewish competitors, and suppression took the form of driving the Jews out of the ghettos, out of cities and princely states. The principality of Baden continued to accept Jews, not as citizens, but as supplicants allowed to live on sufferance, heavily taxed, and pushed into ghettos.

In spite of this tolerance, purchased by the Jews at such high cost, the Christians of Baden periodically demanded the expulsion of the Jews from the state. On one occasion in the seventeenth century the Christians of Lengnau were threatened with fines if they drove the Jews from the village; only thus could the *Landvögt* of Baden restrain the anti-Semitic.

During these years, thousands of Jews wandered hopelessly up and down the valley of the Rhine, driven from one town to the next, to buy a security that might last for a year or for ten. Then the Jews would be driven on again. Among these hopeless wanderers were the ancestors of the family Guggenheim, whose children would come to America seeking the fulfillment of the American dream. How little did those ancestors suspect that Guggenheim would one day establish the family as one of the most important in the United States.

These Guggenheim ancestors at first were nameless to the Christian community. Eventually Christian-derived names were forced on them by the authorities, and this was how the Guggenheim ancestors acquired their surname—from the village of Guggenheim on the Bergstrasse between Darmstadt and Heidelberg. (The name of the village has since been changed to Jugenheim.)

When did the Guggenheims settle in the village of Lengnau in Baden? No one knows. They seem to have come there some time during the seventeenth century, when excitement raged against the Jews throughout the German-speaking world. Baden was still a place of refuge, then the Jews of Baden were beaten and taxed and mistreated, but they were not generally *killed*. So the forbears of the Guggenheims came to Lengnau.

Jews could exist in Lengnau but they had no other rights. When a Jew died he could not be buried there or anywhere in Baden; the Jews had been forced to buy an island in the Rhine to keep their cemetery.

The first mention of the Guggenheims in history was as outlanders: the first name was that of "der Jud Maram Guggenheimb von Lengnauw." The second mention of the Guggenheims came when they fell afoul of the law in the manner that Jews often did, as illegal possessors of real property. In 1702 Jacob Guggenheim was brought into court: It was claimed that he *owned* the house of the late Maram Guggenheimb and that he had, with his brother Samuel, kept a vineyard on Wettinger Hill. For such crimes he could be expelled from the community.

The Guggenheims pleaded that they had tried to sell the house of Maram, without finding a buyer. They had taken possession of the vineyard for a debt, but they had later returned the land to Christian hands.

The two miscreants were forgiven this time but were warned that they must sell the house of Maram as soon as possible.

In that same year, 1702, the ghetto of Lengnau was attacked by a mob of Christians bent on destruction of the Jews and their property. The houses of Jacob and Siseli Guggenheim were burned to the ground. The *Landvögt* fined the villagers 1600 gulden for Jacob's house and 300 for Siseli's, but since the Jews could not own the houses, they did not get the money.

For all the noise about them and all the trouble that came to them, there were not so very many Jews in the villages of Lengnau and Endingen. Perhaps, in all, the Jewish population was five hundred. This population in the eighteenth century represented nearly all the Jews in what is now Switzerland.

Jacob Guggenheim, one whose house was burned, was a man of several talents, a leader in the Jewish community. Somewhere he had acquired a classical Talmudic education. He was an elder in the Lengnau synagogue and was known among his fellows as a scholar of Hebrew studies. In 1732, when the Lengnau ghetto's charter expired (as it did each sixteen years after 1696 when it was first granted), the Christian community of Baden was stirred by a movement to expel all the remaining Jews from the principality. The *Landvögt* had no desire to deprive himself of so valuable a source of revenue, but serious pressures were brought to bear. To remain in Baden the Jews must have a letter of safe-conduct and patronage signed by the *Landvögt*, but the Christian community had persuaded the *Landvögt* to force the Jews to leave their homes before the snows of winter fell.

Jacob Guggenheim and Raphael Pickart were selected by the Jews of the two communities to appear at Zurich before the Diet of the Swiss Confederation. There the *Landvögt's* order of expulsion was read, and only then were the two Jewish representatives allowed to present their case. The expulsion order cited owning of property, breach of the Swiss laws, disorderliness of the Jewish ghetto. In their defense the two Jewish representatives leaned heavily on personal flattery of their ruler, and, finally, agreed on what he wanted—a higher price for the privilege of living in Lengnau for another sixteen years as pariahs, without even the primary right of burial in the community, or the right to own the house under whose roof they slept.

As time went on, the Jewish community gained certain privileges by default. When houses in the community reached a certain point of decay, and no Gentile would buy them, they were offered for sale to the Jews. But the Jews could not repair these houses. No Christian would sell them lumber and they could not buy land on which to grow timber. Anything of value that a Jew could buy must first have been offered to Christians and refused. For example, real estate must be offered three times and refused before a Jew could purchase it.

The restrictions came in surges, which depended on the condition of the economy and the success of the Jews in keeping their heads hidden from the crowds.

Jacob Guggenheim was a strong man, not one given easily to bowing his head before mistreatment. Not long after the renewal of the Jews' charter in Lengnau, Jacob made the acquaintance of a Christian pastor, one Johann Casper Ulrich, who had undertaken the conversion of Jews to the Christian faith. Jacob's son, Joseph, born in the 1720's, was sent by his father to study at the Talmudic School in Metz, and thus the educated Joseph became a primary target of Pastor Ulrich. The pastor invited Joseph to visit his pastorate and his house in Zurich, and interceded for the young man with the authorities so he would not be arrested for violating the curfew against Jews. (Jews were normally allowed to be in Zurich only during a few of the daylight hours, in order to transact business for the benefit of the Christians.)

Eventually Joseph Guggenheim was converted to Christianity, a turn of events that struck horror into the hearts of the Jews of Lengnau.

Joseph's visits to Zurich ceased for his father forbade the travel. Joseph fell ill.

The Christians said the Jews were poisoning him rather than let him become a Christian.

Jacob and his friends accused the Christian pastor of a "breach of hospitality."

The pastor retorted with a charge to the *Landvögt* that the Jews of Lengnau were planning to murder the Christian Joseph Guggenheim.

The Christian pastor won the struggle when Joseph was converted officially and left the Jewish community. In a sense Joseph's loss of the old faith was an augury, for in later years the Guggenheims would drift away from the religion of their fathers in their assimilation into a new society.

But in the middle of the eighteenth century this conversion of a Jew was a serious matter. Jacob's fight brought him into conflict with the Christian community. Efforts were made to have him deported as a troublemaker, along with Salomon Guggenheim. Their thin privilege of residence in Lengnau was continued only after they submitted to the extortion of 600 florins.

In 1760, instead of matters growing better, as the Jews had hoped they might, the conditions of life became almost insufferable. For years the laws about selling real estate had not been enforced and a number of Jews bought property. All this property was reexamined. In the new charter of 1760 the Jews were told that they must sell to a Christian any time an offer was made for *any* piece of property a Jew owned.

The Jew, of course, paid taxes on property; he paid taxes on almost everything.

He paid a tax every time he entered or left the ghetto. This was called the Jew toll.

He paid special peddling taxes.

He paid a tax to avoid serving in the army; he paid the tax even though the army would not accept him if he attempted to enlist.

He paid a tax as a money-lender, and his rates of interest were fixed and examined by the authorities.

In 1760, the Jew of Lengnau was also told by his Christian master that he must not marry a poor person, nor allow poor persons to marry, and that any woman coming into the ghetto must bring with her a dowry of 500 gulden or more. So the Jew's *personal* life was now also regulated. Earlier an attempt had been made to regulate the Jew's marital life, when in 1732, one of the charges made against the Jews of Lengnau was that they dared to reproduce Jews. Jacob Guggenheim had allowed himself the privilege of levity in answering. The Jews, he said, "could not help it that the Good Lord and human nature contrive to replenish the human race." But twenty-eight years later personal regulation was tried again in a different guise.

By the beginning of the nineteenth century, however, some of the fetters on the lives of the Jews of Switzerland had begun to be relaxed. Restrictions on Jews were disappearing in western and southern Europe, and while the Germanic and Slavic states were slower to respond to the feelings of civility and equality that surged across western Europe in the wake of the American and French revolutions, the breeze of freedom did stir even in Lengnau. When Switzerland became the Helvetian Republic in 1798, the Jews were granted limited citizenship in the new canton of Aargau, which replaced Baden as the governing unit and some of the old cultural blocks were removed: The Jews were allowed to traffic in livestock and real estate. The size of the Jewish community had been limited by the charter of 1776 to 108 families; this limitation was removed. Jews were allowed to rebuild, redecorate, and enlarge their houses.

Yet there was a quick reaction. Four years later the Christian community arose and sacked the ghettos in fury against the new rights granted the Jews. In 1803, Napoleon Bonaparte restored the old federal government system in Switzerland and the legal oppression was renewed.

Somehow in all this terror and trial, the Guggenheims of Lengnau prospered. Some were money-lenders, some were peddlers, some were tailors; all trades that could be followed by the Jews. In 1800 the richest man in the Jewish community was Isaac Guggenheim, son of Jacob, and when he died in 1807, his estate was valued at 25,000 florins. Jews being what they were forced to be, most of that estate consisted of gold and silver pieces in a trunk, plus some 117 valuables which he had taken in as security for loans.

This Isaac Guggenheim had a son, Meyer, who married when he was twenty-six years old, and raised eight children. One of them, Samuel Guggenheim, became a hero in Lengnau in 1818 when he rescued two sleeping Gentile children from a burning house in Zurich Canton. Some of this glory was reflected on another son, Simon Guggenheim, who became a tailor in Lengnau. And it was Simon who established the basis for the great Guggenheim fortune and the great House of Guggenheim.

He did so through a single decision made when he was fifty-five years old.

2]

IN 1847, Simon Guggenheim of Lengnau, child of Meyer and grandchild of old Isaac the money-lender, sat ruefully in his tailor shop in the ghetto. Day after day he surveyed the shards of an unsuccessful life. He made clothing for the Jews and for some of the Christian community around him, yet he was anything but a successful man; still he dreamed of success and freedom in a manner that would have been quite beyond the comprehension of his grandfather. Old Isaac died, after all, before the fruits of the American and French revolutions had truly ripened, and for most of his life old Isaac had been subjected to the same strangling restrictions that Jews in Europe had suffered since the First Crusade.

Old Isaac would not have known any other way of life, for humiliation and degradation were the traditional lots of the Jews of his day. But Simon, at fifty-five, the child and man of two centuries, had seen through the windows of freedom at brief moments of his life. Marshal Ney had brought the Republic to Helvetia to give the Jews promise of escape from their private Gehenna. Simon had seen the last of the pogroms at Lengnau, too. He had seen the end of the accordion-like expansion and contraction of freedoms for the Jews. No longer were they totally dependent on the whims of the ruling class and the vagaries of the capitalist economies of Europe.

In spite of the change, many of the Jews of Lengnau had gone away, driven out by Aargau Canton's restrictions under which the Gentiles still insisted that the Jew always be a foreigner in his native land. The term was "tolerated homeless persons, not to be expelled." It was a far cry from citizenship in a country where the

11]

Gentiles had more personal freedom than in any other land in Europe.

In 1847, Simon Guggenheim was a lonely and unhappy man. His wife, Schafeli, had died eleven years before, leaving him a son and four daughters to bring up, and with memories of another daughter dead in childhood. Meyer, the son, was nine years old when his mother died. Now he was twenty, a peddler who traveled in Germany, selling knickknacks and cloth from door to door. He considered himself lucky. Even as a peddler young Meyer was happier and was making more of his life than his father.

Lonely as he was, Simon Guggenheim showed interest in forty-one-year-old Rachel Weil Meyer, whose husband had died, leaving her three sons and four daughters. She possessed a little money, Simon had his shop and a few possessions, but together they could not satisfy the civil authorities that they were wealthy enough to deserve permission to marry.

In old Isaac's day there would have been no solution and Simon and Rachel would have lived out their last empty years, taking solace in sin or their religion. But in the middle of the nineteenth century new hopes had risen in the breasts of the Jews of Lengnau. From America came letters from emigrants, affirming the rumors that to the west lay what was indeed a New World. The Jew in America was not universally loved, said the letters, and he did not find the streets paved with gold, ready for the scooping. Yet the Jew in this new land was free. He had rights; he could become a citizen; he could acquire wealth without being taxed specially because he was a Jew; he could join the army; he could buy a farm; he could trade in livestock; he could use bank credit; he could travel freely from one end of the country to the other without papers or passports, even without questions; he could attend the common schools. He was, to use that revolutionary word of the nineteenth century, a *free* man.

Only dimly could Simon Guggenheim comprehend the details of the letters from Lengnau residents who had gone to the New World, but he could capture the essence—freedom. He also could understand what else fate offered in America, the chance, even at fifty-five years of age, to begin a new life.

Somehow, during the year 1847, the names of the city of Philadelphia and the state of Pennsylvania came into Simon Guggenheim's narrow routine of life, and he learned that here was a large city that *did not even have a ghetto*. He could scarcely believe it.

It was true; in matters of religious toleration, Philadelphia and Pennsylvania were the most liberal of all the cities and states of the new American Union.

This liberality came partly through the accidents of settlement. Originally the Dutch laid claim to this territory, based on the discovery of Delaware Bay by Henry Hudson in 1609, and the exploration of the Delaware River seven years later by Cornelis Hendricksen. This navigator went as far as the Schuylkill, and here on the lower shores soon arose straggling Dutch colonies. The Dutch were joined a few years later by the Swedes, who brought the log cabin to the New World and thus, if for no other reason, earned the respect of their new neighbors. The first permanent town was built at Tinicum, near Chester. It was called New Gottenburg by its founders, Lieutenant Colonel Johann Printz of the Swedish cavalry and the revered Pastor Campanius. With pardonable pride it was also called "the metropolis of New Sweden."

Swedes and Dutch got on well together. They were mutually respectful and tolerant of each other's ways, and also of the ways of the Indians in their region. So the colony began, more than any other, in an atmosphere of toleration. In 1641 when the Puritans of Connecticut sent a colonizing group south to settle on the Schuylkill, their harsh ways soon antagonized both Dutch and Swedes, and the Puritans were sent firmly back to Connecticut.

Violence came to the colony in 1655, but not through the will of the colonizers. As so often happens in history, the jealousy and ambition of outsiders brought the violence and forcible change, for Peter Stuyvesant and the governors of New Netherlands became alarmed at the success of the Swedish colony. In 1655 a fleet of seven Dutch warships swept down on the little settlements along the rivers.

Nine years later when the English sent a fleet to Nieuw Amsterdam and took control of the Dutch colonies, the area that is now Pennsylvania came under English control. It received its name in 1681 when William Penn, son of Admiral Sir William Penn, was given a charter which made him owner of an area between 43 degrees north latitude and 40 degrees north, running west from the Delaware through five degrees of longitude. Young William Penn had joined the gentle Society of Friends and he brought this tolerant faith to the New World with him. As time went on and the colony developed, the heritage of the original Dutch-Swedish cooperation was strengthened. Pennsylvania's tolerant ways attracted refugee Huguenots and other dissident religious groups. Religious and social freedom became an established way of life.

From the upper Rhineland of Germany hundreds of immigrants came to Pennsylvania to settle on the great limestone plain which extends from the Susquehanna to Philadelphia.

Perhaps in his travels in Germany, Simon's son, Meyer, heard of the fabulous successes of the farmers who had come to the new land. In any event Pennsylvania and Philadelphia beckoned the Guggenheims.

The Philadelphia of which the Guggenheims learned in 1847 was the happiest and most peaceful of all American cities. It was laid out by its founders on the plan of ancient Babylon, with miles of pleasant streets and progressive city rulers who were even then preparing to create a metropolitan system to govern the tiny suburbs springing up around the city's fringes.

Until 1825 Philadelphia had been the largest city in America, and the most important port. New York had stolen those titles, but Philadelphia's Delaware and Schuylkill River fronts were still fringed with busy wharves where goods were loaded for every port in the world.

Philadelphia was an important political and cultural and market center. It had once been capital of the nation, a fact which its citizens would not forget. There were more houses in Philadelphia than in New York in spite of the latter city's leadership in population; there were more workers and more industries. An iron industry was growing across the state, and in 1847 the Pennsylvania Railroad was building a rail line that would extend all the way west to Pittsburgh. Philadelphia was a center for the manufacture of rugs and leather goods and a hundred other products vital to the life of the new nation. Steel manufacturing was yet to come, but the improvement of American industry had brought tool and die manufacturing firms, cloth manufacturers and a healthy dry goods trade, with the old firm of Wood, Brown and Company leading all others.

Philadelphia, it seemed, offered everything that Simon Guggenheim could have hoped for in life. So he disposed of his worldly goods in Lengnau, gathered Meyer and his four daughters about him, and joined forces with Rachel Weil Meyer and her family to head for the New World and whatever it might bring. One day late in 1847 the Jewish colony of Lengnau was decreased by fourteen as the two families made their way to the Rhine port of Coblenz and there boarded a river boat which carried them to Hamburg. At Hamburg they secured passage on a sailing ship bound for Philadelphia. One sunny morning early in 1848 the ship made its way into the Delaware River and soon the spire of Independence Hall came into view. The Guggenheims were in the world of their dreams.

3]

SIMON AND the widow Meyer were married and the double family of fourteen settled down in a tiny house in one of the workingmen's districts.

Father Simon and son Meyer knew the tailor's trade, but it became apparent that there was far more opportunity to be gained in going into business for themselves than in hiring out as tailors. It was not a simple matter, even in 1848, to establish a tailor's shop: money was needed for tools and money was needed to pay the rent.

Yet it took no more than a few dollars to equip oneself for another trade. Most housewives in Philadelphia bought their sundry goods from door-to-door peddlers rather than journey to the heart of the city and the dry goods stores. So peddlers they would be.

Simon, the elder Guggenheim, became a peddler on the city streets. Meyer, the younger, bought a back-pack and set out on foot to cover the outlying poor districts of the anthracite region of Pennsylvania. He left on Sunday to begin his travels, to work his way as far as his legs and his goods would carry him half the week, and then to return slowly to his father's table for the ritual celebration of the Sabbath, beginning on Friday evening.

Simon was a religious man and so the family attended the Keneseth Israel Synagogue in downtown Philadelphia. Meyer was not a religious man, and he accompanied the family to the synagogue only to follow the dictates of family piety. Meyer was far more interested in learning the language and in discovering the best ways of getting ahead in this new country. One *could* get ahead, he saw that at the synagogue, where rich and poor Jews alike came to wor-

17]

ship. Some Jews were well-to-do and even lived in *the better districts* of the city. Meyer was eager to join them.

Meyer Guggenheim was a good-looking young man, especially by the standards of the Jewish community, with long dark hair and sideburns. In the coal fields, however, in spite of his pleasant manners and pleasing countenance, he encountered much of the old hatred and discrimination because he was a Jew. But even so, here in the new land he could move out of the ring of hatred and travel to more congenial areas. When he encountered the Pennsylvania Dutch, those Germans whose language he spoke, he was welcomed warmly. When he encountered Quaker and Swede he was not mistreated. The freedom he had discovered in America was imperfect and spotty, but it was real.

As a peddler, Meyer Guggenheim soon realized that he was limited in his earning power by his time and his ability to travel. He was a middleman, a seller of goods who could hope to earn only a few dollars a day. Peddling was a start, but he must leave it if he was to progress.

For Meyer there were two avenues of escape. He tried them both. One was to become manufacturer as well as seller. His most successful item as peddler was a stove polish. Why could he not make his own stove polish? All that need be done was to discover a suitable formula.

Meyer took his stove polish to a German acquaintance, a chemist who lived in Bethlehem, and there secured an analysis of the materials. He came home to his father's house with the formula and suggested that the few hundred dollars they had saved be invested in a business of their own. Simon would get off the streets, take off his pack, and remain at home to mix up the stove polish and put it in packages. Meyer would go out and sell it. He would buy a horse and wagon which would take him out of the peddler class and would enable him to make many more calls in a week than he could make on foot.

The stove polish business prospered, and by selling other products along with his polish Meyer began to accumulate a little money. Then one day in the shop Meyer made an important discovery about stove polish. He wanted to wash his hands, and went to the wash basin. He found that it was full of soapy water. Someone else who had been pulverizing the black lead used in the polish had washed his hands and left the water in the basin. As Meyer threw out the dirty water he saw a thick residue at the bottom of the pan, so thick that he had to scrape it off. When he did so he discovered that the lead possessed an entirely different consistency than usual. The usual lead was troublesome to housewives because it smeared on their hands and was difficult to remove. This residue in the pan was cakey and did not smear easily.

Meyer soon learned that the magic change was due to the presence of soap in the water. He had discovered a far better stove polish than was elsewhere available in the area, and he began manufacturing the new substance.

He bought a sausage-stuffing machine and converted it into a polish-manufacturing machine which cut off the polish in proper sizes. He had been importing black lead from abroad, but he asked businessmen what uses were made of black lead in industry and discovered that crucibles in the iron and new steel mills were made of black lead. When these cracked they were discarded. Meyer visited many of the iron and steel mills of Pennsylvania and arranged to take away the cracked crucibles. He paid nothing for them; the mill owners were pleased to be rid of useless trash. So Meyer now had his materials for next to nothing and the stove polish business became very profitable.

Now came the second avenue of escape from peddling: diversification. Meyer began to sell essence of coffee, which was manufactured by Lehman Meyer, one of his foster brothers. This essence was made by pulverizing coffee beans and adding various strengthening and lengthening agents such as chicory. The rich drank coffee but for the poor it was an expensive drink. Yet by using the poorest quality beans it was possible to make a cheap coffee drink that the working people could afford to buy. Soon Meyer was earning a good profit in the sale of coffee essence, matching his profits in manufacture and sales of stove polish.

Within four years after the Guggenheims arrived in the United States, Meyer had saved enough money and was well enough established in business that he could afford to marry and set up housekeeping in a place of his own. He married Barbara Meyer, his foster sister. At the time of their marriage, celebrated at Keneseth

Israel Synagogue, he was twenty-four years old and she was nineteen.

For four years it had been assumed within the family that Barbara and Meyer would marry. It was simply a matter of time and money. During those four years she had stayed at home with her mother and the rest of the family, occupying herself with womanly chores. She had learned to sew and cook, to buy wisely from the grocer and the baker and the kosher butcher. She had little formal education, but she did have time to study English in her talks in the shops and to better it by use of a small German-English dictionary. On weekends, when Meyer was at home, she helped him with his study of the language, too, more concerned about his progress than her own.

Barbara Meyer was not a beautiful girl but she did have the charm of youth and her auburn hair was so long and shining that her sons remembered it forever. She was married in a gown trimmed with lace which her mother had brought from Switzerland; then she and Meyer began married life in a small house in suburban Roxbury.

Two years later their first child was born, a boy. They named him Isaac. Thereafter, just every two years, another child was born to them; there were eight sons and three daughters in all.

The family's progress in the earliest days in America can be traced through their houses. They moved from smaller houses to larger ones and from poorer districts to wealthier ones. They began in what was little more than a slum, but by 1867 when Simon and his twin Robert were born, they lived in Roxborough, a thoroughly respectable suburb of Philadelphia, in a house with a terrace, with a porch and pillars, and with ample grounds for the six older children to play in. They moved back to the city to Franklin Street, which was not so impressive as the Roxborough house, but Meyer sacrificed a little luxury for convenience. Roxborough was just too far away from the city center when one had to take a jitney or use a carriage to drive to the office.

During these years between 1854 and 1873 the family moved from one house to another about every five years, each more comfortable and more expensive than the one before, until in 1873 when the last daughter, Cora, was born, they moved into a street of affluence, Sixteenth Street, near Broad, into a house with potted palms in the windows. They had achieved, in this move to the west side of North Sixteenth Street, something to which every poor man in America could aspire: the elevation to elegance.

During these years Simon Guggenheim took life more easily. He operated the stove polish factory and Meyer continued to try his hand at many businesses. For a time Meyer operated his own tailor shop. He had dealt in groceries, but he found that manufacturing and wholesale selling were far more profitable and to his liking than dealing in the retail trade.

Meyer had acquired an interest in a mill that made clay fire-bricks, and here the crucibles from the iron and steel mills were broken down and the stove polish was manufactured on an ever larger scale each year. His partner in the mill decamped one day when Meyer was out of town, first selling off all the available polish and collecting all the local accounts receivable. Meyer was dismayed but undaunted. He took his losses and continued his business.

In a very few years the storm of Civil War broke across the country. Meyer Guggenheim was a merchant, not a soldier. Benjamin Meyer, one of his brothers-in-law, joined the Union army as a private, but Meyer was a family man. By 1861, four sons had been born: Isaac in 1854, Daniel in 1856, Murry in 1858, and Solomon in 1861. Daughter Jeannette would be born in 1863; Benjamin, in 1865; the twins, Robert and Simon, in 1867; William in 1868; Rose in 1871; and Cora in 1873.

By the time that Cora was born, Meyer and Barbara Guggenheim had every reason for contentment. Meyer had capital to put away. Barbara was supremely happy; she had her children and a fine husband and every luxury she could wish, including a grand piano. Their house was filled with built-in closets and cabinets of intricately designed woodwork. The furnishings included heavy drapes and potted plants and figured carpets covering the floors. Barbara, after all, was fifteen years old when she came to America, and she could remember, almost as well as Meyer, the squalor and occasional horror of the ghetto. She was now a plump, well-dressed matron with servants to do her work and plenty of time to stroll in the shopping district of Philadelphia and buy what she pleased.

The Guggenheims seldom went out at night together. Barbara almost never went out, except when Meyer took her to the theater or the opera or to dine at some friend's house. These were rare occasions, for Meyer preferred to entertain at home, feasting his friends on shellfish and wine, two symbols of luxury from the old days in Switzerland.

In inland Switzerland, so far from the sea, few Jews could afford to eat the fruits of Neptune, even fewer than could afford to drink wine except for sacramental purposes. All his mature life, Meyer gratified childhood longings and exhibited his affluence with shellfish and wine, his favorite food and drink.

Barbara's life was wrapped solidly in the lives of her husband and her children. Servants or not, she made the sweet German coffee cake for the family on the weekends. She supervised the dressmakers as they knelt before her daughters, pinning up the hems of their tulle dresses. In a way she was embarrassed by luxury; she chose to walk rather than ride down busy Market Street, and she did her own grocery shopping, bringing home the chickens and the vegetables and haggling with shopkeepers in German or her broken English with a quiet good humor.

She did not ask to be entertained. She had little time for entertainment, in these years or ever, with eleven children whose noses must be wiped, who must be cautioned to shine their shoes and keep their cuffs clean.

Barbara was religious. She went to the synagogue regularly. She always had time to work with the ladies' auxiliary. No neighbor fell ill, but Barbara Guggenheim came calling with a pot of chicken soup, and, if needed, more tangible evidences of her neighborliness, including money.

Barbara ran the house; there was never any question about that fact. Meyer ran the business, and he undertook the disciplining of his boys, but the house was Barbara's domain, and over it she ruled as queen.

Since Barbara was religious, she pushed Meyer into the activities of the Philadelphia Jewish community. The synagogue was located in a shabby old church, where the congregation knelt in gloom to contemplate the misery of the Jews. But the synagogue was not enough for Barbara, any more than her private charities. She persuaded Meyer to join the Jewish Foster Home Society, and to help the poor Jews of Pennsylvania who were still so close to them in memory.

Meyer had somewhere lost the faith of his fathers and kept up the pretense of religion only to satisfy his wife. On the Sabbath he took Barbara to Keneseth Israel Synagogue, but he also did business on the Sabbath. He gave generously to the Temple and its causes. He gave to the Hebrew Education Society. He also gave to the Catholic Charities, and for the same reasons. Barbara persuaded him that it was good business for a merchant to give a little.

Meyer had only two hobbies. The first of these was to make money. Then when he became wealthy, he began to cultivate an interest in trotters, as did so many other middle-aged businessmen of the nineteenth century. But while Commodore Cornelius Vanderbilt and Leland Stanford paid $15,000 or $20,000 for a trotter, Meyer Guggenheim bought geldings and mares at $100 or $200 and would not consider keeping a horse for pleasure alone. Vanderbilt's mares occupied a stable on New York's Washington Square, near his house, and were laved and curried by experts; Guggenheim's mares lived in the company stable off Philadelphia's Front Street and on weekdays were used to pull the wholesale house's wagons.

Meyer became the patriarch of the family when old Simon died in 1869, at seventy-six, worn out from a life of hard work and much privation in the earlier years. By 1869, however, Simon could look back on his life with great satisfaction. He was the one who had brought the Guggenheims to America, the one who had made it possible for the family to live in a manner so rich he could scarcely have imagined it twenty years before. No Guggenheim need bow his head or cringe in the city of Philadelphia in 1869. Simon had indeed led his family from Gehenna to the promised land, he knew it, and he died happy because of it.

During the Civil War years Meyer Guggenheim increased his wealth by speculations in foodstuffs and spices. His defaulting partner in the mill had left him a stock of mustard seed and wooden pegs for shoes, both of which seemed useless when he received them, but which proved to be profitable in meeting the expanded needs of the Northern army in the war.

As in the creation of any successful enterprise there was a good share of luck involved in Meyer Guggenheim's progress, but he also had the knack of seeing public needs as they developed, and the experience (gained from his knowledge of European business) and the foresight to capitalize on these developments. In later years Meyer attributed much of his wealth to one faculty.

One day, when Meyer had become a multimillionaire, a relative came to call on him, and flattered him.

"Meyer," said the visitor, "before leaving I must say something that I've been meaning to say to you for some time. I must express my admiration for the way, beginning with nothing, you have risen financially—all by the use of your own good head."

"No, cousin," said Meyer Guggenheim, "I didn't make money with my head. I made it by getting hold of good things and sitting on them. So, you see, I do not owe my prosperity to my head at all, but to another extremity entirely."

That was the earthy Meyer, the man who liked a good salty story told over the wine after the ladies had left their end of the dinner table and gone off to the parlor to talk of babies and servant problems.

As his polish business prospered, he entered others. During the Civil War he formed a partnership with S. Dreifuss and Jacob Loeb, and the firm of Guggenheim, Dreifuss and Loeb opened its store at Front and Arch Streets to deal in general merchandise. He became an importer of spices. He dealt in groceries, and in this business he met a white-bearded Quaker grocer named Charles H. Graham, who was to be important to his future. Meyer's bright, sharp eye caught many opportunities that were overlooked by others. In the 1860's most American families still made their own soap by boiling waste fat and mixing it with lye. Sometimes they made their own lye by burning wood to ash. Commercial lye was produced in America by the Pennsylvania Salt Company, which had a monopoly on the trade. Meyer discovered that a firm in England was producing a caustic alkali, or lye, which was much cheaper to manufacture than the Pennsylvania Salt Company's product. He bought the patent rights for the United States and established a small factory on Wood Street to manufacture his own lye, under the name of the American Concentrated Lye Company. He sold his lye directly to the public through the general store, both wholesale and retail. Soon Meyer's new company was important enough so that the Pennsylvania Salt Company tried to stifle him. First the bigger company threatened, but Meyer did not yield to threat. Next, the Pennsylvania Salt Company called in its lawyers and began suit against the Guggenheim firm for patent infringement. Meyer hired his own lawyers and defended the suit successfully. The Pennsylvania Salt Company then began negotiations to buy him out and to absorb the American Concentrated Lye Company. This was what Meyer really wanted. His partners took stock in the Pennsylvania firm for their interest, but Meyer took $150,000 in cash for his share.

Meyer took cash for one reason: He was determined to become rich and he had been so determined since the moment he arrived in the United States, and to achieve his end he worked longer and harder than anyone he knew. He moved rapidly from one enterprise to another, taking his profits and putting them into new ventures that promised to yield quick turnover.

Early in the 1870's an uncle of Barbara Meyer Guggenheim's started a factory in Switzerland where embroidering was done by machine. Until this time the fine scalloped edgings and laces that American ladies demanded for their dresses and underclothing had been made by hand. Alexander Turney Stewart, the New York merchant, had begun in business as a lace merchant, importing fine edgings from Ireland, and later he had nearly monopolized the trade. Meyer saw possibilities for profit in a machine-made edging that could be sold at half the price of the hand-made variety and still yield a larger return to the merchant. This opportunity dropped into Meyer's lap. His wife's uncle wrote that he had produced a surplus and was sending a small quantity to Meyer to see if he could dispose of it.

Again Meyer was quick to recognize good fortune when she smiled on him. He consulted a friend, Abraham Goldsmith, a Philadelphia cloth merchant. Goldsmith gave him the names of the principal buyers of such specialties and Meyer sent off letters and samples.

The New York firm of Claflin bought the entire consignment and asked for more. Here, obviously, was opportunity and Meyer capitalized on it, even though this enterprise would take him further afield from groceries and would involve the investment of a large share of his savings. Meyer was not thinking about becoming the American agent for his wife's uncle. Not at all. If he was going into the lace business he was going to become a manufacturer.

In making this decision Meyer Guggenheim had very important reasons—eight of them. His sons were growing up, and he wanted to create opportunities for them in a family business that would keep them together. The danger of the boys scattering was already apparent. Isaac, the oldest, had left school at the age of seventeen to go to work in the wholesale grocery business of one of his uncles in Philadelphia and was talking about becoming a traveling salesman. Meyer could not expect all his sons to share his own shrewd appraisals of the business world. He bemoaned the boy's lack of foresight, but he was a good enough judge of character to realize that this break from the home was not unusual and that it might well happen again with the other seven boys.

By the time Meyer had amassed a million dollars he realized that a million was nothing. He had a large family. Dowries for the daughters, even small, sensible dowries, would eat up large chunks of capital, and there would be scarcely a hundred thousand dollars each for his sons. A hundred thousand dollars was not a fortune; a million dollars was a fortune. Long before he knew how he might do it, Meyer dreamed of the day when his sons would have a million dollars each. He could not dream, of course—no one could— that in his own lifetime the boys, with the exception of Robert, who died a few days after a fall from a horse in 1876, would become multimillionaires and that at the peak of their fortune their assets would be valued at nearly half a billion dollars.

4]

THE GUGGENHEIMS of Philadelphia were a close-knit family, and this was the glory of Barbara, who spent all the waking hours of her married life working to that end. William Guggenheim, youngest of the seven surviving sons, many years later described his mother:

. . . The passing years and the bearing of many children took heavy toll of her early bloom. At forty-five she seemed years older than she was. Her figure lost its firm lines; she was graying rapidly; fine wrinkles nested at the corners of her eyes. Still, it is doubtful if she had ever appeared so beautiful to anyone as she then did to her children. They adored her. The gentleness and kindness which were the basis of her character shone through and radiated a beauty that was far more than a substitute for her fading youth.

Barbara Guggenheim was the buffer, and a buffer was needed, particularly for the boys, because Meyer was a stern patriarch. His idea of providing more included discipline. He whipped his sons until they were old enough to leave his household. He used a leather belt, a hair brush, or any punishing surface that came to hand at the moment when his ire was aroused. The older boys stood the punishment manfully, but were secretly ashamed. The younger ones padded their trousers, but were caught, of course, and the punishment was all the more severe. The terms *older* and *younger* were significant in the Guggenheim family. The boys fell into two groups, separated by the birth of their sister Jeannette. The older boys were Isaac, Dan, Murry, and Sol, and they talked and worked and conspired together. The younger were Ben, Simon, and Will, who were regarded by their elder brothers as silly young fellows. The difference was far more than that of age; the older boys grew up in the leaner years; the family had already crossed the line that separates the wealthy from the middle class by the time that Benjamin was born in 1865. The older boys thought in terms of work and business, and all chafed at the education they received at the Philadelphia public schools, for that education was classical in nature and they wanted to learn the ways of business. The younger boys, growing up in luxury, thought in terms of higher education. Ben, the eldest of the young, would go to Columbia University, Simon to a business school, and Will to the University of Pennsylvania.

Life in the big house on North Sixteenth Street was comfortable and pleasant. Barbara had servants to do the housework and she could spend her time with her growing family. Meyer entertained, but Meyer's head was always full of business matters and the people he brought to the house were usually his partners or customers. The Philadelphia Jewish community was large and active, but Meyer was barely a part of it. For a time his boys went to Hebrew school on Mondays, but they did not care for it, and in spite of Barbara's urging, Meyer was not one to tell the boys to keep the old ways of the faith. Although he went to synagogue and the boys attended Sabbath school, and Meyer supported the Temple with generous gifts, he was slowly forsaking his religion and the sons were to follow their father in this respect. For a time several of them attended the Catholic Day School at Broad and Columbia Streets because it was the best school that Meyer knew. In later years it was said that Meyer attended personally to the worldly education of his sons by taking them personally to houses in the red-light district as they reached their bar mitzvah.

The young Guggenheims were not spoiled by their parents. Far from it. They did not receive lavish allowances, but had to petition their father for their spending money until they began earning money of their own. Meyer's one extravagance, if one could call it that, was driving his fine horses. On weekends he would harness a favorite mare to his driving carriage and take Barbara and some of the children out for a ride in the country.

Meyer was a very formal man. His sideburns grew out to become mutton-chop whiskers and as they grayed he became an imposing, even forbidding figure, as far as the family was concerned. To outsiders he was simply a quiet little Jew who never seemed to have very much to say for himself. He was neither prepossessing nor impressive to those who did not know him and appreciate his cool, calculating mind.

Part of this calculation must be laid to Meyer Guggenheim's upbringing in the oppressive atmosphere of Switzerland. He learned there never to trust anyone, least of all a Gentile, and when he came to America it was with an ingrained feeling of responsibility to family—and to no one else. He taught his sons to be suspicious. He was always one to look a gift horse in the mouth—to examine teeth one by one for flaws—for as he told the boys, every apparent opportunity had its other side. It was a harsh world and the key to happiness and safety in this world was money. He never let his boys forget for a moment the importance of money.

Meyer had brought to America many of the characteristics of the European Jew. Culture to him meant music. Occasionally he would take Barbara to the opera at the Academy of Music to enjoy an evening in which he felt he was dispensing culture. For the children, culture was to be acquired at an early age: Each of the older boys was forced to study a musical instrument. Two violins, a violoncello, and a piano were the instruments. In the house in Roxborough each morning at six o'clock the boys were herded into the family basement and the torture began.

Isaac and Daniel played first and second violins, Murry struggled with the piano, and Solomon, youngest of the orchestra, faithfully sawed at the violoncello. It was difficult to know who hated the violin most, Isaac or Daniel. Murry was equally at odds with his instrument, and only Solomon accepted his father's abjurations about the cultural values of music. All accepted their father's orders with respect, however, for that was the way it was in the Guggenheim family. Little Meyer, sideburns aquiver, stood before them and waved his hands like the conductor of a fine symphony orchestra, and the boys waveringly responded with their tortured playing.

Behind the Guggenheims lived a lady who had married at the age when she was already referred to as a "maiden lady," and this lady's patience with musical strivings at six o'clock in the morning was extremely limited. First she attempted to keep out the noise by building an eight-foot fence between her property and the Guggenheims' but no eight-foot fence was equal to the task. Next she complained to Barbara, who tried to soothe her but was forced to admit that although she was queen in the Guggenheim household, Meyer was king, and if he wanted music at six o'clock in the morning, she was powerless to stop him.

The unhappy neighbor withstood her passions for many months, but finally she was reduced to direct action: she called in the police, who came and advised Meyer that his concerts were a breach of the peace.

Morning was Meyer's time to devote to the children, and deprived of this opportunity to enrich them culturally, the father soon lost interest in the children's musical education, much to their delight. As a result, Solomon was the only Guggenheim to retain a solid respect for music and to pursue it. He continued to play his cello faithfully until he moved away from home.

As Meyer went into one business after another and accumulated more surplus, he began speculating in stocks. Nearly all basically conservative businessmen were attracted to railroad shares because railroads at that time represented the best tangible investments and also potentially the most profitable. Late in the 1870's the American railroads were enjoying what appeared to be a halcyon period of profitability. Actually, most of them were being milked dry by pitiless manipulators, but they seemed to be sound investments.

Meyer bought heavily of the stock of the Hannibal & St. Joseph Railway, a small line that hauled into Kansas City. This was the era of railroad building and soon the Hannibal & St. Joseph had competition. When that competition came the investors panicked and the stock plummeted. It dropped from around $100 to $20 a share. Meyer bought and bought some more at the disaster price. Soon he had 2000 shares of the stock, bought at various prices in the uncertain market.

At the time Jay Gould and his associates were putting together the Missouri Pacific Railroad System, which was aimed at dominating the Mountain West and the Mississippi Basin. The little Hannibal & St. Joseph was needed to give them access to Kansas City because their rivals had the other lines. So Jay Gould began to buy. As he bought confidence returned and the price rose until it hit $150 a share.

Gould's brokers scanned lists and buttonholed their confreres to discover who held blocks of shares of the little railroad, and at least once Gould emissaries came to Philadelphia to persuade Meyer Guggenheim to part with his stock in the interest of progress. Meyer held on stubbornly until the stock hit $200 a share and then he sold. It was said that he made a profit of $300,000 on this transaction, not a huge fortune by the standards of the Goulds and the Vanderbilts, but quite a comfortable sum.

When Meyer decided to enter the lace and embroidery business, then, he had the money at hand to do the job the way he wished. His first move was to secure foreign rights to several machine patents which could be used in the manufacture of lace. His second move was to find a young partner whom he could trust to go to Europe and manage that end of the business, while he remained in the United States, supplied the capital, and took care of the marketing. He needed a young man filled with ambition and possessed of a good sound business head.

Meyer happened to know just such a man. His name was Morris Pulaski. He had worked for a time for the firm of Guggenheim, Dreifuss and Loeb, but he had left the business when he saw the Guggenheim boys growing up, because he was convinced that they would go into dry goods and they would become the officers of the company. With some difficulty and only after promises, he had been persuaded to return. Meyer liked the young man and he liked his wife, Lena, daughter of partner S. Dreifuss. Meyer invited Pulaski to become his partner in the lace business, and Morris Pulaski jumped at the chance. The result of their agreement was formation of the firm of Guggenheim & Pulaski.

Isaac Guggenheim happened at this time to be in the right place with the right background to be of great help to his father.

Isaac had been born in Philadelphia on June 6, 1854, six years after his father had come to America and two years after Meyer's marriage to Barbara. He grew up in Philadelphia and Roxborough. He had attended the Philadelphia public schools, and had graduated from the Philadelphia Public High School with honors. He went abroad then, for a brief period, to see the homeland of the family, spending several months in Basle, Switzerland.

Isaac was tall and in his youth he looked more like his father than the other brothers. He had proved himself to be intelligent in high school. He proved himself to be ambitious, for after his return from Basle, he had gone to work for Barbara's brother in the wholesale dry goods business. He might have worked for his father but he sought opportunity in New York as an agent for an outside firm. He had married a girl named Carrie Sonneborn, daughter of a New York merchant, and had settled down to raise a family of three daughters, Beulah, Edyth, and Helene.

Carrie Sonneborn was a little red-haired girl who was full of energy. After their marriage she put on weight until she was no longer little, but her energy persisted.

When the lace firm was formed, Isaac left his other employment to become New York manager of the lace importing business.

The new firm's next move was to establish a factory for the manufacture of lace edgings at St. Gall in Switzerland. In 1873 Morris Pulaski sailed for Europe to manage the factory and he took Daniel Guggenheim with him as assistant. Daniel was seventeen years old. His assigned tasks were to learn the languages and learn the lace and embroidery business.

A scant two years separated Isaac and Daniel Guggenheim in age but there was a vast difference between these two boys in outlook on life. The reason—or part of it—is to be found in the changing circumstances in which Meyer Guggenheim lived during the period of their boyhood and young manhood.

Perhaps Isaac's employment outside of the family had been the stimulant that urged Meyer Guggenheim to broaden his horizons and seek a business in which all his sons might play a part. When Daniel came of age, there was an important place for him in the newly organized business of importing lace and embroideries, the kind of place that would appeal to a young man, for it meant travel abroad and excitement. Daniel went to Switzerland with Morris Pulaski and he remained there for the next eleven years as buyer of laces and embroideries, and as buyer of materials for the factories that were established by the firm. Daniel grew stout of mind and stout of body. A dark mustache covered his slanting upper lip, a mustache that was almost the duplicate of Meyer's, although Daniel never favored the old-fashioned mutton-chop whiskers and kept his sideburns and his chin shaved. He wore his hair close-cropped, for even in his youth it had begun to recede a bit and to turn white, giving him a broad forehead and a look of grave intelligence. He dressed well but not foppishly, paying less attention to his clothes by far than his brother Isaac. The years in Switzerland perfected his German and French and lent him self-confidence in any situation. He had little difficulty in Europe in any way. Jews in Switzerland had achieved full freedom by the time Daniel returned as an American visitor, and a Guggenheim was even mayor of Gailingen, not far from the family seat at Lengnau.

The lace business prospered. Soon several other factories in St. Gall and nearby towns were producing lace for the Guggenheim & Pulaski firm. Later a second company factory was established at Plauen, in Saxony.

From the beginning, Daniel was his father's second in command. Perhaps, as has been indicated in the judgments of Bernard Baruch and others, Daniel had a prescience and sense of business organization that was unmatched by any others among his brothers. From the beginning Isaac took a back seat in the management of Guggenheim companies.

Isaac's great contributions to the Guggenheim fortunes were a slow and steady pace, an unerring eye for detail, and a willingness to work long hours to perfect the detail. One of the celebrated characteristics of the younger Guggenheim males was a preoccupation with pleasures, but this was not true of Isaac.

With Daniel living what they thought was a very romantic life in Europe, the brothers Murry and Sol became ever more restless in their drab Philadelphia high school and they pleaded with their father to send them, too, abroad to learn the business. Soon Murry went to St. Gall to assist his brother and Pulaski.

If there had been no Daniel Guggenheim to take leadership of Meyer Guggenheim's sons in the lace business, the accolade would undoubtedly have fallen on Murry, the third son. Whether he would have accepted it or not is quite another matter, for Murry was one of the quiet ones. Like Isaac, he avoided publicity. Like

Isaac, he lived his later life in quiet splendor. Like Isaac, he was quick to see the reverse side of any proposition, and he acted as a brake upon the vivacity and daring of Daniel. Unlike Isaac, when the chips were down Murry was willing to be daring himself, as he proved toward the end of his life.

Murry had been born in 1858, as the Meyer Guggenheims began moving up in the world and away from the tiny little house in which Meyer and Barbara had set up life together. Like all the other brothers, Murry attended the public schools. It was two years after Daniel went to Switzerland that Murry joined him at the lace center in St. Gall. Murry took quickly to the new life in Switzerland, spending much of his time in the mountains and hiking along the trails above the lakes when he was not working in the account or shipping rooms of the firm. They worked hard in those days, all the Guggenheim boys abroad. Sometimes just before a shipment was to be made to Philadelphia the packing and totaling meant a twelve-hour day. But such a day was followed by a holiday, when Dan and Murry would go off joyfully to a mountaintop restaurant, preferably accompanied by a pair of Swiss damsels.

Murry was not a big man—none of the Guggenheims were large men in body build—but by the time he was twenty he sported a very large mustache and was a dashing figure in white stock tie, dark suit, and patent leather shoes. Alone among the Guggenheim boys he chose his bride from abroad. She was Leonie, the daughter of Jacques Bernheim of Mulhouse in Alsace. Murry met her when she was staying on Lake Lugano and courted her there, sending her chocolates and inviting her to go walking and riding through the parks in the afternoons. They were married in 1887, a year or so before Murry returned to the United States to give full time to the new adventure of the mining and smelting businesses.

Murry was always a thoughtful, precise man, except in one regard: He was most imprecise about his name. Sometimes he was called Murray. Sometimes it was Murry, sometimes Morry, and sometimes he signed himself Morris. He seemed to have no fixed feeling about his name.

Murry was very different from Solomon, the next Guggenheim son, who followed him to Switzerland. Sol was sent to the Institute

Concordia at Zurich to learn German and acquire culture. On vacations he was to help the other brothers in the lace business.

There is a story, told by Milton Lomask in *Seed Money*, which illustrates the independence of Solomon Guggenheim better than any other. When Sol was sent off to school in Switzerland and arrived in Zurich to begin his adventure in education, almost at the first moment he was accosted on the grounds by a group of the older boys.

"What's your name?" asked one of them.

"Solomon Guggenheim."

"You an American?"

"That's right."

"You a Jew?"

"That's right."

"We don't like Jews around here."

"Why not?"

"They killed our Saviour."

"I don't know about that," Sol said, "but I do know I'm going to kill you."

Whereupon he set out to try.

Always, for the rest of his life, Sol had the reputation of being a giant-killer.

The Guggenheims were not interested in outside partners; Meyer's strict training in distrust accounted for that attitude, and so, after a few successful years, pressure was placed on Morris Pulaski to sell out. Pulaski had always been well treated in the company and the offer made to him was apparently a very satisfactory one. When Pulaski left the firm it was reorganized as M. Guggenheim's Sons. Each of the boys who entered the business was given an equal partnership in it, even as a beginner, because of Meyer's shrewd realization that less than equality would breed discontent among the brothers.

Once Meyer was asked why he felt this way:

"True," he said, "when the younger ones first come in they are more bother than they are worth. During this period the older ones must carry the load. But in time all that changes. The day arrives when the older ones wish to retire. Then the younger ones must carry the load. Besides, let us not forget the wives! If the wife of one partner hears that the partner-husband of another is making more money, trouble follows."

The four older Guggenheim brothers developed the lace business; the others were too young. But, following his philosophy, Meyer insisted that the younger boys have opportunity. Meyer Guggenheim's tastes were simple and his generosity to his sons was virtually unmatched among American millionaires. In all things Meyer now tried to guide his sons, to placate them and bring them together, rather than play the stern father.

Meyer had been the stern father much earlier and Isaac had borne the brunt of it. He was first to be punished and he was punished more harshly than the other boys, but that was one of the disadvantages of being first.

When the lace business was reorganized a family crisis was created. As eldest son, Isaac might have expected to be the principal heir of his father. Isaac was the major objector to taking the youngsters in and giving them as much of a share as he had for himself. His point was that he had been working for a dozen years and had contributed heavily to the profits of the lace business. Why should William, for example, who was yet a stripling, be given a full share in the business?

Meyer had come from the old country with a handful of aphorisms to buttress arguments, and he used these unsparingly with his family. The seven brothers, he said again and again, were strong as a bundle of fasces together, but apart they were as weak as a single stick and could be broken as easily. The brothers must stick together, said Meyer. Isaac, the dutiful son, buried his objections, and M. Guggenheim's Sons was formed, to last until after the death of Benjamin thirty years later.

The new low price of manufactured lace did much to increase its use and soon the Guggenheims were making very comfortable profits. All four elder brothers continued to be active. Meyer was not a member of the firm, but his hand was always there to guide them and to stay them when necessary. The product soon became known as "Hamburg edgings" and in the late nineteenth century ladies used row after row of these to adorn their petticoats and dresses. Meyer, with his usual thoroughness, studied the United

States customs regulations on importation of laces and discovered an additional duty of 20 percent on lace imported by the bolt; so he directed the boys to stop putting the lace into bolts and to ship it to him in bulk. He then found new machinery to cut the lace into rows. The lace was delivered to the retailers in five-row pieces. Guggenheim lace had an additional advantage now that Meyer had acted on his information: It was perforated along the lines of the pieces so that all the clerk had to do was tear off a piece of the proper size wanted by the customer.

The boys were very busy in the last few years of the 1870's with this new enterprise. Meyer was busy, too. Lace merchant, dry goods merchant, spice importer, stove polish manufacturer, and stock market speculator, this graying man in late middle age was by this time a millionaire. He did not speak of such matters, even to his sons, and he continued his own hard work in many fields. He went to his factories and his stores every day during the week, wearing his frock coat and careful dress. He gave little thought to luxury; he was still overwhelmingly concerned with the process of making money, not for himself now, but for his sons.

For a man who could remember the Lengnau pogrom of 1802 because he had been there, a frightened, sniveling little Jewish boy cowering in a corner as the mob stormed outside, Meyer Guggenheim had come a very long way.

5]

THEY SAY that Colorado is the Switzerland of America, with her dozens of sharp, high peaks jutting proudly toward the sun in an air so clear it dazzles the eyes of the newcomer; with her lakes so limpid with indigo that they seem to have leaped from an artist's canvas into real life; with her mountain flowers and her mountain sheep and the deep green pastures common only to the high countries of every land.

One might conclude that some affinity developed immediately between the Guggenheims and this counterpart of Meyer's native Switzerland, but it was not the sparkling green of Colorado meadows that brought the Guggenheims to Colorado—it was the dull shine of silver.

The Guggenheims had come to America just before the great California Gold Rush and Meyer had been well aware of the gold fever that swept across America in 1849. He read English slowly then, but each day, all his life, he took an hour to sit down and digest the newspapers so that no item of commercial importance to him should be passed by. In 1849 and later, however, Meyer gave scant thought to the hysterical search for gold in the West. His quest for fortune was to be more pragmatic, within the frames of his experience.

Living in Philadelphia, Meyer Guggenheim learned a great deal about Colorado, and particularly about the Leadville area, because the story of mining in Leadville was linked closely with Philadelphia men and Philadelphia money.

Late in the spring of 1860, as Meyer Guggenheim was grasping for a hold on Philadelphia's wholesale dry goods business, gold hunters doubling back from California crossed the great Park range of the Rocky Mountains and came to Colorado's California Gulch, a deep cut created millions of years ago in the midst of the Rockies by the earth's upheaval. The Gulch was bare, covered only with brush and grass, but beneath the surface along the creek bed the miners found rich panning for gold. In Denver, miners boasted that some claims staked along California Gulch yielded $1000 a day in dust and nuggets. Soon the Gulch was lined with mining claims and the clear water that came from the mountain springs ran through so many dozens of sluice boxes that it came out mud at the bottom of the Gulch.

Summer in the mountains was cool and pleasant but by October the weather began to turn cold; thereafter for eight months the miners either deserted their claims and headed for the shelter of the towns or they froze along the Gulch. But for $18 an ounce some of the men were willing to freeze a little.

By 1866, the surface gold along California Gulch had been mostly worked out and the panners and sluice box men drifted away. Two years later a Philadelphia company organized a mining venture and began working what was called the Printer Boy Lode.

The easterners were welcomed by a luckless storekeeper named Horace Austin Warner Tabor. Tabor had been a stonecutter in New England, a farmer in Kansas, and a Free Soil member of the Kansas Territorial Legislature until that organization was disbanded by order of President Franklin Pierce. In 1859, H. A. W. Tabor had come to Colorado to seek his fortune in the gold fields, and the next year he had opened a general store which was also the postoffice at Oro City, the first settlement in the area that would be known as Leadville. His fortunes rose and fell with those of the miners.

In the middle of the 1860's, when the surface ores of Colorado were being worked out so rapidly, eastern capitalists called on an obscure professor of chemistry at Brown University in Providence, Rhode Island. The Professor, Nathaniel P. Hill, went West to study the chemistry of the ores. In 1864, Professor Hill made the trip to Denver by coach and then traveled to Gilpin County, where the land in question was located. He discovered that the surface ores were located in quartz formations which cracked easily and yielded the precious gold. Where a vein of ore had been found, it was simple enough to bring out the quartz and crush it in a stamp mill. The gold then separated easily from the quartz dust. But not far below the surface of the ground the character of the mineral deposits changed. The miners did not know what the ores were, but they did know that they could no longer stamp gold out of their ore. What they had encountered, Professor Hill discovered, were iron and copper sulphides in combination with gold and silver. These ores did not yield to stamping. An analogy, drawn by geologists, pictured the gold-bearing quartz as a nut that could be cracked to get the kernel of gold. These combination ores were like lemons: One did not get pure citric acid by crushing a lemon; it was necessary to take other steps. So it was with the new ores. But in the mining camps no one knew what steps to take. Consequently, in 1864, while there were some sixty stamp mills in Gilpin County, most of them were shut down because the mills were not yielding even a quarter of the gold in the ores.

Professor Hill made two trips to Colorado to examine these odd ores. He made a trip to study the metal smelters and refineries in Wales. He went to Freiberg, the German university that specialized in mining engineering. He came back to Colorado bringing a metallurgist from the smelters of Swansea in Wales, gathered Colorado ores, and took a second trip to Europe to work them over with the experts at Swansea. The eastern capitalists paid for the freighting of seventy-two tons of ore from the Bobtail Mine in Central City to the Missouri River, where the ore was transferred to a boat, then to a ship at New Orleans, and taken to Wales. There Professor Hill and his backers discovered that the gold and silver in the ores could be extracted by smelting, and Hill came back to Colorado to settle and direct operations of the Boston and Colorado Smelting Company. He built the first smelter in the United States, at Black Hawk, Gilpin County, Colorado, and began smelting in 1867.

The Printer Boy Lode, organized in California Gulch by the Philadelphians, was most successful, and although it was operated only during the summer and autumn months it managed to yield its backers a quarter of a million dollars in gold in a few years. A smelter, which was called the Malta, was built near the conjunction of California Gulch and the Arkansas River. With this and other smelters belching black smoke into the clear sky, the mining industry of Colorado began to revive.

It was a new kind of mining. When the old hardrock man panned for dust and nuggets or crushed the rock, his investment was very small. With the need for smelting, the need for capital increased. One could stake a claim and pick out ore without much expense, but then, if the assay of the ore proved that it would be profitable to smelt, it would be necessary to begin driving shafts and to bring in wagons and teams of mules to carry the ore to the smelter.

In 1869 while the smelter men were learning to deal with the Colorado ores, five prospectors staked a claim in California Gulch. One of them was A. Y. Corman. After a few months of discouragement, four of the miners gave up and moved on, leaving the claim in Corman's hands. Corman worked the claim faithfully, but with little success. Like so many miners before him, he was looking for the glitter of gold, and while he found some gold in his mines— enough to keep him going—he had to work through tons of heavy rock to do so.

In 1874 a pair of promoters named W. H. Stevens and A. B. Wood came to California Gulch with a plan to bring water from the Arkansas River headwaters along California Gulch. They heard that the miners were complaining about the heavy boulders in the creek and the heavy dirt that made it hard to pan for gold. On a hunch, the speculators took some of the rock for chemical analysis, and learned that it was carbonate of lead, which carried not only gold, but also silver. The pair kept their discovery secret until they had patented nine claims along the Gulch, each claim 300 feet wide and 1500 feet deep.

When the news broke that the heavy rocks were carbonate of lead, the interest in California Gulch took a rise. Now, knowing what to look for, the mining men began to make progress. The first important carbonate strike was made by the Gallagher brothers on Iron Hill near Stray Horse Gulch. Then came others: the Adelaide, the Pine, and the Charleston mines. All these mines began to yield good profits to the men who worked them, but there was nothing very spectacular about the finds, and the cost of mining and refining was such that interest was still relatively mild. L. Z. Leiter of Chicago, once partner of Marshall Field in the dry goods business, bought the valuable Wood claims along California Gulch for $40,000

By 1877, California Gulch was no longer half-deserted. There were several hundred people working claims in the mining district with varying success. H. A. W. Tabor's general store no longer seemed to him to be on the verge of failure.

Tabor was always willing to grubstake a miner for a share in the findings, even though most of the time the miner spent a month or two eating his beans and bacon and hardtack and then became discouraged and moved on, while Tabor held the unpaid bill. In the spring of 1878, storekeeper Tabor agreed to grubstake a pair of former shoemakers who had come to the gold fields. These men, August Rische and George T. Hook, agreed to give H. A. W. Tabor a third interest in whatever they might discover.

Ten days after Tabor had made his investment of a few dollars worth of supplies, Rische and Hook reached the twenty-five-foot level of a shaft they had named the Little Pittsburgh mine. There they struck rich carbonate ore, and in one week of mining they brought forth enough ore so that the partners split $8000 after the smelting costs were paid. Later, the Little Pittsburgh produced as much as 100 tons of ore a week with a value of $200 per ton—or $20,000 a week in silver. Inside of a year Hook had sold out to Rische and Tabor for $98,000. Rische sold his share to two other men for $262,000. Tabor later sold his one-third share for a million dollars.

This kind of mining changed everything in California Gulch. The town of Leadville sprang up, to be called "the Carbonate Camp," and soon it was not a town but a city. From a few hundred miners and their families in 1877 the population of the district grew to 1500 by 1878, to 5000 by 1879, and to 35,000 by 1880 when the full impact of the success of the Little Pittsburgh had reached the world.

Many people in the East were excited by the prospects of California Gulch. A lucky few came west, and still a luckier handful found fortune in the silver fields. After he sold the Little Pittsburgh, H. A. W. Tabor bought another claim—some say it was a false claim, salted for sale with specimens of rich ore—and the "false" claim proved to be a bonanza. Tabor began mining $100,-000 a month in ore. The bonanza lasted for a decade, and brought Tabor a fortune of $12,000,000.

In 1877, A. Y. Corman gained a little hope with the discovery of the carbonate ore. He restaked the claim on the old mine in California Gulch and named it the A.Y., after himself. He also staked another claim immediately above the A.Y. and named it the Minnie, in honor of his wife.

He kept digging his shafts but it was hard work for a miner who was not young. He must line it with timbers to prevent cave-in and timbers cost either work or money. To A. Y. Corman they meant sawing and chopping, for money was hard to come by in his camp. What he had came from the few grains of gold he was able to pan out of the Gulch.

In 1879, lured by the stories of the Carbonate Camp, Charles H. Graham left his grocery business in Philadelphia and traveled to Leadville to buy a mining property. He had little money and so soon he had several partners. One was George Work and another was Samuel Harsh, both Philadelphians. A fourth partner was Thomas Weir. The four bought out A. Y. Corman's two claims, the A.Y. and the Minnie, for $4000. Since the only one of the four who had very much money was Harsh, he paid out the bulk of the cash to Corman, and took notes from the other three.

In time, those notes came due. If they could not pay, the three other partners would all lose their shares of the mine to Harsh. Work and Weir apparently had no chance of raising the money, but Graham recalled his past association with the little Jew, Meyer Guggenheim, who had made so much money in the wholesale grocery business. Graham went to Guggenheim for a loan, and showed Meyer how the rich strikes in the Carbonate district bracketed the A.Y. and the Minnie. Meyer was intrigued by the possibilities of silver mining and agreed to finance Graham's share, lending him money without interest, but only if he could buy a half-share of the mine for himself. It was done. Meyer took over the interests of Weir and Work and with an outlay of $5000 he was half-owner of a silver mine.

Meyer was not really gambling much. The A.Y. was a paying

proposition. Graham and the others began extracting good ore in July of 1880, and in the last four months of that year they were shipping 200 tons a month to the smelter—all profitable ore.

But Meyer had scarcely made his investment when troubles began. The A.Y. and the Minnie both became flooded, and the work had to stop. Graham and Harsh wrote from the West that the mine could be pumped out, but it would take money. If that was the case, Meyer decided, he must go to Leadville and see these mining properties for himself before making any decisions.

Meyer Guggenheim, the slender, middle-aged Swiss Jew with the thick accent and whiskers parted at the chin, took a train for the West, and in a few days was panting along the streets of the high-altitude city of Leadville—Cloud City, they sometimes called it, because it was located 10,000 feet above sea level. In his frock coat and city hat Meyer was as strange a sight to the miners of Leadville as they were to him. It was a boom town, there was no question about that. Leadville boasted 51 grocery stores and 27 barber shops. It also housed 120 saloons, 115 gambling houses, and 35 houses of prostitution lined up along Tiger Alley. (For fifty dollars a man could employ the services of a lady tattooer.)

Meyer Guggenheim came to Leadville on the Denver and Rio Grande Railroad in a Pullman Palace Sleeping Car. He came down the main street, Harrison Avenue, past the Tabor Grand Hotel, past the Tabor Opera House, past the Tabor Bank of Leadville.

On the street he was jostled by drunken miners and prostitutes, walking arm in arm along the sidewalks. Along the side streets he could catch glimpses of the freight wagons and the eight-mule teams that hauled the heavy ores to the smelters. It was summer but it was cool and he drew his coat around him; had he come a little earlier in the year he would have found the miners in fur caps, with six thicknesses of scarving around their heads and necks, wearing three flannel shirts, three pairs of woolen drawers, vests, pants, coats, and boots over their shoes.

At a newsstand, seeking his daily paper, Meyer learned with gratification that Leadville had its own *Deutsche Zeitung*. It also boasted a healthy Jewish community. David May and Moses Shoenberg kept an auction house and community clothing store at 108 Harrison Avenue. There were six Jewish pawnshops in town.

There was not yet a synagogue, but the Jews met on the Sabbath in a store, and at the rooms of the Rocky Mountain Lode 322 International Order of B'nai B'rith.

It certainly was a Tabor town, as Meyer could see. Not only had he passed H. A. W. Tabor's magnificent Opera House and Bank and Hotel, but he was soon to learn that Tabor was president of the Leadville Illuminating Gas Company, the Leadville Improvement Company, the Smelter's Supply Company, the Leadville Mining and Stock Exchange, and several mining companies.

Meyer saw something else: His partners in the mine also were engaged in other enterprises. Samuel Harsh, who was acting as superintendent of the A.Y. and Minnie, was also a partner in Harsh and Cary, a firm that advertised itself as specializing in the sale of mines and real estate. The firm also acted as agents for Gibbs and Starrett, manufacturers of pumps, boilers, and mining supplies. Charles Graham, the other partner, was clerking in the establishment of Hickman and Graff, commission merchants whose store was located at Chestnut and Pine Streets.

It was just as well that Meyer had come to Leadville to look over the mines before deciding what must be done. Every man in Leadville, obviously, was very much concerned with his own interests, a state of affairs that Meyer was quite willing to accept. Graham, he learned later, was also in the livery stable business in Leadville. It paid to look after one's own affairs.

Samuel Harsh took Meyer out above the town to California Gulch where the mines were located back to back. The men peered down seventy feet into the murk of the A.Y.'s main shaft, and could see nothing. Meyer was ready to ask questions, but Harsh picked up a stone and dropped it into the shaft. Meyer, too, could hear the splash as the stone hit the water.

Harsh was a mining engineer, and so was Thomas Weir, who had stayed on, after selling out his interest, to handle the books for the company. Harsh's brother Albert was also working for the mine. They advised Meyer that pumping equipment was needed, and that it would cost money. Meyer expected that, but he was not willing to take Harsh's word for it. After a few days in Leadville, Meyer went to Denver, where he scouted around, and finally hired

Charles Hill, another mining engineer, to come in and supervise the "unwatering" of the A.Y. and the Minnie.

Four oilwell pumps were brought in for the A.Y. and the Minnie, each driven by a twenty-five-horsepower engine. Not only was the Number One shaft of the A.Y. pumped out, but two more shafts would be sunk, and each would be kept dry with pumps.

With his employee Hill to protect his interests in the mine, Meyer Guggenheim returned to Philadelphia. Harsh could not keep up his end of the cost of the improvements and he agreed to sell to the other partners for $50,000. Meyer thus acquired a larger share in the mine, and became majority owner with control of the property. He could rest easier after that transaction.

The pumping of the A.Y. and the Minnie did the trick. In the last four months of 1880 the mine had averaged ore shipment of 200 tons a month; in 1881 after the repair was done the miners began taking 50 tons a day out of the A.Y. alone. Soon the shafts were going deeper.

Meyer Guggenheim, in Philadelphia, waited eagerly for the regular reports of Superintendent Harsh, which usually included requests for more money, for a change or a repair. Meyer continued to invest money in the mine, but he was growing restless, because for the first time in his life he was dependent on the judgments of other people.

Then, one Friday morning as Meyer sat in his office at the dry goods store at Front and Arch Streets, a messenger brought him a telegram from Leadville. The miners working the A.Y. had struck a bonanza.

6]

ALMOST AS soon as Superintendent Harsh announced to Meyer Guggenheim that he had a rich mine in the A.Y., the superintendent was forced to transmit the doleful tidings that the mines of Leadville were shut down by angry strikers.

The strike came about for reasons not unusual in the American capitalistic economy: With the news of the rich silver discoveries, thousands of men flocked to Leadville seeking fortune; the oversupply of labor depressed the market; the mine operators grew concerned about the incursions of eastern promoters; the mine managers decided to cut wages.

In the earlier days the common labor rate had risen to $5 a day in Leadville. The mine managers, Samuel Harsh among them, met at the Clarendon Hotel and agreed to post a wage scale of $2.75 a day for common pick and shovel labor. A year earlier the mine operators would not have tried to do this, for the population of 5000 in 1879 meant that all available labor was needed. Now, with 35,000 people in the district, there was a surplus of workers and some of them were offering to work for less than the going rate just to get jobs.

In this past year the miners had come face to face with an unpleasant truth: The mining business was not what it had been in the days of the California placers, or even in the early times in California Gulch. In the new mines men did not pick the ore out of the mountains and take it to the bank. They picked out rock, made valuable only by application of chemical processes, and so the importance of the miner was greatly diminished. Any "bohunk" could work in a Leadville mine and do all that was required of him. In self-protection, in 1879 the miners organized a union, and in the spring of 1880, as Meyer Guggenheim's A.Y. mine was pumped and ready to begin producing ore, the miners voted to strike the mines rather than accept the wage cut. Their point was that the mine owners were growing richer than ever; the price of silver was rising monthly, following the passage of the Bland-Allison Silver Act of 1878. That law required the Secretary of the Treasury to buy at least $2,000,000 worth of silver every month and coin it into silver dollars. The silver men had been holding out for unlimited coinage of silver, which would have meant that every ounce taken out of the mines would go into circulation. The Bland-Allison Act was a compromise, but a compromise which caused the price of silver to rise steadily.

The miners realized, too, that the great days of H. A. W. Tabor were ended as far as they were concerned, unless they found an entirely new mining district. By 1879 the eastern capitalists had moved in and by 1880 they had taken options or made outright purchases on all the free land around California Gulch. The miner who came to Leadville in 1880 with a pack on his back did not stand a chance of striking it rich. If he brought his family, he found that building lots along Harrison and Chestnut Streets were selling for $3000 to $6000 each, and those in the outlying districts of town were not much lower. If he stayed in a boarding house he found that it cost him seven dollars a week for his room. With dinners at fifty cents in the restaurants, it cost at least a dollar a day for his meals. He must supply his own clothing and tools, pay his medical expenses, and see to his own recreation. All this on $2.75 a day? What if he had a family as many men now did? Others in the family must work or the family would starve.

The miners met in the last days of May, and voted to strike all the mines of Leadville. On May 27, the great strike began. H. A. W. Tabor called for the forces of law and order, which he controlled, and they protected the mines and fought the miners in the streets. The miners organized into militia groups and protected the mining halls. The strike was finally broken, but when it was broken the nature of Leadville was changed. Mining had become big business.

Following the end of the miners' strike, the A.Y. still did not pay off immediately. During the shutdown, water had again seeped into the shafts and had to be pumped out. It was autumn of 1880 before Superintendent Harsh indicated that the A.Y. was producing ten tons of ore a day. The A.Y. ore sometimes ran fifteen ounces of silver to the ton; sometimes thirty ounces. At the price of silver in the autumn of 1880 this meant the A.Y. was producing $200 to $400 a day in silver plus the lead, which ran between 20 percent and 6 percent of the weight.

Meyer had sometimes complained about this mining adventure because it was so expensive. One day on a visit to Leadville he had noted that Graham's dry goods store was stocking up on Guggenheim and Pulaski lace edgings. "And that's about all I'll get out of Leadville," he had said. When the strike came, Meyer did not understand the refusal of men to work at common labor for $2.75 a day; that was as much as a skilled mechanic earned in Philadelphia. Meyer did not know that meals and lodging and everything else cost three times as much in Leadville as in Philadelphia. It would be fair to say that Meyer did not take a sociologist's interest in this problem. The boy of the ghetto could scarcely be asked to take a long humanitarian view when he had struck it rich by luck and his own shrewdness.

One thing was sure, the Leadville investment had paid off and was worth pursuing. Meyer Guggenheim traveled to Leadville again. Philadelphians were now very much interested in the Leadville mining district, and several of Meyer's acquaintances had become involved in various properties, such as the Silver Cord Mining Company and the Sovereign Group. When Meyer returned from the Cloud City on this occasion he found that he was a celebrity in his adopted city. A newspaper reporter came to interview this mining magnate and was told the story of his investment. He had bought the mine with Graham for $4000, he said, and his profits in September were exactly $17,231.52, or more than 800 percent on the investment.

"Is your mine for sale, Mr. Guggenheim?" the reporter asked.

"No, sir, the mine is not for sale," Meyer answered. "I would not sell my share for half a million cash money. I have made a thorough investigation of the property and if what the geologists tell me is true, we could get three or four millions cash money out of the mine. I think it is better to work such a property myself than to form a company."

What Meyer referred to in that interview was the propensity of mine owners in the 1880's to strike it rich, then form a stock company to exploit the claim. This practice was encouraged by the fear of most owners that the vein might play out at any moment. A mine might be producing $2000 a day during one month, and then might never produce another ton of ore valuable enough to pay the smelting costs.

When the Philadelphia newspaper clippings reached Leadville, mine Superintendent Harsh denied that Meyer's $17,000 figure represented a month's production from the mine. It represented the entire gross proceeds, he said. Given the price of silver and the declared assay content of the ore, this could not have been true. Meyer's figure did check out, considering the value of the lead.

In 1881 and 1882 the A.Y. produced an average of fifty tons of ore a day, and the Minnie, which was newly exploited, began to add to that total. It was apparent to Meyer that he and Charles Graham had more than a seven days' wonder in hand, and he began thinking about the future. At one time, when interviewed in Denver, Meyer had spoken his thoughts aloud. "I have seven sons," he said, "and each will have a million dollars." If this statement sounded boastful, it was now also apparent to the public that it was possible. The Dunkin mine, near H. A. W. Tabor's Matchless, was said to be worth at least $2,000,000, and the Guggenheim properties were more valuable.

Meyer continued his commuting between Philadelphia and Leadville, but he laid plans for the future years that involved his sons. Isaac, the eldest, who had married Carrie Sonneborn, had moved to New York City to manage an office of Guggenheim & Pulaski; thus had Meyer curbed his eldest son's desire to be off in business for himself. Daniel, Murry, and Solomon were all in Europe, either studying or working in the lace business. Benjamin was going to college in the autumn, and the two boys, Simon and William, would be growing up soon. Meyer persuaded Benjamin to study metallurgy at Columbia University, and in summer the boy was sent to Leadville to obtain practical experience in the operation of the A.Y. and the Minnie under Superintendent Harsh.

The Leadville to which Ben journeyed in the summer of 1882 was aptly described by Oscar Wilde, who came there that year.

From Salt Lake City one travels over the great plains of Colorado and up the Rocky Mountains on the top of which is Leadville, the richest city in the world. It has also got the reputation of being the roughest, and every man carries a revolver. I was told that if I went there they would be sure to shoot me or my travelling manager. I wrote and told them that nothing they could do to my travelling manager would intimidate me. They are miners—men working on metals, so I lectured them on the Ethics of Art. I read them passages from the Autobiography of Benvenuto Cellini and they seemed much delighted.

I was reproved by my hearers for not having brought him with me. I explained that he had been dead for some little time, which elicited the inquiry "Who shot him?" They afterward took me to a dancing saloon where I saw the only rational method of art criticism I have ever come across. Over the piano was printed a notice

PLEASE DO NOT SHOOT THE
PIANIST
HE IS DOING HIS BEST.

The mortality among pianists in that place is marvelous. They then asked me to supper, and having accepted, I had to descend a mine in a rickety bucket in which it was impossible to be graceful. Having got into the heart of the mountain I had supper, the first course being whiskey, the second whiskey, and the third whiskey.

I went to the theater to lecture and was informed that just before I went there two men had been seized for committing a murder and in that theater had been brought onto stage at eight o'clock in the evening and then and there tried and executed before a crowded audience. But I found these miners very entertaining and not at all rough.

The miners, of course, had put on a show for the effete Englishman, but Leadville *was* a rough, tough town. The dance halls were filled with prostitutes who charged fifty cents a dance. Between dances the miners entertained themselves by playing three-card monte, mine manager standing next to mule skinner. In the storage room of the Comique Saloon, the bartender locked up the drunks in rows between the whiskey barrels. Nelson and Company, the undertakers and embalmers, were busy men.

Still there was more than roughness to Leadville in 1882. The "oculists and aurists," Wyand and Hillis, had established an office at 107½ Harrison Avenue. The city supported six elementary schools, a high school, and Professor Joseph Luce's School of Mines at 316 Harrison Avenue. (Professor Luce was a practical scholar: he also ran an assay office at the same address.) There was still no synagogue but there were seven churches, two Masonic lodge chapters, and local units of the Knights of Pythias and the Odd Fellows. There was even in existence a Leadville Temperance Club which met at the Methodist Church on Tuesday evenings.

Ben Guggenheim went to Leadville to take in all the sights and to settle down to learn the mining business during his college summers. By the second summer he was working as bookkeeper at the A.Y., and this was a busy job. The mine consisted of three shafts on ten acres of land. Shaft No. 1 was 166 feet deep and still going down. Shaft No. 2 was 165 feet deep. Shaft No. 3 was 350 feet deep, so deep that an air compressor was used to keep that shaft's air clear. As many as 100 men were employed at the A.Y., although this number varied with the seasons. Ben made out the payrolls and kept track of expenses and income for the mines.

The following year Meyer put up the cash for construction of a concentrating mill on Iron Hill where the A.Y. and Minnie were located, and Thomas Weir, who had been so close to a fortune as a partner in the A.Y. and the Minnie before Meyer came along, was hired as manager. Ben Guggenheim spent part of the year in Leadville, living at 134 West 6th Street. The next year Ben returned to Leadville again during vacation. The Minnie was now an important property in its own right and had its own manager, J. L. Loomis. The A.Y. was so important that its offices had been moved down from Iron Hill to East 4th Street.

This year Benjamin made the acquaintance of Edward R. Holden, who ran an assay office in the basement of the post office building with a partner named Arthur Chanute. Chanute was the originator of the business. He had come to Leadville in 1882 and has been joined there by Holden the following year. Holden was the ambitious one, however. He soon opened a small smelter at the corner of Leiter Avenue and Elm Street, which specialized in milling and smelting for small mine operators.

The year 1885 marked an important change in the mining operations of the Guggenheims and Charles Graham. Thomas Weir was made general manager of the A.Y. The A.Y. and the Minnie were combined and Benjamin Guggenheim was bookkeeper for both mines, a job he decided to keep in the autumn instead of returning to Columbia University.

The Jewish community of Leadville was growing rapidly. The synagogue Temple Israel was built at the southwest corner of 4th and Pine Streets, and soon there was a Ladies' Hebrew Benevolent Society, which organized an annual Jewish Strawberry Festival. Benjamin Guggenheim, however, played no role in the Jewish community. Like all the Guggenheim sons, he was concerned with becoming an American and a capitalist and was not interested in his Jewishness.

In 1885 Ben's brother, William Guggenheim, entered the University of Pennsylvania, where he attended the Wharton School of Business. Simon, having persuaded his father that he need not attend a university, had completed a brief course in business college and had gone off to Spain to absorb languages and European culture. William learned business methods; then he, like Ben, switched to metallurgy, for his father indicated that the mining business would be where Will would be invited to make his million dollars.

In the 1880's Meyer and Benjamin Guggenheim's names appeared in the Leadville city directories, although Meyer was never a resident of Leadville. They became familiar figures in the mining center; Meyer, with his businessman's dress and jutting whiskers, was known as "Guggy" in the Cloud City, although not without respect for his business acumen in gaining control of one of the bonanza mines of the district. The respect was apparent in the legends that grew up about the Guggenheims. One legend said that Meyer had been a poor peddler who came to Leadville selling laces and gained a piece of the mine in trade. Another said that Graham or some other merchant had been unable to pay a business debt to the Philadelphia wholesaler, Meyer Guggenheim, and that he had taken the mine for the debt. Another said he was a tenderfoot who bought a salted piece of mining property and made it pay off. Still another tale described Meyer as a wealthy Jew from Holland who came to the United States and struck it rich immediately. Ben later added to the rumors: He said that he had been sent to Leadville to collect a bad debt and that he had taken the A.Y. and the Minnie for the debt.

Meyer never contradicted a rumor, never added to or subtracted from the public stories. He was content to stand behind the scenes, manipulating the affairs of his mining company. His managers, not he, belonged to the Operators' Association. His managers, not he, were named in the many suits that were brought in Lake County, by and against the Guggenheims.

The suits came often. The Guggenheims sued to evict miners who had built shacks on the claim, so that a tailing pile could be built on the sites of the shacks. When the injunction was granted, but the sheriff refused to act, Manager Weir hired men to come in and tear down the shacks. Then the miners sued the Guggenheims and Graham for damages. Since there was big money in mining there was big money in litigation and it was never-ending.

Other arguments, which did not reach the courts, concerned Meyer just as much as the suits. He was in constant conflict with the county about taxes. He fought (as did all the other operators) with the railroads about freight rates. The railroad operators were capricious and greedy in their fixing of rates. He fought with the smelter operators about the prices they charged for the smelting of the Guggenheim ores. The smelters worked on a system of "penalties," which meant that ores taking extra work to break down cost the miner more money. The ores of the A.Y. and the Minnie were difficult ores and Meyer paid healthy fees for the smelting. Further, he was annoyed at the practices of the smelter operators. After the smelters came to Colorado, the men who engaged in the business adopted the scheme of taking the ores, smelting them, and then paying the mine owners for the precious metals, less the cost of smelting. This practice was helpful to the small mine owner. In one delivery and one transaction he cleared himself of the burden of his ore. But to a mine owner like Meyer Guggenheim, who had plenty of capital and no need for shortcuts, the smelter operators' practice was nothing short of robbery. The smelter operators took a man's ore, charged what they wished for smelting, and then arbitrarily paid the price of the moment for gold, silver, lead, and zinc.

For their profit the smelter operators might hold that metal and speculate on it. The mine owners were then cut out. Furthermore the smelter operators might charge the mine owner penalties for the presence of such metals as zinc and copper, and then take those same metals and sell them profitably on the market.

By 1887 the Guggenheim mines had produced 9,000,000 ounces of silver and 86,000 tons of lead. They employed 130 men, and two miners in a single twelve-hour shift could pull down enough ore from the stopes to pay all expenses for the day. The mines were earning one-half to three-quarters of a million dollars a year. Meyer contemplated these facts and figures, and he also considered what his profits would have been had he not been paying so much to the smelter operators. Thereupon, he began to investigate.

7]

IN LEADVILLE the skies at night gleamed red and purple from the fires of the smelters that ringed the mountainside, and in the daylight hours the smoke poured out from the tall stacks of the smelters.

The first smelter of Leadville was the Arkansas Valley, which had been built in 1877. Another was the Grant, established by a young metallurgist who had been trained at the finest of mining schools in Freiburg, Germany. The Grant smelter had burned in 1882, just as Meyer was going into business, and James B. Grant had relocated it in Denver. It was later known as the Omaha and Grant, because the metal was shipped from the smelter to a refinery at Omaha. There were other smelters in the area, and Meyer tried them or investigated them, every one, in his constant search for advantage that would increase his fortune.

The mining business was a full-time job, Meyer had realized in 1881 when the prospects of the A.Y. and the Minnie had seemed so bright. He then completely disengaged himself from the lace and embroidery businesses, turning them over to his four elder sons in the form of the M. Guggenheim's Sons partnership, in which he had no share. Sometimes he borrowed money from the partnership. More often, he lent money to the partnership. But it was the business of the boys; he had given it to them, and they were making it profitable.

By 1887 Meyer Guggenheim was thoroughly disgusted with the expensive mine-smelter relationship and was eager to do something about it. Benjamin Guggenheim had become friendly with Edward R. Holden in Leadville. Holden had gone to Denver in 1886 and, in partnership with C. B. Kountze, president of the Colorado National Bank, and another banker named Dennis Sheedy, had built a smelter at a place called Globeville, not far from Denver. Holden commuted between Globeville and Leadville, sampling the ores at Leadville and shipping the most profitable ones to his smelter at Globeville. But this system led quickly to difficulties because Holden reported to the mine owners on his samples taken at Leadville and the Denver partners made their own samples at Globeville, and the two did not always agree. What was the mine owner's rightful share of payment for his ores? This question, which had been nagging Meyer Guggenheim for years, began to trouble the smelting partnership. To settle disputes, a referee was called in when a mine owner and a smelter operator could not agree, and his decision was binding, but the mine owners claimed that the smelter operators controlled the referees.

Holden's quarrel with his banker-partners reached the stage where he wanted to leave the company, but he could not afford to do so. Then he met Meyer Guggenheim, who wanted to learn about the smelter business. Holden informed Meyer that the smelter operators made 150 percent profit. In fact, he said, they made all the profits there were to be made in mining. Meyer knew that this was not true, but he was willing to listen more.

"So," he said, "if smelters make the money there is in mining, what's the use of having a mine unless you have a smelter?"

"None at all," said Edward Holden. "Try it."

Meyer decided to do so.

He bought $80,000 worth of stock in the Holden smelter and began to investigate smelting from the inside. His one provision was that his mining son, Benjamin Guggenheim, should have a job as timekeeper with the smelter, and this was done.

Meyer then decided that smelting held the profitable future, not mining. The mine operator took every chance and might not ever strike a good vein. If he did strike one, the vein might peter out. And if he had valuable ore he was at the mercy of freight car and smelter operators. The smelter man dealt in every conceivable metal and he was in control of the ore. Meyer decided that the smelter business was for him and for his sons.

The four older boys were all back in America. Daniel and Murry were married, Daniel to Florence Shloss and Murry to Leonie Bernheim. Daniel's first son, Robert, was two years old in 1887 and Murry's son Edmond would be born the next year. Of the elder group Solomon was the only one still a bachelor; he would not marry for several years.

These older boys were well satisfied with the money they were making in the lace and embroidery business. Meyer believed it was a dying trade, because the Swiss were now competing strongly with his family's factories. Smelting was new in America and the West was young and seemed to be filled with endless mineral resources.

When they began, the Guggenheims knew absolutely nothing about smelting, and like most other miners they found it hard to understand why smelting was necessary at all. Meyer had wondered why he could not simply crush his ore under stamp mills, then pan out the gold and silver, or wash it with amalgam plates so that mercury would pick up the precious metals.

The answer was that by far the greatest majority of ores carried the valuable metals locked in a chemical combination, not a physical combination. Thus, they could not be released by stamping. They demanded the use of the smelting process.

Here is how those early smelters worked.

The ores were put into a furnace, along with layers of coke, lime, and iron ore, all of which were essential to the mixture. Each must be measured scientifically so that when heated the mass did not choke up the furnace or create too much slag. There had to be enough iron, for example, to fuse the siliceous ores, or they would run together and cake like molten glass. Once the metallurgical charge, or combination of coke, lime, and iron ore, was established, then the ores to be treated were put in with the charge and the whole was heated to a very high temperature—so high that water must be used in jackets surrounding the furnace to keep the furnace from fusing.

In the heating process, or roasting, the sulphurs in the sulphides were carried away as fumes and the metals sank by force of gravity to the bottom of the molten mass. The waste, or rock, was on the surface, and could be drawn off in slag pots and thrown onto the tailings pile, or dump. The base metal, perhaps copper, perhaps lead, sank to the bottom, and it gathered the silver and gold. It was then only necessary to tap the furnace near the bottom, and draw off this metallic combination. This combination was then sent to a refinery, where the gold and silver were separated from the copper matter or the lead bullion.

Meeting with his older sons, Meyer suggested that M. Guggenheim's Sons be expanded to include the smelter business and that when the three younger boys were ready for the business world they could handle this end of the firm's affairs. The older boys, who knew nothing about mining or smelting, were not impressed, especially when Meyer said that each of the seven, no matter what his experience, should be given an equal partnership.

Daniel had shuttled back and forth between Switzerland and Philadelphia until 1884, when he came to New York to settle down and take charge of M. Guggenheim's Sons as senior partner. That summer he had married Florence Shloss, who was then twenty-one years old to his twenty-eight. In 1885 their first child, a son, had been born.

Meyer's second son had moved into a house in New York City, and from that had moved to another as the children came along to increase the family. For a time the Daniel Guggenheims had lived in a pretentious town house at 12 West 54th Street, just off Fifth Avenue, which was then a millionaires' row, with the mansions of Astors and Vanderbilts standing sentinel along the Avenue.

(Simon and his family later owned the house at 14 West 54th Street, a stone house on a twenty-foot lot next to Daniel Guggenheim's twenty-foot-front house at 12 West 54th Street. When the Simon Guggenheims were in town, Florrie and Simon's wife Olga could and did lean out their back windows and talk on pleasant days, with their heads very nearly touching.)

These were typical New York houses of the well-to-do. The kitchen and laundry rooms were in the basement. The dining room was at the back of the house, overlooking the garden, and the servants managed meals by sending the food upstairs in a dumbwaiter. The formal parlor opened off the halls in the front of the house, with a study or a sewing room off to one side, and upstairs on the second floor were the rooms of the adults, with the children and servants on the third floor.

Now Meyer proposed to give all sons an equal share in the business; to give Will, who was still a student at the University of Pennsylvania, an equal partnership with Daniel, and with Isaac, who had been learning the textile business since he graduated from Philadelphia High School with honors nearly twenty years earlier. How could Meyer justify such a plan? The two young brothers, Benjamin and William Guggenheim, were wild, there was no question about it, and this only added to the doubts in the minds of the older brothers.

In their youth, Benjamin and William looked very much alike, and quite unlike any other members of the family. Both were slender, with prominent sensuous lips, and they had more than the usual Guggenheim snub nose that Daniel had made so famous. They shared features more delicate than those of any other brothers. (Simon, who was born between Ben and Will, had the heavy jaw and mouth of the older brothers.) And as they looked alike, so in many ways did Benjamin and William behave like one another and quite outside the pattern of the Guggenheims. These were the two, Ben and Will, who went to American colleges to be trained in metallurgy.

Yet training was the least of it. Experts could be hired.

Isaac was the least enthusiastic about his father's plan. Isaac was ever the most conservative of the family and he objected to diverting efforts from the embroidery and lace businesses to the smelting business. His objections were always against rapid movement in any field, and sometimes he was correct, as later in the Caracoles tin speculation in which the Guggenheims moved too far too fast and found themselves up against impressive and difficult competition from a world tin combine headed by British industrialists. (Eventually the Guggenheims would make money out of tin, but not quickly, and not easily, as Isaac warned.)

Now in the smelting crisis, Meyer reminded the boys that he had installed them in business, that he had bought out Pulaski to give them the entire lace company. Again he recalled the Aesopian fable of the man with a bundle of faggots which could be broken one by one but not if all were bound together. The seven sons, working together, would have the strength of a phalanx; alone they were nobodies. Further, said the shrewd Meyer, looking back to his old philosophy, even if the sons might agree to various levels of profitability from the partnerships, the wives of the sons would never agree. If Isaac's wife bought a grand piano, Daniel's wife would want one, too, and she would not be able to understand why she could not have one. No, said Meyer, if M. Guggenheim's Sons was to survive as a partnership it must become an equal partnership and it must involve all the boys.

Meyer was strong and the boys were stubborn. They were not convinced, they were overpowered. They finally agreed to take the three younger sons into M. Guggenheim's Sons as equal partners in the new venture but not in the old. The lace and embroidery business would be kept separate. Meyer would bear the risk by financing the new smelter, and if there was a loss he would bear it. The older boys, in other words, simply agreed to extend their partnership to cover the smelter business without assuming any financial responsibility.

Having settled the route of the future, Meyer went to Denver to confer again with Edward Holden. In January, 1888, Holden announced the formation of the Denver Smelting and Refining Company, with offices at 1657 Arapahoe Street in Denver. Edward R. Holden was president and general manager, and Benjamin Guggenheim was secretary-treasurer. The capitalization of the company, Holden told the press, would be $500,000. The next step was to build the biggest smelter in the world.

The residents of Denver—and all Colorado—were impressed with Holden's announcement. Quietly, Meyer Guggenheim began to consider sites for the smelter. Denver was the first city on the list because it was the transportation center of the state. Also under consideration were Leadville and Pueblo. Meyer's connection with the enterprise was scarcely known. He was never a man to seek any attention. He found that he worked much better in the background, using men like Holden to front for him.

Holden continued to talk to the press. The new plant would be the most complete in the United States, he said. It would have six smokestacks and it would be capable of treating 400 tons of ore a day. The plant alone would cost $200,000.

When the city fathers of Pueblo read their newspapers and

learned what Holden planned, they began to talk among themselves. Pueblo was already an important smelter town. General William B. Palmer was making it into an important steel center with the Denver and Rio Grande Western Railroad. Jay Gould, proprietor of the Missouri Pacific, chewed on his cigars and told the world that he was going to make Pueblo the biggest city in Colorado. The city fathers asked Holden to come south and take a look at their region.

Holden and Ben Guggenheim went to Pueblo. There the Board of Trade presented its case. Denver was too far away from the coal, coke, and lime that the smelter needed, they said. There was plenty of coal in the Arkansas Valley as far as that was concerned, and the Arkansas River flowed right through Pueblo. Leadville suffered from discriminatory freight rates, they said, and from high labor costs. (Benjamin Guggenheim certainly knew *that* was true.) Colorado Springs, also a hopeful contender, just did not have anything to offer, said the Pueblo men. Holden and his secretary-treasurer were not so certain about that, but Pueblo did have a better labor supply.

Pueblo also was centrally located, at the foot of the mountains, within easy access of Leadville and the Cripple Creek mining district. Pueblo was on through north-south and east-west rail lines. From Pueblo the smelter could handle the ores of all the Southwest and even of Mexico. And, said the Board of Trade officials, they could assure Holden that labor costs would be kept down in Pueblo and that construction of the smelter would be far cheaper than it would be either in Denver or in Leadville.

On March 7, 1888, Holden and Ben Guggenheim returned from their visit to Pueblo. A reporter from the Denver *Republican* asked them if they had yet decided on a site for the proposed smelter. "Not positively," said Holden, "but it will not be Denver."

That statement brought excitement to the business community of Pueblo, but also some worry. What use was it to put Denver out of the running, if Pueblo were to lose the smelter to Colorado Springs or even to Leadville?

On March 27, President Holden and Secretary-Treasurer Guggenheim returned to Pueblo. They were met at the station by the

Policeman's Band and one other brass band and were escorted in a triumphal parade up the main street of the city. The mayor was there. The county commissioners were there. The entire Board of Trade's bevy of officialdom was there. Every banker in town was on hand, smiling a banker's smile.

Bankers and businessmen smiled a little less broadly when Holden presented the Guggenheim proposition. If the city would furnish the land, and if the citizens of Pueblo would put up $25,000 in cash as a bonus to the company, Denver Smelting and Refining would bring its smelter to Pueblo. Work on the plant would start within one week.

It was a hard bargain for the town, but the town needed industry. They could easily donate a few acres of sand flat outside the city limits. This land could support only a handful of cattle in good years and in bad years the acres were nearly useless. The land was not so much a problem, but to raise a $25,000 bonus was something else again. The Board of Trade men and the bankers swallowed hard a few times and then decided to call a mass meeting, without announcing the purpose except to say that it concerned the smelter proposition.

The mass meeting was held at 10:30 on Thursday morning, March 29, at De Remer's Opera House. Two bands were again on hand. There were speeches and there was music and there was much gaiety. Then the letter from Holden, containing the Guggenheim proposition, was read to the crowd. A committee was appointed to solicit funds from everyone in the Opera House before the meeting ended. The mayor subscribed $100. Governor Alva Adams, a Pueblo man, gave $500.

At the end of the meeting Holden and Ben Guggenheim discreetly disappeared, and Board of Trade volunteers set out to canvass every business in the city to raise money. Another mass meeting was held on Saturday, and the mayor announced that all but $2000 had been raised. Speeches were made and the bankers and businessmen were urged to dig just a little bit deeper and put the deal over. They did. That very day a telegram was sent to Holden in Denver telling him that the money had been raised and that he could now come down and begin to dig the foundation.

The Guggenheims managed to squeeze a little more out of

Pueblo before the final decision was made: The city council met and agreed to suspend all taxes on the smelter for ten years; the county commissioners met and agreed to do the same. On Tuesday, April 10, Holden and Ben Guggenheim held a press conference in Pueblo to announce that everything was settled and the smelter would be built in Pueblo. Furthermore, because it was being built in Pueblo, the name of the company was being changed. But the fact that it was changed from Denver Smelting to Philadelphia Smelting and Refining Company shows how little the spirit of the West had sunk into Meyer Guggenheim's consciousness.

So the first shovelful of earth was dug and the building began in earnest. The schedule called for the smelter to begin operations on October 1, 1888.

The smelter builders did not manage to keep to schedule. In later years the engineers blamed much of this on Meyer and Ben Guggenheim. One said: "The old man and Benny were, both of them, always wanting to change the plans or proposing innovations that metallurgically would have been ridiculous. The greatest work in building the Philadelphia was pester. Wherever I turned there was always a Guggy in the way with questions and suggestions."

The engineers might complain and their listeners might laugh at the thought of the little Jewish tenderfeet trying to learn the mining and smelter business. The fact was that the Guggenheims *were* learning as quickly as anyone ever learned these businesses. Ben already knew a great deal, from his experiences at Leadville and his curious wandering among the smelters of that city and of Denver. Meyer was content to forget the technical aspects, which he never would master, and to follow the precepts of good business management. This attitude was responsible for many of the changes in the smelter planning. Meyer wanted, if possible, to refrain from using established smelter apparatus because these machines were sold on a royalty basis and he did not want to pay someone else forever out of his profits. A new type of hearthless furnace was devised for the Pueblo smelter. It was not very successful and had to be replaced with the traditional variety. There were other troubles, and when the smelter went into operation there were heavy losses. Once the furnaces did begin to work, the price of silver fell from $1.25 to under a dollar an ounce. Then there came further difficulties.

All the seven brothers began to take an interest in the smelting business in 1888, either eagerly or reluctantly. The older boys were appalled at the early losses, and the cost, which came originally to $300,000, or 50 percent more than Meyer had bargained for in the discussions with Holden. Isaac took charge of the New York office. Daniel began to study freight rates and similar problems. Murry studied the legal questions of smelting, and Solomon studied markets. Benjamin was already in Pueblo. Simon was brought home from Spain to scour the West and Mexico in search of ores, and even young Will went into the business that year.

During his summer vacation from the University of Pennsylvania in 1888 William was given the option of going abroad. He chose, instead, to go to Colorado to work at the mines in Leadville and the half-built smelter in Pueblo. The fact was that although William had agreed to switch over to study metallurgy, at his father's request, he did not care much for chemistry or the other scientific studies. He realized, however, that the family was becoming deeply involved in the metals business and that he ought to gain some practical experience. He went first to Leadville and a job in the laboratory and assay department of the mine. He lived at 31 Delaware Block in the town, and every morning he drove a light, two-wheeled straddle cart up the mountain to the mines in California Gulch.

By 1888, Leadville had slowed down considerably from the days of Oscar Wilde's visit. Usually William came down the mountain in his tricky straddle cart, left cart and horse at the livery stable, and went to dinner at the Saddle Rock, his favorite restaurant. After dinner he would walk around town for a bit and then go to bed. There was not much time for any other activity when one worked a twelve-hour day. Occasionally William went down to the Tenderloin district, which was still in Tiger Alley. Mollie May, the first queen of the red light district, was no longer the leading madam and there was no need for so many houses now, but there were still enough of them to suit the miners and to provide gossip for the ladies of the churches. One of Will's haunts was Ben Loeb's saloon. At one end of the rough, board room a stage had been erected, and around it were scattered tables and chairs. Along one wall was a long bar. Above, a balcony ran completely around three sides of the hall, divided into alcoves which might be curtained off for those who desired privacy. The girls of the establishment entertained on stage in spangles and feathers and net stockings, and then mingled with the patrons, sometimes retiring with them discreetly to the alcoves. Ben came here to drink hard liquor with the other miners and to whistle at the girls when they struck his fancy.

He remained in Leadville only for two months that summer, then traveled to Denver to work in the public assay office of Henry E. Wood for a month and learn about ores that were unlike those of the A.Y. and the Minnie. He lived at the Windsor Hotel, the pride of Denver, and in the evenings visited Denver's red light district. In Leadville the area was called The Row. In Pueblo it was called Peppersauce Bottoms. In Denver the houses were called *Maisons de Joie*, and in Denver young men were thrown out of the *Maisons* nightly for conduct unbecoming gentlemen, which could include anything from being sloppy-drunk to insulting the madam by referring openly to her profession, or by calling the girls whores.

That summer, William Guggenheim took one brief trip to Pueblo to visit the smelter as it was being built. Then he returned to the University of Pennsylvania.

The next year a new superintendent was appointed to oversee the technical aspects of smelting because none of the Guggenheims was yet proficient in this part of the business. The smelter was still losing money—some said at the rate of $50,000 a month— but there were many reasons for this loss.

In 1889, William graduated from the University of Pennsylvania with a diploma that said he was educated in metallurgy and mining. With the children married and scattered to New York and the West, Meyer and Barbara Guggenheim had left Philadelphia and moved to New York so that Meyer could supervise the business activities of the youngsters, and Barbara could be near the grandchildren. William spent a few days at the new family house and then he headed West, too. He would now go to Pueblo to become assistant to the superintendent of the smelter. In a few years, the older brothers estimated, Will would know enough to take over the technical end of the business.

The older brothers had been away from home when William

was growing up, and so they must be pardoned for misunderstanding the youngest of the Guggenheims.

When Will arrived in Pueblo the six blast furnaces had been built. Each furnace could handle about sixty tons of ore. Roasting furnaces had also been built to handle sulfide ores. The smelter had actually been in operation since December, the year before.

Just before William was sent to Pueblo, a family conference was held in New York City in the M. Guggenheim's Sons offices. Around the table sat the elder brothers with very long faces. They believed the losses of the smelter business threatened to destroy their father's fortune. Several of the older brothers ventured recriminations about entering the smelting business instead of limiting themselves to the comfortable and predictable trade in laces and embroideries. Only Meyer was thoroughly optimistic. Here is William's later account of his father's demeanor at that meeting:

He was no longer young and the wealth which was being swept away was more the fruit of his labors than that of his sons. He sought to dissipate their fears and to instill in them the confidence with which he himself faced the future. He could not believe that his instinctive touch for success had failed him at last. This venture, like all his others, must succeed. Very quietly he went about reassuring the doubters. The loss had been enormous: that there was no denying; but they must not be discouraged. He impressed upon them the fact that everything he possessed was in back of them in this—even the A.Y. and the Minnie mines would be sacrificed, if necessary, to carry on to a successful conclusion. They all knew what the mines meant to their father: to him they were the chief source not only of his income, but also of his interest in life. His offer to toss them into the scales in their support allayed the panic which had seized them and clinched the point. They began to plan again, determined that they would not be beaten in their ambitious undertaking.

Meyer was again showing the boys the way, although popular beliefs had him quite out of the business affairs by this time.

It had been in the autumn of 1888, when all the children were grown except the last two girls, and they were away at convent school, that Meyer had decided that he and Barbara would move to New York, which had become the center of the Guggenheim business world. Although Meyer refused to become a member of M. Guggenheim's Sons, he supplied it with cash and paternal direction from the boardroom in the office on Broadway. The house to which he and Barbara moved was a solid, upper-income town house on West 77th Street, off Central Park and just opposite the American Museum of Natural History. It was a mansion, although not as pretentious as the mansion of that other lace merchant, Alexander Turney Stewart. Meyer did not have any taste for collection of works of art or the building of marble palaces. Until the day he died his great interest and solace was the fortune he had established and increased, and he gloried in watching his sons increase it further.

There, of course, was the reason for Meyer's insistence that the boys continue in the smelter business. By this time he could indulge himself in trotters of any price, but he was half ashamed of this second hobby. His first hobby and his love had been the acquisition of fortune for his boys, and by this he meant *all* his boys, down to the youngster William.

William Guggenheim arrived in Pueblo that summer and made his way out to the hot flat where the smelter was located to take his post as assistant to the superintendent. Immediately, he began to find fault with the manner in which the technical operations were conducted. He said the superintendent knew nothing of metallurgy, and he complained to Holden that the man's operations of the furnaces were causing much of the loss in smelting. It was true that the metal yields from the ores of the Philadelphia smelter were nothing like those of the neighboring Pueblo smelter, which had been in existence for a decade.

The superintendent was discharged and another was brought in, a man who used the orthodox principles in smelting. Matters improved. But the price of silver did not come back, and the Philadelphia smelter was caught with ore contracts that had been made months earlier, stipulating the high prices of that period. Now, with a falling market, every ton of ore that was smelted meant new losses for the smelter. Even when there were no contracts, between the time of agreement and smelting of the ores the prices fell, and still the smelter lost money.

In the autumn of 1889 came a new disaster. That summer the

men who worked the furnaces had asked that their twelve-hour shift be cut to eight hours during the hot summer months because twelve hours in front of a furnace in the blazing Pueblo flats were more than a man could bear. The Guggenheims and Holden agreed to this proposal, with a concomitant cut in wages. In the fall, the men decided that an eight-hour shift was proper year around, and they insisted on it. The company refused. The men struck and were out for two months. During this period more ore stacked up in the yards, and the price of metals dropped again. There were more losses. When the plant was reopened in the fall, the twelve-hour day was brought back, but this did not repay the Guggenheims for the time and money expended. At home, the older brothers grew more worried.

The second superintendent of the smelter left, claiming that William was interfering too much with his conduct of his work. A quarrel arose between the Guggenheims and Edward Holden, and Holden offered to dispose of his 49 percent interest in the smelter. He was concerned about the losses and did not have the capital to sustain more loss. He offered his stock at a very attractive price—or a price that would have been attractive if the smelter had been profitable. In New York the boys debated about what they would do, but Meyer did not hesitate. He advanced the money to buy Holden out, and Holden then went off to Glenwood Springs on the western slope of the Rockies, to operate another smelter and to tell many tales about interference of the "Guggies" which, he said, was driving the Philadelphia smelter to ruin.

In order to buy Holden out in Pueblo, Meyer had to sell his interest in the profitable Globe smelter in Denver. C. B. Kountze and Dennis Sheedy bought that up and were well satisfied. Meyer was pleased, too, because now the Guggenheims owned their own property outright, and that was the only way that he liked to do business.

Murry came back from Switzerland to the United States with his statuesque wife and their first child, Edmond, and they went to Colorado where Murry would supervise the activities in smelting. Officially, his title was president of the Philadelphia smelter. Actually, he was the Guggenheim brother in charge of western operations at that point, with Ben as manager of the smelter under him.

The fractious Will was to come in as general assistant at the smelter and then move on to Mexico, and Simon came to Denver to become chief buyer of ores and supplies for the Guggenheims, and chief contact man with the western miners.

When Murry and Leonie arrived in Colorado, Leonie must have been appalled at the rawness and redness of Pueblo, growing as a manufacturing town, where the tall stacks of the steel mills and smelters stood high above the railroad freight yards, spewing forth a constant stream of yellow flame and black greasy smoke. On hot days the smoke and heat hung low over the town and the atmosphere was nearly unbearable. Murry retreated from grimy Pueblo, fifty miles north to the quiet luxury city of Colorado Springs, which had been laid out in geometric beauty by the engineer's pen of General William Palmer, founder of the Denver and Rio Grande Railway and the big steel mill that defaced Pueblo's skies. General Palmer had built his private castle back in the hills behind the city and had retreated there himself, annoyed by the recalcitrance of humanity. Colorado Springs was unique, much like a Swiss city transported to America, for it nestled on the shoulder of the Rampart Range of the Rocky Mountains and here the air was sweet and clean.

William had begun with a title, but did the work of a laborer. At first he had worked as a scaleman, at $100 a month, weighing the ore cars that came into the smelter. Then he had become yard foreman, in charge of storage and distribution of the ores and smelting materials. He was also manager of the sampling mill, and it was in this capacity that he had begun finding fault with the operations of the smelter. In the autumn of 1889 the price of silver seemed to stabilize at 93 cents an ounce, having fallen from $1.30 (the *stability* of price was what counted in the smelter business, however). The labor market was stable again, now that the union men had lost the strike for the eight-hour day; the flow of ore was regular. The snarls in the technical operations of the smelter had been ironed out. Now under Guggenheim ownership and management the brothers would show whether or not they could succeed in the smelter business.

8]

WHEN BENJAMIN GUGGENHEIM became manager of the Philadelphia smelter in Pueblo, he brought in Herman Kellar, a graduate of the University of Pennsylvania School of Metallurgy to be superintendent of the plant. Young William Guggenheim became Kellar's assistant. Under Kellar the smelter began to pull out of the unprofitable position it had always occupied, and in New York City the elder Guggenheim brothers relaxed a bit. Their fortunes were no longer threatened. Actually the brothers need never have worried. The smelter could have been sold at almost any time, and the A.Y. and the Minnie were declared to be worth $14,000,-000. Meyer had turned down an offer of $10,000,000 for them late in the 1880's.

Yet, even when profits began emerging from Pueblo, all was far from serene in the smelter. The Guggenheims had made contracts for ores that carried a considerable amount of barium, which was very difficult to process. Ben Guggenheim and Superintendent Kellar agreed to change the formula for smelting to handle these complex ores. After the change, the slag, or waste, was running heavy with useful metals and even some silver was being lost. In such a situation it was necessary to re-treat the slag to capture the valuable metals, and this would cost the smelting company money. Ben Guggenheim objected. Kellar said that Will Guggenheim had exceeded his instructions in changing the formula. William, as a full partner, objected to censure. Not long after this difficulty, Herman Kellar left the smelter to join the Arkansas Smelter in Leadville, and the growing number of mining men who spoke of "too many Guggies" in the business.

William, of course, wanted the superintendent's job for himself. He was only twenty-two years old and had been with the Philadelphia smelter for about a year. He got the job. Now it was up to him to prove that he could hold it.

Fortunately for William, in the spring of 1890 Congress was preparing to pass the Sherman Silver Purchase Act, which would force the Treasury to buy 4,500,000 ounces of silver every month and to issue paper money to pay for it. This inflation would bring a rise in the price of silver to $1.25 an ounce, and already prices were rising. Nearly anyone could operate a smelter profitably, so if William made mistakes, they could be forgiven in the high Guggenheim return from mines and smelter. Also, although William retained the title of superintendent of the smelter, Benjamin brought in August Raht, a graduate of the Freiburg School of Mines, to take charge of the furnaces. Raht was reputed to know more about American ores than any other man alive. He asked a very high price for his services, and Meyer was aghast. But Ben said he was the best man in the business, and this was just what Meyer wanted. August Raht was hired, and soon his middle-sized frame, surmounted by a big head with white clipped beard and handlebar mustache, was seen all around the smelter. He peered into everything. Within a few weeks August Raht had developed a method of smelting the difficult ores of California Gulch more profitably than had ever been done before. Given the good fortune of the passage of the Sherman Silver Act and also, in 1890, the threat of the McKinley tariff, which would put a high tax on foreign lead, the Philadelphia smelter profits rose to $50,000 a month, or $600,000 a year. Even conservative Isaac could find nothing to complain about.

As Edward Holden had indicated, the smelter men held the keys to profit in the mining industry. It seemed that they could hardly lose, no matter what happened. Consider the case of the Philadelphia smelter and the Mexican ores.

In 1889 Simon Guggenheim had gone scouting for ores up and down the mountains. He had gone to Mexico and had arranged for a contract with some independent mine owners to smelt their silver ores in the Pueblo plant. These mines were located in the Sierra Mojada and Santa Eulalia districts of northern Mexico.

This Mexican ore was very useful to the smelter owners because it was cheap to purchase and heavy in lead and contained large quantities of other chemical elements that made it mix well. The use of this good cheap ore put the smelter owners in a position to give more favorable rates to American mine owners whose ores were more refractory, and for those who had the same kind of ores, the rates were very low indeed.

Mine owners, not smelter owners, caused the Mexican ores to be heavily taxed under the proposed McKinley tariff. But the smelter owners were not hurt, because the tariff would raise the price of American lead. Also, the threat of the McKinley tariff was indirectly responsible for the expansion of the Guggenheims into the international metals field.

Well ahead of the Guggenheims in consideration of Mexican investment was the Consolidated Kansas City Smelting and Refining Company, which maintained smelters at El Paso, Texas, and at Argentine, Kansas. This company had bought mines in the Sierra Mojada and Santa Eulalia districts of Mexico, and smelted its own ores and the ores of others on the American side. The McKinley tariff would deal a serious blow to the Kansas City Smelting and Refining Company. All the ores from the south carried much lead and the tariff of one and a half cents a pound on the lead in the ore took the profits out of smelting silver. The tariff threat also created consternation among the Mexican mine owners, because they had no important smelters in their own country. How would they get their ore treated?

Mexico had first been brought to the attention of Meyer Guggenheim in New York and Philadelphia in 1887 by Colonel A. J. Robinson, then of the Louisville and Nashville Railway. This was a time when Meyer was just beginning to interest himself in smelters but before he was ready to act. The older boys were still, at this point, arguing against heavy involvement in the metals industry.

Whatever encouragement Robinson received from Meyer, he did go to Mexico and secured a concession to build a railroad, and began building the Monterrey and Mexican Gulf Railroad from Trevino on the international boundary to Tampico, through Monterrey and Ciudad Victoria.

Even before the passage of the McKinley tariff, the Mexican

government became annoyed with United States policies and announced that it would place an export tax on all metals sent out of the country. Faced with double taxation, the situation of the Consolidated Kansas City Company was serious. Consolidated Kansas City *depended* on Mexican ores, while the Guggenheims' Pueblo smelter simply used Mexican ores along with western United States ores.

In northern Mexico, mining and railroad men talked incessantly about the tariff. When Simon Guggenheim went south he was buttonholed by Colonel Robinson, who recalled his acquaintance with Meyer and suggested again that Simon bring his father and brothers to see the minerals potential. David Kelly, the purchasing agent for ores in Monterrey, said the same. At this time, in the *Engineering and Mining Journal*, a young mining engineer named Edgar L. Newhouse suggested that what was needed was a smelter industry built in northern Mexico to tap the rich ores. Newhouse had been a chemist and assayer for Consolidated Kansas City and later had gone to Mexico as ore buyer for one of the company's subsidiaries. He left Consolidated before too long, but he had gained a thorough grounding in Mexican mining and political affairs.

The "McKinley" tariff, which was responsible for all this agitation, had been first recommended by President Benjamin Harrison in his inaugural address on March 4, 1889. Representative William McKinley reported the bill out of the House of Representatives Committee on Ways and Means on December 17. The bill was passed by the House in May, but the Senate held it until September, 1890. Then it was passed, signed, and became law.

In the interim, as the debate was continuing in Congress and the nation, Edgar L. Newhouse came to meet Daniel and Murry Guggenheim, who happened to be in Pueblo at a time when Newhouse was in the area. Much had happened in the past three years to change the thinking of the elder sons about the metal business.

Isaac had not been convinced of the importance and profitability of mining, and he continued to operate the lace business from New York, but Meyer's second son, Daniel, had been quick to realize the potential, and he had stepped into leadership of the family enterprise with the assurance and power of a born general. Daniel was now thirty-four years old, short, medium of build, with prematurely graying hair. His years in Europe had given him a grand manner, a fine assurance, and an appreciation of wines, music, literature, and women. Daniel had the presence and the ability to realize that the metals business held far more than embroideries would ever offer.

Murry, who was president of the Philadelphia Smelting and Refining Company, had also developed as a businessman. He was now director of one of the largest banks in Pueblo. He still lived in Colorado Springs where the fine mountain air was unsullied by smoke from his smelter, and he represented the eastern brothers in financial decisions that had to be made in Colorado. Of the other brothers, Sol had become supervisor of sales for the smelter metals, and the three younger brothers were engaged in day-to-day operations in the family mining and smelting enterprises. In a matter such as expansion, Dan and Murry were the men to see, for they had a fine sense of business adventure that made their father proud.

The meeting with Edgar Newhouse came in 1890, after he had left the Consolidated Kansas City smelter and was writing and talking about Mexican ores and the opportunity for American smelter-building in Mexico. Murry was in Colorado Springs and Daniel had come West for a visit that summer. While Newhouse was riding a train from the East, he had the good fortune to encounter Alfred Geist, chief metallurgist of the Philadelphia smelter. Newhouse was actually bound for Colorado Springs for a holiday, but after he and Geist began talking in the smoking car and each learned that the other was a mining man, their talk became so stimulating that Geist persuaded Newhouse to come to Pueblo to see the two Guggenheim brothers in the company offices.

These were the days when the Guggenheim brothers were committed to a policy of unanimous agreement before making a fundamental decision, yet there was nothing amiss in a long exploratory trip to Mexico, even if it was unusual for Daniel to change his plans so abruptly. Daniel, Murry, and Newhouse went to El Paso the very next day. Then the party went to Mexico and the Guggenheims were convinced that here lay opportunity. Both agreed wholeheartedly to the Mexican venture.

On conclusion of the tour the Guggenheims decided that they would locate two smelters in Mexico, one at Aguascalientes to serve the southern half of the country and one at Monterrey to serve the north. The decision was conditional, and the condition was that they receive a favorable concession from the Mexican government.

Edgar Newhouse was acquainted with General Porfirio Díaz, President of the Mexican Republic in 1890. Díaz had been president since 1877, when he brought a temporary end to the feudal warlord system under which Mexico had been half-governed—no more than that—for more than a score of years. Díaz was a dictator. He was also, in his own way, a patriot who believed that the future of Mexico could not be realized without large amounts of foreign capital. Díaz had surrounded himself with wealthy men of the same view. They called themselves the *Científico* party and they were dedicated to the creation of a modern system of industry and transportation.

Dave Kelly, the Guggenheim man in Monterrey, was acquainted with General Bernardo Reyes, governor of Nuevo Leon and military chief of northern Mexico. The Guggenheims began work, using all these contacts. From northern Mexico the word preceded the Guggenheim group and it was soon known what they wanted to discuss when they reached the capital. It was fortunate that this had happened because it gave the administration time to consider and prepare. When the group arrived in Mexico City, a call was paid on Emeterio de la Garza, an attorney who was well connected with the government. Some days, then, were spent in sightseeing and in acceptance of entertainments. The future of Mexico came under discussion often and the Guggenheims indicated that they, too, believed that foreign capital could hasten the industrial development of the nation. Most of the men with whom they talked realized that this foreign capital must be attracted by conditions that would make high profits certain. Naturally no man or group could be persuaded to come to Mexico to throw away money.

Finally Daniel Guggenheim was invited to the office of President

Díaz in the National Palace on the Plaza Zocolo, the center of the old Aztec city.

They sat down to talk, the heavy-faced, bull-necked Mexican peasant who had become a general and a leader of his people, and the smiling Daniel Guggenheim who now called upon every reserve of charm and culture he had amassed in his years of constant upward movement in society. This moment was a grand one for the Guggenheim family; here was a son of a man who had begun life as a detested Jewish peddler, now sitting as an honored guest in the office of a chief of state. Each man controlled what the other man wanted, so it was not difficult for them to reach agreement that day. Díaz wanted more Mexican smelters; Daniel wanted to come to Mexico. So it was arranged.

The Guggenheims would import machinery and erect as many as three smelters. The machinery could come in free of duty, and there would be no tax on the output of the smelters. Daniel Guggenheim was also authorized to undertake exploration and exploitation of all kinds of mines.

This notable agreement was reached and put on paper on October 9, 1890, before the full effects of the McKinley tariff were felt (the law had been passed by the United States Senate only in September). The Guggenheims had acted swiftly and surely and had outreached their competitors, particularly the Consolidated Kansas City Company which had been the chief rival for Mexican ores.

Even with this advantage there was much to be done and it must be done quickly. There were competitors, other concessionaires. One was the Nuevo Leon Smelting, Refining, and Manufacturing Company, which had been organized by Spanish and Hungarian capital. Another was the Compañía Minera, Fundidora y Afinadora de Monterrey, a Mexican enterprise.

Daniel Guggenheim's party traveled to Monterrey. At first the Guggenheims attempted to negotiate with the governor of Coahuila State, in which the major known ore deposits lay. They had gone to the wrong man, however, for the one with whom they must talk was General Reyes. Having learned this, Daniel did as was expected, and soon he and the bluff military man reached a settlement on a working level. It provided for exemption from all municipal and state taxes on the capital Daniel Guggenheim might invest in the establishment of a smelter in Monterrey. To receive this concession, the Guggenheims must build a smelting plant at a cost of at least 300,000 pesos within eighteen months, and to guarantee their good faith the Guggenheims must deposit 4000 pesos which would be forfeit if the concession was not taken up.

This agreement was made on December 12, 1890, and Daniel and his party left for New York. So far, he had invested two months of his time, travel expenses, and about $1000 of the capital of M. Guggenheim's Sons, and in return had sewed up a valuable mining and smelting concession if the others of the firm agreed to undertake the venture. The risk he had taken so far was negligible. The risk proposed was considerable and demanded a consultation of all the senior partners in New York, especially that most senior who was not a partner at all, Meyer Guggenheim. Daniel learned that there was no question at all in Meyer Guggenheim's mind as to the direction in which the boys must head. They must expand and persevere to control as much of the mining and smelter business on the North American continent as was possible.

9]

IN 1890, after Daniel and Murry returned from their visits with President Díaz in Mexico City and General Reyes in Monterrey, the brothers sat down to decide who would go to Mexico to oversee the Guggenheim interests there. Solomon was the next in line for a position of responsibility, because Isaac was now handling the finances of the lace business, Daniel was overseeing the entire mines and smelters business as senior partner in New York, Murry was the western manager and was in charge of sales, and Simon was the mining representative in Denver. So it was decided that Sol should have the responsibility of the Mexican operation. He had charm, culture, and a sparkling way about him. His was the longest and curliest mustache. His was the brightest eye. Solomon was afraid of nothing on earth and probably of nothing off it; Daniel could not have found a more level-headed manager for the family interest in Mexico had he searched outside the fold. Sol went to Mexico, where he was soon carrying a revolver around in his belt, but with his abilities and his charm he was never to use it.

The Mexico to which the Guggenheims committed themselves in the early months of 1891 was not the Mexico of cool nights and hanging gardens that Daniel had enjoyed in the capital, nor even the Mexico of green jungle and luscious fruits that existed along the east coast. It was blue-fringed mountain crests where a man roasted in the sunlight and froze beneath the moon, where water turned to ice in the buckets at night and the dust blew into the cracks in his lips by day. Monterrey was a dingy little adobe town whose boasts of modernity ended with the railroad station and the electric light plant, and did not include street paving or sewers.

The men of the town hid beneath their huge hats and talked about the coming of the *yanqui* while their wives pounded the corn with mortar and pestle and took the family wash to the creek to scrub.

Monterrey was a city of 25,000, mostly illiterate people descended from the Indian tribes who had once hunted these grounds. The city lay at the foot of the mountains, entirely surrounded by tall peaks except for the broad valley that opened at one end. Above the city rose LaSilla, the saddle, named because of the broad depression between two peaks. The farms around the city were anything but estates. The soil was good but the men who ran thin cattle and ragged goats along the hills lived as their grandfathers had lived before them, bedeviled by the gritty north winds that swept down the mountains, drying the air.

There would be a hotel—there was promise of one near the town's central square—but in the winter of 1891 what passed for a hotel was no more than a dirty travelers' inn, an oversize limestone house with an extra room or two for the occasional wayfarer. In the evenings, at least, the town's people came to the plaza for their one recreation. For an hour or so the men sat on benches in the square in the cool of evening and smoked and gossiped and read the provincial newspapers, while the girls and the matrons walked around the plaza, displaying their charms.

Now, to Monterrey came Solomon Guggenheim, gentle but stubborn. The other brothers had fitted into their places in the Guggenheim scheme already, and he had good-naturedly made half a place by seeing to this detail of business and that one. Now, at thirty, this was his chance to show his strength, and he proposed to make the most of the opportunity.

At home in New York at 71 Broadway, where the Guggenheims kept their desks in one huge partners' room, Daniel and Murry ironed out the financial and business details, and when the American and Mexican lawyers were through with their work, the Guggenheims had organized the Compañía de la Gran Fundícion Nacional Mexicana, or the Great National Mexican Smelter Company.

In Monterrey the knowledgeable Dave Kelly introduced Sol at the Foreign Club and helped him become acclimated. They were joined by Henry Dieffenbach, a metals buyer for a New Jersey refinery before he was hired away by the Guggenheims. Outside the city they selected a site for the plant where there would be enough water for operations. They purchased and leased land. They began looking for ore, a task at which they competed with the other smelters and the Consolidated Kansas City. They slept on flea-ridden straw mats in mountain huts, ate tortillas and frijoles day after day, suffered dysentery, insect bites, and heat rash, and some-how made enough progress that it could be said the work was get-ting done. They leased the *Cedral* mine for iron, the *Reforma* for lead, and the *Encantada* and the *Parena* for silver. They made con-tracts with the Mexican National Railway and the new Monterrey and Mexican Gulf Railway for freight and sidings. Kelly knew every mine owner in northern Mexico, and he went around with Sol, talking and smiling and being entertained, to tell all the good news about the proposed smelter and to secure commitments so that the new enterprise would have enough ore when it began firing those big furnaces. Dieffenbach worked with the lawyers to establish water rights in this dry land where water meant every-thing.

In New York, Daniel bought machinery and all the building supplies that must be imported, with the calm assurance that the prohibitive Mexican duties on machinery had been waived in the Guggenheim concession. Murry returned to Colorado to find an operating manager who would go to Mexico, build the smelter, and then settle down there to run it for the Guggenheims.

The Philadelphia smelter in Pueblo was running along sturdily and very profitably. Not long before, Murry had hired Alfred Geist away from the Pueblo Smelting and Refining Company to be gen-eral manager of the Philadelphia. Now Murry proposed that Geist move to Mexico and establish the new smelter, taking William Guggenheim along as assistant. Geist agreed. Land maps and other information came up from Monterrey and the engineers and metal-lurgists began to draw plans for construction of the Monterrey smelter.

The weeks passed and the work continued. In studying the smelter problems, Geist also began to learn something about the wild country for which he was headed, and he began to have sec-ond thoughts about the venture. He had lived in Pueblo for a long time. He had built up a comfortable household and position in the community. Now he was being asked to move to a new, foreign, wild country where there was not even a decent hotel or restaurant. General Manager Geist decided that if he was to uproot and take such risks, he must be made a partner in the firm. He presented this idea to Murry and Murry forwarded it to New York.

Geist might have asked for twice as much money as he had been promised. He might have asked for a pension for life or almost any other guarantee of personal security, and the Guggenheims, needing him as they did, would have been willing to pay. But partnership was another matter. The Guggenheims had all the experience with outside partners that they wanted. The relationship with Holden had left a bad taste in Meyer's mouth. Further, he and his seven sons sensed the huge potential of the metals industry, and with so many of them to share the profits, they were absolutely unwilling to grant a partnership to any outsider.

This discussion arose very late in the preparatory period, and when it was finally resolved by Geist's resignation, time was pressing, so that the Guggenheims decided to get along as best they could with the people on hand. William had been serving as Geist's assistant in the planning. Young as he was, still in his early twenties, he *was* a member of the partnership and he had done at least a satisfactory job of handling himself in the crisis period in the Philadelphia smelter when Holden had quit and two superintendents had followed him.

It was recognized in the family that William was headstrong. He had quarreled with many employees, including Edgar Newhouse, who had been brought to Pueblo as purchasing agent for the Philadelphia smelter. One day Newhouse discharged a foreman in the ore department. William rehired him, and Newhouse quit, then went into business for himself in Pueblo as a buyer and assay office operator. The Guggenheims rehired him now as superintendent of the Philadelphia so that William could go off on his new venture.

William was headstrong, of course, but all the Guggenheims were headstrong, and William did have youth, courage, and some sound metallurgical knowledge plus a little experience in the field. Ben, in charge at Pueblo, finally suggested that William be sent to Monterrey to supervise the construction of the smelter according to the plans that had been drawn. He would be under the general supervision of Sol and Kelly and Dieffenbach, and he could hardly get into much trouble, providing he left the ladies alone. In Pueblo, William was already known as Prince Billy because of his courtly ways and his attentions to the girls of the houses in Pepper-sauce Bottoms.

William made demands of his own. He wanted to have the title of General Manager for Mexico. The brothers debated, but finally they let him have his way. Titles made no difference in the Guggenheim pattern. Dan was running the New York office without a title and Murray would continue to run the entire Colorado operation without more than the presidency of the smelter. Sol could could certainly cope with young William, title or not.

William Guggenheim went to Chicago for a few days to check on the machinery that had been ordered for the Monterrey plant and see that the orders were complete. Then he returned to Pueblo and with two assistants set out for El Paso, where he would transfer to a Mexican train and go to Monterrey. One of the assistants was a skilled carpenter, who would supervise the Mexican laborers as they put up the buildings. The other was an engineer named Van Yngling, a gloomy Scandinavian who took the job because of the high pay, but predicted that he would not come back alive from the wild country below the border, where the only things worse than the gangs of bandidos were the rattlesnakes.

William arrived and was taken under Dieffenbach's wing. He was eager to begin construction work at once but difficulties arose almost as soon as William came across the border. In the concession that had been granted to the Guggenheims the government had agreed to waive export taxes on the bullion the Guggenheims exported from their smelter. Mexican operators protested immediately upon learning of this concession because the native producers paid a 5 percent tax. If the Guggenheims could export their bullion without tax then the native industry was threatened.

This argument was raised in Mexico City and even the *Cientifico* partisans could not shout it down. The entire concession was held up by the Secretary for the Promotion of Industry while the problem was reexamined.

Now the machinery from Chicago arrived at El Paso. William

ordered it transshipped across the border, but the customs officials of the Mexican government said that the heavy import duties must be paid because the concession was not in force. The machinery was placed in an El Paso warehouse and there it sat.

In Mexico, Attorney Emeterio de la Garza began making a round of calls at various government buildings, devoting his energies to the clearing of the difficulties. Such matters took time and it was two months before a solution could be reached: The bullion would be allowed to leave the country untaxed up to 204 ounces of silver per ton, with the 5 percent tax levied on all above that figure. The machinery could come in untaxed.

Now there was nothing to delay the shipment of the machinery to the Monterrey site—save one small matter. The smelter was a mile from the Robinson railroad and in spite of Robinson's promises that his spur would be built in plenty of time there was still no spur or siding.

The responsibility for construction of the siding had been given to a Scottish civil engineer who spent most of his time at the Foreign Club drinking tequila and aguardiente. William did not know what to do with him. Every day the engineer would put him off. One night William took the engineer to dinner and joined him in a drinking bout afterward. William was not much of a drinker, and after several hours he collapsed and was taken home to bed, where he remained for a day and a half recuperating from the effects. On the third day, when he was able to come out and look at the sun, albeit shakily, he encountered the Scottish engineer, who informed him blithely that the spur line had been finished while William was lying in bed. The engineer had taken a shine to his drinking companion.

It was no trick then to begin construction, because the freight yard of Monterrey was filled with cars of lumber, and corrugated iron and bricks from a Laredo brickyard. William, engineer Van Yngling, and the other Americans involved in the construction moved out to the smelter site to be on the job all the time while the work continued. William moved into a shack near the boiler houses and ore sheds. It was constructed to be a company store, but now it served as office and bunk house for him. A few yards away from this shack of two-by-fours, planking, and corrugated iron roof was another almost like it, except larger. This was the cookhouse where the workers ate when they were on the job. The cookhouse was under control of a Chinese cook who made the daily mess of beans and tortillas. At night, William and the cook were the only men on the property, for Van Yngling and the carpenter occupied an old stone house about a half-mile away. William said that this was the loneliest period of his life and that the shacks of Monterrey, six miles away, looked to him, at night in his bunk at the company store, like the buildings of a great city.

Will Guggenheim had his faults, but he was capable of inspiring his men to work for him. In Pueblo days Will had aspired to become an amateur actor. He had helped create a Miner's Playhouse in Pueblo, and had undertaken one role himself as leader of a line of miners who played the roles of chorus girls. He had removed himself from the chorus line only when he achieved the exalted position of assistant to the superintendent of the Philadelphia smelter, and found the chorus line beneath him. Now Will had a captive audience, the Americans who worked for the Guggenheims in Mexico. He could not organize amateur theatricals here, but he indulged his histrionic sense by calling the men together and giving them long lectures on metallurgy. After one incident, however, the men accepted even this odd behavior.

It began when one of the windstorms called "northers" swept down on the mining men and covered the smelter site with a blanket of dust. Hours later when the dust cleared, William looked at the first smokestack to be erected. It had been brought almost to completion by the Mexican masons, but they had been using the Laredo brick, and now Will discovered that the brick was inferior, the mortar more so, and that the stack had cracked at the base and was leaning, perhaps dangerously. Will asked the masons to go up inside the stack and check it. They would not go near it and they predicted that within a few hours the entire structure would crash. Will looked it over and said it was perfectly sound. The masons looked blank and would do nothing.

Will then entered the flue chamber and began to climb the ladder, which was made of small iron bars set in the brick. He climbed to 150 feet and checked the stack all the way. It was sound enough, except for the trouble at the base. When he came down, the shamed masons looked over the work and discovered that they could repair the crack and bring the smokestack almost, if not quite, into proper alignment. (It never was quite corrected, and was a conversation piece at the smelter for years afterward.)

Given such a display of bravery, the men looked up to William Guggenheim with all his brashness and all his playboy airs. They rather liked him, although he was irresponsible in many matters, for he had dash, and that counted for much in this tough and dangerous country. The Guggenheims—Sol and Will—did not think much about the danger of living in Mexico, until one day when the smelter was nearly completed.

Van Yngling, it was said, had aroused the animosity of a Mexican peon who lived not far from the stone house on the mining property. The engineer occupied a room on the top floor of the house, and the carpenter foreman lived on the bottom floor. One night the carpenter was sitting up reading, when he heard screams upstairs followed by the scuffling of feet, and when he looked out the window, he saw four men in sombreros and serapes scurrying across the courtyard in the moonlight.

The carpenter rushed upstairs and found Van Yngling lying in a pool of blood, dying from some thirty stab-wounds. He rushed out of the house and ran the half-mile to the shack where Will Guggenheim was sleeping and told him that Van Yngling had been murdered.

Will jumped up, used the telephone that connected the smelter with Monterrey to summon a doctor, and went back to the stone house with the carpenter. Van Yngling was still alive, but he died just after the doctor came.

The next day every American worker in camp was ready to leave, and the carpenter insisted on going back to Colorado. He did so but the others were persuaded to stay when General Reyes sent a detachment of troops to find the culprits who had killed the engineer. Reyes reported to Sol that the men had been shot. Sol wanted to know if they had been tried and found guilty. No, said General Reyes. They had been shot.

Thereafter Sol and Will Guggenheim always carried revolvers when in northern Mexico.

The American staff was persuaded to stay, but only because the

Guggenheims adopted a paternalistic system. They established a recreation hall, a sports field, and very comfortable permanent quarters on the site of the smelter. Included in the recreation hall were an auditorium for Will's polemics and a bowling alley. The Guggenheims attempted to bring in a similar paternalism to cover the Mexican workers, but found that there was a difference. A common laborer in Monterrey in 1890 received 25 centavos a day. The Guggenheims needed a great number of laborers, so they raised the wage and soon they were paying a peso a day. Other employers complained, but not the workers. Yet the Guggenheims were not happy, because they had as much trouble with labor as ever. The Mexican laborers discovered that by working for the Guggenheims at a peso a day, they only had to work a quarter as many days as they would have for anyone else, and that is what they did. Finally, the Guggenheims were driven to offer free housing and special prices at the company store to any man who would work twenty-five days a month.

Considering all the difficulties encountered, the Monterrey smelter went up very quickly and very satisfactorily. It began operation in 1892 and the first month's profit was reported to be $60,000. No months of smelting losses were to be suffered here; the Guggenheims had learned the smelting business. In the first year the entire capital expenditure of the Monterrey smelter was recovered, and thereafter that particular smelter went on to earn enormous profits for M. Guggenheim's Sons. Eventually it was to be increased to the same size as the Philadelphia smelter in Pueblo. Each would employ 1600 men. Each would handle 3600 tons of ore every day. But in Pueblo the smelter workers were paid two dollars a day in gold and in Monterrey the workers were paid either a dollar a day in silver or forty cents in gold. At that time the Pueblo payroll would be $19,200 a week and that of Monterrey would be $3840 a week for the same work.

In 1893 T. S. Austin was hired to come to Monterrey and take charge of the *Gran Fundicion Nacional*, the northern smelter. Led by Daniel in New York, the Guggenheim brothers decided on the basis of the first few months' operation that they would build their second smelter. Sol went to Aguascalientes and began the buying and surveying work again. Will came to supervise the construction of the *Gran Fundicion Central Mexicana*, and a year later this, too, was in operation, yielding handsome profits. The company now opened a purchasing office in Mexico City and hired agents in Zacatecas, Guantajuata, Pachuca, Catorce, Matchuala, and Las Charcas, who kept in touch with mine owners and bought ores for the new smelter. Sol bought the Tepezala copper mines for the family, giving the Guggenheim Mexican smelters a new direction.

The Mexican adventure occupied Sol off and on throughout the 1890's. When he was at home in New York City he lived with his father and mother on West 77th Street because he was a bachelor. In 1895, however, he married Irene, daughter of Henry Rothschild, the merchant who was later to go into the brokerage business. Three daughters would come into this family, Eleanor, Gertrude, and Barbara. There would be no sons, but Solomon would accept that tragedy gracefully, unlike his brother Isaac.

Solomon was often sent off to do the brotherhood's chores abroad, with the fullest confidence of Daniel and the others. Even before his Mexican adventure he was the brother who disposed of the Guggenheim financial interests in the embroidery business, selling off the factory at St. Gall and the factory at Plauen. One might say that Solomon established in these transactions the generous Guggenheim employment policies which were consistent with Daniel's later socialistic, or at least technocratic, theories on the responsibilities of labor and capital. Solomon, in closing the Guggenheim investments in lace, forced the new owners of the lace mills to employ all the Guggenheim workers as a condition of the sale, and the Guggenheims bestowed bonuses on the people who had served them faithfully. Then they left Europe.

Solomon showed the same business acumen and general kindliness in Mexico, and was immensely popular there. At about the same time that he was expanding the family's horizons in the mine field, under August Raht's direction, the Philadelphia smelter in Pueblo began smelting copper, too. The Guggenheims were moving rapidly in many directions, and old Meyer's prediction that each of his sons would have a million dollars seemed likely to come true. The Guggenheims had arrived.

10]

Forty years had passed since Meyer Guggenheim had arrived in the New World, a penniless immigrant from misery and persecution. A few glimpses behind the façade of the family indicate how the Guggenheims had prospered in following the American dream.

By 1890, Meyer was a relaxed, happy man. He was sixty-two years old and he seemed to have everything a man could want. His girls had gone away to Paris to be educated by Madame Bettlesheimer, who ran a finishing school for Jewish girls from the Continent and America. Yet tragedy had already visited the family again. Jeannette, Meyer's oldest daughter, had been married to a bright young businessman named Albert Gerstle. There had been a fine wedding and celebration at the big house. The young couple had been happy for a while, and then, in 1889, Jeannette had died in childbirth, leaving a stricken husband and an infant daughter.

To counterbalance the tragedy, there was the happiness of the others. Rose, in particular, made a love match. She had scarcely returned from Madame Bettlesheimer's when a young man named Albert Loeb began coming to the house just off Central Park. Young Loeb, the second son of Marcus Loeb, was working in Wall Street. Albert Loeb's uncle Solomon was one of the founders of Kuhn-Loeb, the growing brokerage house, but Albert was struggling in another establishment. Meyer did not mind; he quite approved of young men struggling for their living, at least in the beginning, and soon the young man became a regular visitor at the house. Rose and Albert were married in February, 1891, and went off for a glorious honeymoon to the South, where they had their picture taken on the porch of Mount Vernon.

Cora, the youngest, would marry Louis Rothschild of a New York merchandising house. The boys were either married and raising families or they were working in the smelters of the West and Mexico.

Meyer now kept a "community stable" a few steps from the house at 36 West 77th Street. He called it a community stable because this term was a sop to his conscience. After the move to New York, wealth established, he had begun to extend himself. He bought the barouche and trotting rig he had wanted for years and he bought real trotting mares and sped through Central Park nearly every clement day. Meyer called the stable "community" because he was ashamed to be indulging in so much extravagance, and he masked it by inviting all the boys, and the daughters and their husbands, to use any and all of the carriages or horses.

Friday night was family night at the Guggenheims'. Dutifully all sons and daughters donned their best suits and dresses, the men in their stiff high collars and the ladies in their stays and bustles, the children in their long woolen stockings and high-buttoned shoes, and they came to the house of Meyer and Barbara on West 77th Street for the Sabbath dinner. Meyer would speak to each grandchild, and, depending on age and sex, would give the child a pat on the head, a kiss, or a coin.

Usually the old man was quiet and smiling in the presence of his grandchildren—but not always. One day, Meyer went out and bought himself one of the newly invented electric runabouts to show how modern he could be. For weeks afterwards, the grandchildren were treated with rides around the block in the new car.

And then, in times of stress, old Meyer could be as tough as nails. When the children came to the house and entered the portals that passed the redstone front beneath the big bay window, they were expected to be on their best behavior. But as with youngsters, the illusion was often more apparent than the reality.

After dinner, when the women adjourned, the children were usually left to their own devices while their elders gossiped. One night Daniel's son Harry and Murry's son Edmond began playing in the hall, and in the course of their roughhousing broke a finger off one of the furnishings—a white marble statue. They broke off other fingers then, in experiment, and for several weeks kept breaking parts of the statue experimentally on their Sabbath visits to the grandparents. Then, one night, their destructive tendencies carried them even further and they ravaged a new silk hat belonging to their Uncle Isaac. When this damage was discovered, so was the other, and Grandfather Meyer's wrath was marvelous to behold. He ruled—and it was carried out—that from that day forward only one of the two miscreants would be allowed in the house on any Friday night. All those in good odor in Meyer's house would eat at the big long table beneath the crystal chandelier, and then the children would be dismissed, the women would gather about Barbara and talk of household affairs and listen to the player piano, and the men would adjourn for privacy to Meyer's library where they would smoke cigars and discuss the latest news from the stock market and the metal markets of the world.

Occasionally the proud family would sit for a portrait. One such was taken just after the senior Guggenheims moved to the house on 77th Street. It shows Meyer surrounded by his family, he in a neat tailored suit with edges of piping on his double-breasted long frock-coat, soft collar, and big square bow tie, his hair gray and his mutton-chop whiskers gray, but his guardsman's mustache dark and sleek. Meyer was a more handsome man than any of his sons, then or later. The older boys, Isaac and Daniel, were beginning to put on weight. The younger three had their father's eyes, but their mother's chin and mouth, and the combination was not prepossessing. Another picture of Meyer and his seven sons was taken a few years before Meyer's death when all the boys were working together in the mining and smelting businesses. Soon they would part company and Benjamin and William would go their own ways, but for a little while Meyer had his dream of M. Guggenheim's Sons, a family partnership of multimillionaires working together.

Old Meyer wanted his children around him, so he arranged for Rose and her husband to live in a whitestone house at 123 West 75th Street. Rose then lived the happy life of a well-to-do Jewish matron in Manhattan just before the turn of the century. Barbara was too shy to mix well in the new Jewish society of New York, but her daughters had all the polish that a year or two of Madame Bettlesheimer's tours of the Loire chateaux and the many hours spent at easel and piano and in the Louvre could give them. They were much at home in the wealthy atmosphere of West Side New York.

Rose was a good mother to her children, although they were raised largely by the servants. When any child was sick, no one could keep her from her children or from having her own way during the crisis.

There were family expeditions, rides in the horseless carriages along city streets, and occasional rides on the new West Side subway.

In 1890 and thereafter, Meyer amused himself by playing the stock market, driving in Central Park or along that frightening raceway known as Riverside Drive, and attending the opera, particularly when Gilbert and Sullivan's comic operas were playing somewhere in New York. Usually he wore a Prince Albert coat, day or night, and usually he was seen smoking a cigar.

During the summer months the various Guggenheim families took houses at West End or Long Branch, New Jersey, which were fashionable summer resorts for the wealthy during the administrations of Ulysses S. Grant. The really fashionable families of New York had moved on to Saratoga and then to Newport and Long Island, but some of the older families and many of the Jewish families still came to Long Branch. The houses were usually big frame houses, yellow or white, with broad porches and well-clipped yards. Daniel liked chicken yards, Solomon liked luxury and lived in a big house on Rumson Road. It made no difference to Meyer and Barbara, they visited every one and did not keep a house themselves in the country.

Daniel had become a leader in the Jewish social group of New York City and Long Branch. This Jewish social world of the nineteenth century was separated from the rest of American society by a "vague barrier" (that term is borrowed from Harold Loeb, old Meyer Guggenheim's grandson, son of Rose and broker Albert Loeb.) The vague barrier, in the nineteenth century, was the wall of their Jewishness, which kept the Guggenheims and other Jewish families from mixing with their economic equals, the Gentiles who were leaders of the business world. Among the Jews of New York there was also a hierarchical structure, a Society, although it never achieved the heights of ridiculousness and pretentiousness of the Society of 400 Families, created by the New York newspapers. At the peak of this social structure stood the wealthy representatives of Jewish families that had come from the Rhine River valley in the 1840's—at the time when Simon Guggenheim emigrated. These were the Seligmans, Lehmans, Lewisohns, Loebs, Borgs, Beers, Walters, Helmas, Strauses, Gimbels, Greenhuts, Kahns, Bloomingdales, and Baruchs. Some members of this society were in business, some were in the professions. Only a handful were in industry, and among these the Guggenheims were the unquestioned leaders, although they were mavericks. The Guggenheims conformed only partially to the mores of the Jewish society. Most of them, Daniel included, became members and financial supporters of the fashionable Temple Emmanu-el on Fifth Avenue, but all the Guggenheims were marked by the unwillingness to confine their activities within a strictly Jewish social atmosphere. They might be confined there for a time, and like Daniel they might never achieve any respect for the conspicuous consumption or wealth of the Vanderbilts, but they sought wider horizons than those of Fifth Avenue. Meyer himself never paid any attention to Society of any kind.

Less pretentious than the Gentile families of wealth, the Jewish families did keep to themselves. There was social distinction between the families who went to Far Rockaway and those who went to New Jersey, for the latter had more standing. One young Jewish snob once advised a Guggenheim child not to visit a particular Jewish family because they kept their summer house in Far Rockaway. In the 1890's the Guggenheims all went to New Jersey, and their relatives all went to New Jersey, taking houses that befitted their means. For a time Daniel rented a gingerbreaded Victorian cottage not far from the sea at West End, complete with garden and chicken yard. Doctor Baruch, who was then old Meyer's physician, lived down the street. Meyer would come and stay with the family.

Old Meyer's visits were relished by the adults, for he brought good sense and a feeling of well-being. The children of the families recalled his visits with less pleasure—sometimes with outright terror. Meyer was at his best at meals, sitting at the head of the table, enjoying his double mutton chops. As far as the children were concerned he was at his worst in the afternoon hours. Barbara was content to sit out on the long porch of the house she happened to be in, taking the sun and reflecting on the good life. Meyer could never bear such inactivity. Harold Loeb recalled typical visits, when old Meyer, formally dressed as always, would stump up and down the long wooden porch, killing caterpillars on the ceiling with his cane and brushing them off into the garden.

During these long marches, any child who happened to come in sight was ordered into the magisterial presence of his grandfather, where he or she was plied with questions regarding school, summer activities, and general deportment. Loeb could recall half a century later the feeling of being questioned by a drill sergeant, and the story was the same for all children in all families. At Daniel's, Meyer once shocked all the ladies by speaking up loudly in the presence of the children of the condition of the chickens in Daniel's handsome chicken yard.

"Scrawny," Meyer called them. And he raised his stick and asked the heavens and all about him if they wanted to know why.

"Too many roosters" snorted Meyer in answer to his own question. And the ladies blushed, and the little children wondered why they were swished out of their grandfather's presence so rapidly.

In 1898 Albert Loeb bought land between Cedar Avenue and the railroad in Long Branch and employed an architect named Robert Lyons to design a southern colonial mansion, which was called Rosedale.

Behind the house at the end of the drive was a stable where a coachman named Thomas held forth, caring for four horses: one for riding, one for the hansom, two for the Victoria, and then various combinations for the vis-à-vis, the brougham, and the gamecock. The children had a nurse and then a governess. They learned piano and the finer graces.

The ladies of the family got on well, although even now the Guggenheims were beginning to live in their own spheres of interest, brought together largely by Meyer and Barbara on the week-ends.

Albert became Meyer's broker, but the Loeb income never rose the way the income of the Guggenheim brothers began to rise at this period.

After a few years, as his millions began to mount, Daniel built a big summer house at Elberon, New Jersey, so big and so preten-tious that it must have a name, and so he called it *Firenze*, which had the characteristics of being high-sounding, faddishly Italian, as well as being the Italian translation of his wife's first name.

Daniel and Florence had three children. Meyer Robert had been born in 1885, Harry Frank was born in 1890, and Gladys Eleanor in 1895. They were to grow up as very wealthy youngsters in the very top echelons of Jewish society.

As Daniel became extremely wealthy, a slight schism in the fam-ily did develop. Rose, in particular, began to feel like a "poor rela-tion" of the rich Guggenheims. She complained that her pearls were smaller than those of her sisters-in-law, her dresses from Mrs. McNally's were less expensive and not so numerous as Florence Shloss Guggenheim's.

One day Florence (Florrie, she was called in the family) came to see Rose at the house in the city. Behind her walked a footman carrying a large box. Rose inquired, and was told that it was a pres-ent for her oldest son, Harold. He was called in to watch the box being unpacked. Inside it was filled with tissue paper and when that was undone a tweed riding suit was revealed, the breeches fixed with suede pads to protect the twill from rubbing. There was a pair of handsome brown boots, a riding crop, and a hard hat.

Harold took the treasures upstairs and tried them on. They fit perfectly. He was very pleased with himself until he came back down and heard Aunt Florrie telling his mother that Harry had outgrown his outfit and how nice it would be if Harold could get some use out of it. Harold walked in the door and announced that the trousers hurt, and so Aunt Florrie took the treasures home again, for another nephew. Wealthy or not there was no waste in the Guggenheim family in the 1890's.

With the expansion of the Guggenheims, Murry came East again to head the merchandising and selling of Guggenheim ores.

This became his specialty, although he was also as expert at finance as Daniel. He left the exercise of executive power to Daniel for he had no wish to be in the limelight.

Murry was not an entirely retiring person. Daniel had built his Italian palace near Long Branch, New Jersey, for summer living, and so did several of the other brothers, but Murry topped them all with the construction of a *marble* reproduction of Le Petit Trianon at Versailles.

Sol, like so many of the Guggenheims, enjoyed living in the grand manner. His summer house at Long Branch was colonial in style. In New York City he lived on Fifth Avenue, and later moved to apartments in the Plaza Hotel. He had a shooting lodge in Idaho, and a shooting preserve on Long Island. Both got him into trouble eventually. At one time it was claimed that his Idaho property was nothing but a bear trap, where the Guggenheims baited animals. (He was also accused of holding a lodge on the edge of Yellowstone National Park and luring protected animals into shooting distance. These charges were shown to be without foundation; they are important only to indicate some of the feeling against the Guggenheims in the West in the years after 1907.)

Later, on Long Island, Solomon came into conflict with the ubiquitous Robert Moses, who intended to build a park and parkways on the south shore of Long Island. Solomon maintained a bird shooting preserve there, which he leased, and when Moses came to him in his nicest manner and demanded that Sol give it up, Sol's hackles rose and he refused. As usual, Robert Moses had his way, but not without delay, and not without a fight. The Guggenheims had become men of property and they would struggle to protect it—a far cry from the ghetto of Lengnau.

Meyer Guggenheim, social leader of American Jewry, amused himself on his summer visits by talking business with his sons in the evenings as well as by marching up and down the porches during the daytime.

But after summer, sometimes in the fall and winter, Meyer would take the elevated railroad downtown to Wall Street to drop in at the office of M. Guggenheim's Sons, where he kept a roll-top desk. Until his death Meyer would keep the A.Y. and the Minnie mines in his own name. They were leased out for $50,000 a year, which Meyer split with his old partner Charlie Graham. (Graham was out of mining, too, and had gone into railroading. He was president of the Red Mountain Railroad Company.) Yet in spite of Meyer's ownership the offices of the A.Y. and the Minnie were finally moved to Denver, where they could come under the eye of Simon, the Denver representative of the sons' firm. The boys were taking hold.

Meyer Guggenheim's innate distrust of outsiders, his inheritance from the Swiss ghetto, contained the secret that would bring to the Guggenheims one of the great fortunes of America. The secret was that unity meant control and power.

In the early days of Meyer's search for fortune he was allied with others, which meant a spread of power. When he became a spice importer on his own, and manufacturer of lyes and dyes, he headed in the direction of power and fortune. The A.Y. and the Minnie mines, shared with Charles Graham, brought large sums of money, even fortune, but without the means of sustaining fortune. Money itself had a way of dissipating, losing value or importance. Money invested in government bonds brought security and a growing need for security. Money invested in stock market speculation brought greed but not always fortune: witness the case of Daniel Drew who died broke after having amassed much money and earned a reputation as the wildest speculator in Wall Street. Money invested to control an enterprise, no matter how small, brought complete power over that enterprise and created the base for great fortune. Naturally, money alone was not enough. Basic business management and the time and efforts of those who had the money were also necessary. Lessons in capitalism were being written all around the Guggenheims in the 1890's: Daniel Drew was dead and half forgotten; William Henry Vanderbilt had withdrawn much of his strength and attention from the New York Central Railroad before he died, and his sons were withdrawing further, setting the stage for eclipse of what was in the 1870's the largest fortune in America; J. Pierpont Morgan, with a banking establishment that was far from the largest in America, had become the most important banker in the nation because he controlled his bank absolutely.

It is doubtful if Meyer Guggenheim or his sons read the lessons being written around them. They had no need to do so, for Meyer sensed this basic fact of the capitalistic society: with power one can always employ the best brains in any field.

In 1893 the Guggenheim metals properties consisted of part of the A.Y. and Minnie mines, the Philadelphia smelter in Pueblo, the *Gran Fundicion* of the north in Monterrey, the *Gran Fundicion Central* in Aguascalientes, the Tepezala copper mines of Mexico, and a number of mine leases in northern Mexico and elsewhere.

Nowhere was the importance of control better illustrated than the story of the A.Y. and the Minnie. Early in their partnership, Meyer had agreed to give Charles Graham operating control of the mines because Graham was on the scene and Meyer was flitting here and there in his search for fortune. Graham took this license seriously. Although at various times the younger boys worked at the mines, Graham was in charge and his word counted. Thus, after the Philadelphia smelter was built at Pueblo, and Ben Guggenheim came to Leadville expecting to contract for all the ore output of the A.Y. and the Minnie, Ben received a serious shock. Graham told Ben to submit sealed bids just like the rest of the smelter men. He would take the highest bid for the ore. Ben had expected to be able to see the bids of the other smelters and then bid against them, or at least to have the Meyer Guggenheim share of the ore. Graham said no, and Meyer backed him up, because it was Graham's responsibility, and the A.Y. and the Minnie were not a part of the M. Guggenheim's Sons properties; they belonged to Meyer alone.

Henry R. Wagner, then an ore buyer for the Globe smelter near Denver, was in Leadville one day when sealed bids were opened and the Globeville smelter won the ore of the Minnie, which was then the big producer. Ben and Edgar Newhouse, who was his ore buyer, had been waiting at the Vendome Hotel, expecting to get the business. When Globeville got it, they swore vengeance, and the next time bids were taken Ben bid so high he received all the ore—but then he was angry because he had to bid so much.

Charles Graham had nothing against Ben Guggenheim, he was simply protecting his interest and Meyer's. Here was a lesson in power. The Guggenheim brothers learned this lesson well, and did not engage in partnerships with outsiders. That is why, when Gen-

eral Manager Geist suggested "partnership" as his price for undertaking the management of the Mexican property, it was as if he
had run smack into a stone wall.

In 1893, when the Aguascalientes smelter was completed and the
Tepezala copper mines were producing for them, the Guggenheims were in stronger position vis-à-vis their competitors than
most outsiders could imagine. Wittingly or unwittingly, they had
established their smelters geographically and had established their
mining properties geologically, so that they were able to take advantage of diversification—at a time when the word was scarcely
included in the industrial dictionary. In the events of the next few
months, this position of the Guggenheims proved to be extremely
fortunate.

Until 1893 the western mining country prospered. Ores were dug
out of the mountains of Colorado, Utah, Montana, California, and
Mexico faster than the smelters could handle them. Colorado led
all the other regions, and by 1893 metal production in that state
was valued at $30,000,000 a year, with one-sixth of the people in
the state working in mines or allied industries.

Passage of the Sherman Silver Act in 1890 had created a false
sense of prosperity in the United States and an artificial boom in
silver, for the purchase of silver by the government and the forced
issuance of paper and silver money was nothing less than a raid on
the United States Treasury by special interests. Eventually the
price had to be paid.

In the fall of 1890, with the swiftness that follows a spark in a
powder factory, the Baring Brothers banking firm of England
failed. The Baring failure really had nothing to do with America or
American finance. It was caused by overconfidence and reckless investment in Argentine securities (especially railroads), and the
later collapse of the Argentine treasury. When Baring Brothers was
struck, however, every banking house in England was affected and
British investors began unloading the American securities they had
purchased in order to raise money to meet obligations at home.
Those American securities were redeemable in gold, so the gold of
America began flowing across the Atlantic. At the end of two years
or so, New York's bankers were concerned that soon the United
States Treasury would no longer be able to pay its obligations in

gold. In May, 1893, the stock market came crashing down and many banking houses began calling loans. The tentacles reached out to every part of the American economy, and businesses of all kinds failed for lack of cash, particularly gold. Silver now glutted the market until bankers came to hate the very sight of it, and in the fall the Sherman Silver Act was repealed.

With this repeal the price of silver broke, for as soon as the United States Treasury stopped buying silver the British government of India closed that nation's mints to the free coinage of silver. Suddenly, instead of an unlimited market, the market for silver producers seemed scarcely to exist at all. China cut down its coinage. The price of silver had been about 92 cents an ounce because of the Sherman Silver Purchase Act. After the act was repealed, the price dropped to 47 cents an ounce.

The strength of the Guggenheim position then became apparent to the world. In the United States the miners of low-grade ores had to stop mining. Their profit margin was wiped out in the price fall. And because the ore supply fell off, many smelter owners were hurt. They cut prices, preferring a reduced profit to closure, and the cut-throat competition began. By August, 1893, all the Pueblo smelters except the Philadelphia smelter were shutting down some of their furnaces, but the Philadelphia kept in production because Simon Guggenheim had been traveling around the West, buying various kinds of ores, and not confining himself to silver. He could do this because of the Guggenheims' various operations in the United States and Mexico.

Alone among the Colorado smelters, the Philadelphia kept up full production in the next few years. At the end of 1893, while the mining industry was generally depressed, the business of the Philadelphia smelter was so good that Benjamin moved the headquarters of the company from Pueblo to offices in Denver's Equitable Building, a more central location.

One reason for Guggenheim prosperity in 1893 was the possession of their interest in Mexico. Cheap labor there made it possible for the Guggenheims and the other smelter owners to produce silver profitably with the world price at around 50 cents an ounce. The Guggenheims were careful, too, not to be caught in the box of holding ore purchased at a high price while the world market price dropped. They renegotiated all their agreements with Mexican mine owners so that payment for the ore was made on the basis of world price fluctuations. Will Guggenheim even called on Don Jose Yves Limantour, Mexican Minister of Finance, and persuaded him to *increase* the Mexican coinage of silver money. His argument was that an increase in the minting tax (which the Guggenheims were willing to accept) would give the government more revenue, and the increase in consumption of silver would provide more employment in the smelters. The Mexican government increased its coinage and flooded the Orient with silver dollars, and the Guggenheims and the other Mexican smelter men prospered.

In New York, the headquarters of all Guggenheim operations, Daniel Guggenheim was quick to recognize the changed direction indicated by events. If the firm's resources were spread widely in profitable metals enterprises around the world, the diversification would protect the profits, because one nation's loss in the world of finance often turned out to be another nation's gain. Furthermore, the opportunity now presented itself to go one step ahead in the metals industry, and carry out the final refinement process in plants that would also be in Guggenheim hands.

The principle of refining can be shown by what happens to a lead-silver combination (this was largely the combination with which the Guggenheims were concerned at this time). The bullion of lead and silver (with some gold) was put into a softening furnace where it was melted. Then it was transferred to desilverizing vats where zinc was added, melted with the mixture, and the whole was stirred. The mixture was allowed to cool slightly but not enough to let the lead harden. As it cooled the zinc rose to the top in a scum, gathering the gold and silver. The scum was skimmed off the lead, and then the zinc was burned off in retorts, leaving the silver and gold. These, in turn, were separated by sulphuric acid in fine-grained white cast-iron pots. The pots were heated and the sulphur dioxide fumes that resulted were carried off, the pots were cooled, the liquid was poured into vats, and cold acid was ladled in to precipitate the silver. The gold, which was not soluble in sulphuric acid, was left in the bottom of the white iron pots.

In the earliest days of American mining, as noted, ores had been taken to Wales for smelting, and after smelters were built, ores were still taken to Wales for the final process of refining. With the purchase of the Mexican properties, there was an opportunity for the Guggenheims to enter refining. The Monterrey smelter and Aguascalientes smelter each had rail connections to Tampico, where ore could be loaded aboard ships and taken away cheaply for refinement. Why not refine it in America rather than send it abroad? The Guggenheim brothers agreed to extend their business that step further, and in 1894 began construction of a metals refinery at Perth Amboy, New Jersey, located in a drained swamp between the tracks of the Lehigh Valley Railroad on one side and a dock capable of taking ocean-going vessels on the other. Once the Perth Amboy refinery was built the Guggenheim position was stronger than ever.

The calculations for profits in the metals business were complicated, involving the question of mixtures of metals in the most efficient manner to separate the elements with the least expense and loss. One secret was constant flow of metal ores to the refiner. Another was proper mixture of ores in a reduction tank. These were matters for experts and the Guggenheims had the experts: men like August Raht, who experimented successfully with new methods in copper smelting, and Edgar Newhouse, who traveled the continent buying ores. The Guggenheims supplied the impetus, the financial management, and the capital, and they rented the technical brains they needed. They were now on the road to empire.

11]

AFTER THE beginning, for the most part the Guggenheims created their own luck or at least the conditions in which good fortune simply increased the profit of their enterprises. It was not an accident that when other smelters were banking their fires, in 1893 and 1894, the Philadelphia smelter in Pueblo was going full blast. Few other companies had as many men in the field dedicated to the tying up of mine output as the Guggenheims. Simon Guggenheim, at twenty-seven, headed this part of the organization, but he had the technical assistance and direction of half a dozen other men.

In Mexico, the Guggenheims leased the San Antonio iron mine, adding a new ore to their list. They maintained leases on silver mines, including the Reforma mines where a second large vein of silver was found after the first had been exhausted.

Given so many aspects to their business, the Guggenheims were able to find more ways of making profits. For instance, in the beginning of the Mexican adventure they had relied on a bank in Mexico City to handle their foreign exchange problems. Soon the volume of business was such that it was profitable to open a full-time business office in Mexico City to manage this problem. The family was extremely successful and was acclaimed—everywhere save at home in New York.

In other places in the world the Guggenheims were welcome in the highest reaches of society. This was particularly true in Mexico, where the brothers had important friends. One of the most important of these was Emeterio de la Garza, the Guggenheim attorney. When de la Garza's eldest son was married in Mexico City, William Guggenheim was chosen as one of the young man's honorary fathers, godfathers to the children, called *padrinos*. The other *padrinos* included a justice of the Mexican Supreme Court and Don Porfirio Díaz, the dictator himself. William was popular in Mexico City; Daniel was even more popular, for the Mexican leaders knew that he was the chief operating officer of the family concern.

By 1895 it is said that the Guggenheim smelters were bringing in profits of a million dollars a year. These were not stock market figures but actual cold cash. The Guggenheim concern was a private partnership and it issued no financial statements to the public, but in the metals business the company was known, respected, and envied.

The year 1895 was the year in which the smelter owners of Colorado and the railroads came together and agreed to cut freight rates and smelter rates in order to put the mining business back on its feet. An action that coincided with discovery of gold ore at Cripple Creek and Victor, which brought about a new mining boom—and more business for the Philadelphia, as well as the other smelters in Pueblo, the closest smelting center to the new ore strikes.

In 1896 William came north from Mexico to become a vice-president of the Philadelphia smelter with offices in Denver. Simon continued as secretary-treasurer and Ben was still general manager; Murry was spending more of his time in the East.

The next year Simon was made vice-president and William was listed as treasurer. The change was not particularly important, but it did indicate William Guggenheim's restlessness and his inability to settle down to any one aspect of the mining business. He and Simon went on a long trip to British Columbia, to investigate a lead discovery in the Kootenay mining district. When they returned, Benjamin announced that he was going East to manage the Perth Amboy refinery, and that Simon would be in charge of the Colorado properties. William, who had rather expected the responsibility for himself, went back to Mexico again. Simon, with his ready smile, took up residence at the Brown Palace Hotel and made himself popular with gifts of food and clothing to the poor children of the city.

In 1898 the Guggenheims began thinking about broader mining

operations, and Simon hired mining engineer Henry R. Wagner that summer to travel to other countries in the Western Hemisphere and look for ores for the Guggenheim smelters. He offered Wagner $500 a month and expenses.

Wagner's first assignment was to travel to Bolivia to investigate the output of the Huanchaca Mining Company which was seeking a loan of £300,000 from the Guggenheims. The company offered a company-owned railroad as security for the loan, and—most important—offered the Guggenheims an exclusive smelter contract in return.

Wagner went to Bolivia, and discovered that the mine was a good producer, although it was old and deep (12,000 feet). It was connected by a narrow-gauge railroad to Antofagasta, and the railroad seemed to be in good condition. He cabled back that if the Guggenheims wanted the output of the mine, the arrangement seemed fair enough. Then he went to Valparaiso, Chile, where the Huanchaca company maintained its headquarters, and met with Antonio de Urioste, manager of the mine and its properties.

The Guggenheim brothers in New York met and discussed the proposition. Will and Ben were there, sitting at opposite ends of a long conference table, and arguing. They seldom agreed on anything. These were the two smelter experts and the other brothers listened, somewhat bored. The brothers almost invariably sided with Benjamin, whose judgment over the years had proved to be excellent.

In this case, the decision was also a business decision, which meant that the words of Daniel and Murry were given most weight. They suggested that they might be able to get much better terms from Manager Urioste if they brought him to New York. Wagner advised them privately by cable that Urioste was not going to change his mind about the terms of the agreement, and that they might as well sign. From New York, the brothers cabled that they would not sign an agreement except in New York.

When Urioste heard of the Guggenheim decision, his brown face broke into a broad smile and he hailed Wagner as his true amigo. He packed up his wife and his six children and his two servants and in May, 1899, they all arrived by ship, accompanied by

Wagner, to stay at the Waldorf-Astoria Hotel and see the sights of Nueva York.

For two months the Uriostes investigated the wonderful metropolis, while the brothers Guggenheim tried every wile to secure better terms from the mine manager. He smiled, said he was willing to sign the contract any day on the original terms, asked about a restaurant or two, and suggested that they meet again mañana. Daniel exerted all his charm. H. Randolph Guggenheimer, senior partner of the Guggenheims' law firm of Guggenheimer, Untermyer, and Marshall, tried to get Urioste to change his mind. Samuel Untermyer used all his graciousness. Louis Marshall spent hours of his time on the problem. And finally after two months, the Guggenheim brothers admitted defeat and signed the original contract that Urioste had been willing to sign in Valparaiso. The cost of the celebrated Guggenheim stubbornness in this case was $25,000 in legal fees and expenses to Guggenheimer, Untermyer, and Marshall, $5000 in expenses and salary for Wagner, and a $5000 hotel bill for Señor and Señora Urioste, six small Uriostes, and two servants, plus the cost of transporting the ménage back and forth from Chile to New York. Like everyone else's, Guggenheim judgment was sometimes fallible.

The Huanchaca experience was less than a total success. The ores of the Huanchaca mine were difficult to smelt, they contained zinc, antimony, arsenic, and tin, as well as silver. To smelt such ores, a content of 15 percent lead was necessary for the proper mixture; in the ores on hand such a lead content was available, but in the contract for smelting that the Guggenheims had finally signed with Señor Urioste there was no provision for shipment of lead ores. The Guggenheims built a smelter to handle the ores of the Huanchaca, and then discovered this woeful lack.

Henry Wagner, who was the Guggenheim man in South America, suggested that they revise the contract to secure a provision about the ores. The Guggenheims, however, decided they did not want to revise the contract. The decision was made at the long table in the partners' room at 71 Broadway in New York City, and it was made in the usual fashion, after a long argument about technical matters between Ben and Will, while the other brothers and

Meyer sat fidgeting. The smelter at Antofagasta was in operation and the mix was wrong. What was to be done? The trouble, as Daniel pointed out, was that the contract they had was very favorable and the prices of metals were going up. So any change would undoubtedly cost them more money. It would be cheaper to bring in lead and copper ores for the Antofagasta smelter than to change the contract.

It was left that way, a most unsatisfactory situation for Wagner, who was in charge of the Antofagasta smelter. During the first six months had not the Antofagasta smelter paid $100,000 in profits? Wagner argued that this would not continue, and he was right. Within a few months the cost of shipping in ores and the problems involved took the Antofagasta smelter out of the black-ink column and into the red. The Guggenheims then decided to bring the ores to Perth Amboy for treatment, and in the difficulties, Wagner resigned. The Guggenheim future in Latin America seemed very dubious at that moment.

12]

WHILE THE Guggenheims suffered their troubles in Latin America, the other American smelting men were suffering much more in the metals depression of the 1890's. A number of western smelter operators talked of a combination and agreed to cut prices and, through joint action, forced the railroads to cut rail freight rates which had always been disparately high in the West. The smelter operators of Colorado formed a smelter association which met with increasing frequency in the crisis months to discuss increasingly serious problems. As important Colorado smelter men the Guggenheims were approached in the initial attempt to form the association, and they joined but simply ignored the rules. More serious attempts were then made to bring the Guggenheims into the fold. At one point William was offered a post as secretary of the association, but his brothers firmly declined the honor for him.

This Smelters Association of Colorado was organized to fix prices and stifle competition, and for a time it did so, the Guggenheims lending their name to the movement although they did not attend meetings. Then the Guggenheims discovered that the stifling of competition was stifling them as well and they withdrew, signing up mine owners all over the state and far outside it, paying better prices for ore than the Association members. They had, in fact, never depended as heavily on local mining as did the other smelter operators and that was one reason that the Philadelphia smelter was going strong when others in the state were banking furnaces instead of profits.

All over America, in the 1890's, combination was rapidly replacing competition. It had happened in steel, had happened in the railroads, and would happen again. Indeed, the most effective combiner of businesses in the nation was J. Pierpont Morgan, who believed firmly in the conservation of profits and opposed the wastefulness of competition. Morgan's view was accepted by hundreds of businessmen and industrialists.

In the metals industry of the West, a huge combination was assembled in the Amalgamated Copper Company, which took a handful of competing copper mining businesses and put them together in a multi-million-dollar trust.

In 1898 a group of eastern capitalists were led by Henry H. Rogers, who had formed the copper trust, into forming a national trust of smelters. The Wall Street brokerage firm of Moore and Schley was called in, a firm that had important connections in New York banking. (Grant Schley was the brother-in-law of George Baker of the First National Bank of New York. Schley and Moore were so highly regarded that a few years later in the Panic of 1907, J. Pierpont Morgan would save them when they were threatened with destruction, because he liked them, because they were properly connected, and because their salvation was important to the good name of the business community.)

Moore and Schley began traveling West and South to visit various smelter operators. One of the first men they visited was E. W. Nash, President of the Omaha Smelter. They showed Nash how dangerous competition could be turned into profitable cooperation, if only the smelter men would combine their efforts. Nash was persuaded and he spent the winter of 1898–1899 persuading others. By March, he had secured the promises of eighteen of the largest smelter operators in the United States that they would come into the combination. Two smelter firms at Leadville would join the trust, two at Pueblo would join, the Omaha and Grant would come in, as would the Globe and the Durango. The Consolidated Kansas City would join and bring in its Argentine smelter and the El Paso smelter and sampling mill. Refineries at Omaha and South Chicago would join. Smelter operators at Philadelphia, Salt Lake, East Helena, and Great Falls would all throw their assets into the common pool. In all, the largest and most important smelter firms in the country were included—except for one: the Guggenheim smelter, the Philadelphia.

Unlike the other smelter operators, the Guggenheims were now working on an international business basis, and it was not to their advantage either to split their business or to take it into the trust intact.

When the Guggenheims were approached, Meyer said, "They would *control* my smelter." And as far as that was concerned, he had given his answer. The Guggenheims had not suffered the loss of General Manager Geist over the question of principle and partnership to give in now to a combination.

Moore and Schley and their representatives painted a rosy picture: no more scrambling for ores; they would put in their physical assets (and it was understood that these would be overstated) and they would take out stock in the new supercompany. Half the stock would be preferred stock paying 7 percent dividends; this was guaranteed before the common stock paid a penny. Half the stock would be common, which held voting control. The Guggenheims said no. They did not mind the competition. They did not care for stock, they cared for their smelter business.

Among the other smelter companies, a number chose to take cash and get out of the smelter business rather than continue in a field that would be dominated by one huge firm. The promoters paid out $19,000,000 in cash, eliminating a number of small competitors. The larger firms stayed in, however, jumping their capitalization as they threw it into the pot, until finally the American Smelting and Refining Company was formed. The incorporators declared that the company's assets and trading power made it worth $65,000,000. So 325,000 shares of preferred stock and 325,000 shares of common stock were issued at a stated value of $100 per share. A. H. Danforth, once a Guggenheim man, said he suspected that $12,000,000 would more than purchase all the actual physical assets of the entire combination. Yet no matter the numbers, if the trust was able to control the smelter business of the United States, it could be worth whatever its backers said it was worth for it could control the price of metal. Control was the key to everything; capitalization, operations, and the profits of the company.

Henry H. Rogers, who conceived the monopoly, might have been warned when the Guggenheims flatly refused all approaches to bring them into the combination, but he was too far along in the dream by that time to think rationally.

"It is proposed," said the trust prospectus, "to combine all the principal smelting works in the United States with the exception of the Guggenheims'."

On April 4, 1899, the trust was formed. The syndicate organizers, Rogers, the copper merchants Adolph and Leonard Lewisohn, and Moore and Schley kept nearly 20 percent of the common stock of the new combine—65,000 shares—for their efforts in arranging its birth. The smelter men could hardly complain, because they had far inflated the values of their properties, under the winking eyes of the promoters. On the market, Moore and Schley initially offered ten shares of stock in the new company—American Smelting and Refining Company—plus seven shares of preferred stock, for a total of $1000. It was understood that this offer was only temporary—those who subscribed to the stock before issuance day, when it was thrown on the open market, would have these benefits. Theoretically, on issuance day the stock would sell at $100 a share, but the promoters explained confidently that it was bound to go much higher since the corporation represented almost total control of the smelter industry of the United States.

So the promoters had 65,000 shares of common stock, the smelter men, among them, received 305,000 shares in common and preferred stock, and about 170,000,000 shares were subscribed, with 110,000 shares left in the treasury.

In other words the public was to contribute something over $10,000,000 for a minority interest in the smelter trust, the combined assets of which were worth $12,000,000.

The promoters made the scheme work, in spite of all warnings of common sense. By the middle of March, the bargain subscriptions were closed and the stock was selling at $115 a share.

The first president of American Smelting and Refining was E. W. Nash, in honor of his energetic efforts to help bring the other smelter men into line. Henry H. Rogers, Leonard Lewisohn, and John Moore all managed to be represented on the board of directors. Others on the fifteen-man board were old smelter men: Anton Eilers, August Meyer, the head of Consolidated Kansas City, D. H. Moffatt, Dennis Sheedy, the Globe Smelter man, and J. B. Grant, Denver banker and smelter man who had pioneered in Leadville. Most of these people knew the Guggenheims well, several of them had been associated with them or competed with them in years past. Moffatt was a railroad owner. Grant had been governor of Colorado. They were important men, and Rogers was the most important of all. In a way it was a great tribute to the standing of the Guggenheims in the business world that they would dare put themselves up against so powerful a combination of men.

American Smelting and Refining's officials denied that it was a trust from the very beginning. They said in their defense that there were many independent smelters and refineries, and while this was true, the real truth of their claim lay in the fact that they were unable to secure the participation of the Guggenheims. This they could not do except on old Meyer's very harsh terms of Guggenheim control.

Control by the Guggenheims? Turn the smelter trust over to one family that possessed only one smelter in the United States, plus a single refinery at Perth Amboy? The smelter men snorted in derision and settled down in the spring of 1899 to put their house in order and force the Guggenheims to come to terms. That 110,000 shares of stock left in the company treasury was available for the Guggenheims if they wished to cooperate. At the going rate of the stock it represented probably ten times their capital investment in smelter and refinery.

Meyer Guggenheim and his sons were not unaware of the risks they faced in opposing the scheme of so powerful a man as Henry H. Rogers, associate of William Rockefeller and manipulator of the copper industry. They indicated this awareness of their danger almost immediately by their own course of action. Until now the Guggenheims had played a family game in business and finance. Now, as Daniel and Murry and Ben could see, they were faced with multi-million-dollar competition, and it would be wise for them to secure some strong allies, even if this meant, in part, sacrificing some of the family's independence. Money must be assured, and the price must be paid, although it need not be a sale of the Guggenheim independence.

The Huanchaca venture had taught the older Guggenheim sons that if they were to go afield in their expansion of their business, they had best have the groundwork well laid and have a strong organization at their fingertips. Smelting profits in the United States were on the decline, even for so well supplied a company as the Philadelphia. In 1899 most of the necessary lead for the Philadelphia was coming from the Coeur d'Alene district of Idaho and the Horn Silver Mine in Utah. Perhaps not immediately but eventually the Guggenheims could expect a vigorous struggle by the trust to take over this output.

Daniel was soon in touch with William C. Whitney, Grover Cleveland's first Secretary of the Navy, who had inherited millions of dollars of the fortune created in Standard Oil by Oliver H. Payne. The Whitneys moved in the circle of the Vanderbilts and Astors and Belmonts. This, in itself, was no particular recommendation to Daniel Guggenheim, except that it gave entrée to large fortunes and sources of power. What Daniel wanted were men of wealth who would be willing to risk large sums for potentially large returns. In Whitney he found the man he wanted, and in the Guggenheims, Whitney found the opportunity that he wanted for investment, adventure, and an opportunity for his son, Harry Payne Whitney. From their discussions emerged the Guggenheim Exploration Company, or Guggenex, which was incorporated by Isaac, Murry, and the metallurgist of the Perth Amboy plant. Whitney was a large stockholder—how large was not revealed.

As with any Guggenheim property, by looking at the table of organization, an outsider had absolutely no indication of the power structure or even the purpose of the operation, as a rule. Guggenex was capitalized at six million dollars as a New Jersey corporation. Its purpose was to explore and deal in lands, mines, and mineral resources anywhere and everywhere in the world.

Typically, it was the older brothers and their father who made the decision to bring the family into Guggenex. The younger brothers were not consulted. When William and Ben learned about the new company they were very much annoyed, and complained that the Guggenheims ought to confine themselves to their single concern, M. Guggenheim's Sons, and not become involved in corporate finance. The others insisted; William and Ben then withdrew from further participation in Guggenheim enterprises. William never did accustom himself to thinking in terms of huge financial enterprise. He was always the mining engineer, and play-boy, although he had developed an irritating habit of taking credit for the accomplishments of all who worked with him, too. He also took the position that the Guggenheims endangered their inde-pendence by this move, not understanding Daniel's view that in order to protect the independence of the parent company more financial resources must be brought around the perimeter of the firm. Ben's position was basically the same. Daniel was not sorry. He never forgot that there were seven sons, each an equal partner, each draining off large sums from the profits, so that a vast amount of income was needed to create the necessary capital reserves to keep the family firm going. Two dropouts—two big spenders— would not harm the Guggenheim position.

Many capitalists in America and abroad were persuaded to take small shares of Guggenex stock, including Sir Ernest Cassel, the British financier, and, through him, King Edward VII of England. The Guggenheims had indeed come a long way from the ghetto of Lengnau.

The incorporators of American Smelting and Refining always looked hurt and spoke unhappily when they heard the common charge that they had established a smelter trust in America. As noted, they were on solid ground in denying that they had estab-lished a trust—the truth was that they had tried to establish a trust and had not been very successful in their undertaking. The primary test of a trust is to be a consolidation of companies into one huge supercompany that eats up all competition and becomes godlike in its field. By that definition, the American Smelting and Refining Company in its first year was a dismal failure, and its panicked members held together only because they did not fully understand their failure, and because they had nowhere else to go.

From its very beginnings, American Smelting and Refining was in trouble. The former presidents of the various smelter companies remained in their home territory for the most part, with the thought that they would continue as resident managers of their smelters and refineries, and that life would go on much as it had in the past except that prices would be fixed and they would not have to fight for their shares of the smelting and refining business. Almost as soon as the board of directors was selected, however, it became apparent that there were too many smelters and refineries located too close together, and that they were competing in a way that threatened the well-being of the entire supercorporation. Some smelters had to be closed. Among these were the Grant Smelter in Denver, the Argentine, the Great Falls Smelter, and the Bi-Metallic Smelter in Leadville. Suddenly the men who had spent their lives in these smelters found that they were no longer kingpins.

The center of the new corporation was located in Colorado, and in Colorado the smelter owners had been struggling with organized labor for a dozen years. In the spring of 1899 the Colorado General Assembly passed a law prohibiting employers from working their men more than eight hours a day without paying overtime. The law became effective on June 15.

On that day the manager of the smelter at Durango in the southwestern part of the state posted a new wage scale and announced that his men could work as many hours as they pleased. Of course they did not have to work more than eight hours a day, but when the men read the new wage scale, under which they were to be paid by the hour instead of by the day, they discovered that it had been neatly calculated so that they must work eight hours at straight time and four hours at overtime each day in order to make as much money as they had been making before the eight-hour day became a part of Colorado law.

This plan was adopted by the other members of the smelter trust, and within a few days the miners' union—the Western Federation of Miners—struck every smelter of the American Smelting and Refining Company in Colorado.

The Guggenheims were not angelic in their labor relations, but they were intelligent, and they agreed to accept the eight-hour day subject to a court test of its constitutionality. The American Smelting and Refining Compnay smelters might have done the same, for their lawyers were carrying the case to the Colorado State Supreme Court as quickly as they could do so, but the smelter men were rough and ready citizens who were not willing to be "told" by the unions how to run their business.

With the trust's smelters shut down, there was only one place in the Rocky Mountain West for the mine owners to go with their ores, and that was the Philadelphia smelter in Pueblo. The Guggenheims had all the business they could handle, and the ores piled up in their bins and on the freight sidings. The strike continued for nearly two months, ending with a 10 percent raise for some workers and the return of the twelve-hour day. The smelters opened again, but in the meantime some mine owners had decided to switch their contracts to the more stable Guggenheim operation. The smelter trust men had hammered away at the Guggenheim control of the Coeur d'Alene lead, and the Guggenheims now moved into the Missouri lead district and contracted for enough lead for the future to give them insurance that they would never have trouble smelting silver ores. Eventually, the Colorado Supreme Court declared the eight-hour-day law unconstitutional, and the Guggenheims, without a struggle, were in the same bargaining position that they had been in before, while the smelter trust had lost prestige with the public and had incurred the enmity of the union.

The officials of American Smelting and Refining made more enemies in the West in a year than the Guggenheims had made in all the time they operated in Colorado. The trust raised its prices and told the small miners that they could go hang as far as the smelter operators were concerned. The Guggenheims salved the small operators' feelings and took their ores. The smelter trust members posted a notice saying that they would hereafter pay only $19 an ounce for gold. The mint bought gold at $20.67 an ounce, which gave the smelter operators an exorbitant profit, and everyone knew it. The Guggenheims retaliated in behalf of the small miners by paying $20 an ounce, which still brought plenty of profit. (The miners paid the smelting charges before they received their proceeds from the pure ore.)

The officials of American Smelting and Refining announced price increases for smelting, and mine owners in the West complained that there was no competition and that the smelter owners were forcing the small miners out of business. Talk was begun about a whole new chain of smelters to be spread across the United

States by the Guggenheims. The Guggenheims were not foolish enough to even consider such a program; they had carefully built all their smelters after the Philadelphia *outside* the United States, where labor costs were lower and profit margins were much greater. They did nothing to quell such rumors, however, and many a pleasant smile was smiled in the partners' room at 71 Broadway as the brothers read the pages of the *Engineering and Mining Journal* and perused the New York financial journals for the latest rumors.

The Guggenheims did deal the trust a few telling blows. They stepped up smelting operations in Mexico and flooded the world markets with silver and lead, which made difficulties for American Smelting and Refining. The Guggenheims bought lead mines in Missouri and leased others, and in the summer of 1900 they glutted the market with American and Mexican lead and dropped the price, which forced American Smelting and Refining to drop its prices.

It seemed incredible that the Guggenheims, with only one smelter in the United States, could overpower American Smelting and Refining, and they could not have, had American Smelting and Refining been organized on a truly sound basis.

In that summer of 1900 Rogers and the other spirits behind American Smelting and Refining announced that the Guggenheim properties *must* be brought in. In one year the trust had run up $7,000,000 in debts, after first exhausting its working capital, and it now had on hand $14,000,000 in inventories which looked less promising every day as the Guggenheims kept the world markets glutted and let the prices fall. All summer long, questions were asked and negotiations were held with the Guggenheims, and in the late summer an offer was made. The Guggenheims would surrender their plants and mining possessions, and they would receive 110,000 shares of American Smelting and Refining stock.

Daniel, Murry, and Ben Guggenheim conferred with Meyer when they received this offer but they did not really intend to take it. At the end of the fiscal year profits of $3,500,000 were reported by American Smelting and Refining Company, or about 5 percent of stated worth of the trust. That did not seem to be a bad figure at all. Then the Guggenheims, who did not release official figures, let it be known that Guggenheim properties had earned $3,600,000 in that same period, working with three smelters and one refinery plus a smelter under lease in Chile. With about a quarter of the facilities, the Guggenheims said they earned $100,000 more than the trust.

The officials of American Smelting and Refining, headed by E. W. Nash, came back again to see the Guggenheims and reopen negotiations. In December these executives announced to their board that they had found a basis for agreement with the Guggenheim brothers. The capitalization of American Smelting and Refining would have to be increased by the board by issuing $35,000,000 in new stock, raising the capitalization from $65,000,000 to $100,-000,000. The Guggenheims would receive $45,200,000 in American Smelting and Refining preferred and common stock, or 452,000 shares. For one-third of this amount, the Guggenheims would give American Smelting two-thirds of the original working capital that ASARCO had spent in the last year—$6,666,666.66 of the $10,000,000 that had gone in the struggle to secure the monopoly —and the Guggenheims would also turn over $9,000,000 in cash and solid credits. As for the other 300,000 shares of stock they were to receive, that was for the three smelters, the Perth Amboy refinery, the various contracts the Guggenheims held, including Huanchaca, and "good will." Of course, most of this value was "good will" or the ability of the Guggenheims to whip the trust.

It was a complex financial arrangement, but in return for $15,000,000 in hard cash and credits, the Guggenheims were taking nearly half the total ASARCO stock (including the new issue to be authorized by the board of directors). They would have 452,000 of the total 1,000,000 shares, nearly half of the common and preferred stock that would be then outstanding.

At the moment of the deal, the trust's common stock was quoted at 60 and the preferred stock was quoted at 100. Thus, for some $15,000,000 in cash and credits and physical assets that were worth perhaps $3,000,000, the Guggenheims secured stock that was worth more than $36,000,000 on the market.

They were not giving up their mines in Colorado or Mexico or Missouri; or a steamship line they had built to haul ores from Tampico to Perth Amboy; or the Guggenheim Exploration Company, in which M. Guggenheim's Sons owned control. In other words, the Guggenheims were promising that they would not compete with the smelter trust in smelting, but they were not turning themselves over to the trust. It was argued by outsiders that *all* the physical properties of the Guggenheims could be reproduced at that time for $5,000,000, and they were giving up just about half their assets, but of course, the physical properties of the American Smelting and Refining Company were not worth anything like $65,000,-000 without Guggenheim property, so that argument was self-defeating. What the outsiders did not know, any of them, was that some of that huge profit of the Guggenheim smelters had come because Guggenheim mines were showing no profits, so the smelters could have it all for purposes of display. That would be learned later. What was known in 1900 was that Guggenheim smelters were working at full capacity, and this was worth a considerable sum to the American Smelting and Refining Company, whose smelters were not.

The Guggenheims were investing $15,000,000 in cash, or what was as good as cash, and *this* was the key to the arrangement. The smelter men knew they were in trouble and they did not know how much longer the American Smelting and Refining Company could go on without a new supply of working capital. Neither did they know where else to turn for capital.

The arrangement was generally accepted by both sides just before Christmas, 1900, except for H. H. Rogers, Leonard Lewisohn, Moore, and Schley, all of whom were involved in the original promotion of American Smelting and Refining. These four men had now established the United Metals Selling Company, which had been the exclusive metals sales agents of ASARCO.

Rogers, Lewisohn, and Moore were members of the fifteen-man board of directors of American Smelting and Refining. They objected to giving the Guggenheims so much stock for so little in assets, but were forced to yield because they had no alternate plan for raising the needed cash. All was going smoothly until one day Daniel told a reporter that one of the great advantages of the merger was that ASARCO would be able to use the selling organization of the Guggenheims. When Rogers, Lewisohn, Schley, and Moore read this report they were stunned. This move would threaten a business that was to them far more lucrative than

ASARCO. Rogers grew furious and began a suit to void the merger. He also took a more characteristic action; he called into his office one of the important brokers of Wall Street who specialized in "bear" activities, or the artificial depression of values of a given stock. Wrecking, they called it, and it was a well-known specialty of David Lamar, who had done it before for H. H. Rogers. In the first two weeks of February, thousands of shares of American Smelting and Refining common, held by the conspirators, were suddenly thrown on the market. Panic sellers followed, and in one day 100,000 shares were dumped, causing the price to drop $7 a share, from 62 to 55.

The Guggenheim cash position was not as strong as it might have been, because they were committed to turning over some $15,000,000 in the merger, but in recent months the Guggenheims had acquired powerful allies, including William Whitney. Whitney agreed that it would be useful for the Guggenheim interests to control American Smelting and Refining and agreed to back them. Suddenly the thousands of shares of stock found buyers at the low price. In a few weeks some 60,000 shares were sold on the market to the Guggenheims and their allies. Once the stockholders of ASARCO approved the Guggenheim deal, the family would control the company with 502,000 of the total 1,000,000 shares.

In the middle of February, 1901, a meeting of the stockholders of American Smelting and Refining was held to act on the board's proposal that the company's stock be increased to the 1,000,000 share figure, to take in the Guggenheims. The majority of the stockholders were perfectly willing to do this, but the Rogers faction managed to secure an injunction against the increase.

Then came a struggle in the New Jersey courts. The Rogers men claimed that the Guggenheims had inflated the value of their properties for the purposes of the exchange of assets with American Smelting and Refining. No one mentioned the previous estimates of inflation of the values of the properties that went into American Smelting and Refining, which were worth perhaps one-sixth of the valuation placed on the capital stock.

The Guggenheim attorney, Samuel Untermyer, showed that the Guggenheim properties had earned $3,600,000 in the preceding twelve months, which meant 8 percent on a capitalization of

$45,000,000, which the Guggenheims now claimed. Untermyer did not say anything about the assignment of the mining profits to the smelters for the purpose of showing this large profit.

The Rogers faction charged that the Guggenheims had attempted to bribe the board of directors of American Smelting and Refining by offering more than 100,000 shares of stock to these directors at rates substantially below the market price of the stock. If this were true, the Guggenheims must have begun their negotiations with American Smelting and Refining only to secure a huge profit on their investment and then become a part of the trust, for the sacrifice of so much stock would have kept them from having an absolute majority. Once the charge was made, the bribery attempt, if there ever was one, fell through, and the Guggenheims were left with the prospect of backing away from the trust, or seeking to control it.

In March, the New Jersey courts held that Rogers and his friends had failed to prove their case, that $45,000,000 was not an excessive price to pay for the Guggenheim properties, considering the industry involved. A higher court soon overturned that decision and issued an injunction against issuance of the new stock by American Smelting and Refining. The decision was widely hailed in the press as a victory for right and justice over the trusts. The reason was that with the formation of the United States Steel Company by J. Pierpont Morgan, there had come to the United States the first billion-dollar trust, and Americans awakened at the turn of the century and decided that they were being sold down the river to big business. President McKinley expressed serious concern about the trusts, and had set the government wheels in motion to begin investigation of the business community. A few months earlier, when the Guggenheims battled the American Smelting and Refining Company openly in Colorado and Missouri and Mexico, they were hailed as the champions of the people against the bloated capitalists. In the spring of 1901, however, the Guggenheims were depicted by the newspaper cartoonists as the most bloated of all American capitalists.

Many months had passed since the initial truce was made between the Guggenheims and the smelter trust, and the *entente cordiale* that existed had shown itself in the profits of the two companies. Relieved of competition, since they fully expected to become parts of the same firm, both companies had increased their profits greatly. Guggenheim profits for 1900 were said to be $4,500,000 and ASARCO's were nearly $6,000,000. Such increases had been brought about by cooperation.

For example, a famous "ore filching" case was resolved amicably this year. In 1899 the Guggenheims had purchased the Encantada mine in the Sierra Mojada of northern Mexico. The property adjoined a rich silver lode that belonged to Consolidated Kansas City. Shortly after the Guggenheims began working the mine, Consolidated Kansas City filed suit charging that the Guggenheims had dug their shaft through into Consolidated Kansas City's property, well below ground, and were mining Consolidated Kansas City ore. This expensive suit dragged on for more than a year until it was finally settled in the cordial atmosphere that accompanied the agreement to bring the Guggenheims into ASARCO.

The court defeat of the ASARCO-Guggenheim merger left the Guggenheims with an important decision: Would they continue to try to fight Rogers, with the Standard Oil billions behind him? Would they withdraw and go back to their old ways of doing business during the struggle with American Smelting and Refining? When the struggle began, the Guggenheims were a close-knit, homogeneous business group, carrying on their affairs in the manner that Meyer had prescribed for them so many years before. In fighting the trust, Daniel had organized Guggenex, the lace and embroidery business had been sold off to provide elbow room, and the Guggenheim pattern was subtly rearranged. The Guggenheims were now big businessmen. Until 1900 the Guggenheim name had scarcely ever appeared in the newspapers outside the West and the technical mining journals. *The New York Times* ignored them. After 1900 the Guggenheims suddenly became known in every American community. The struggle with the trust had brought them to public attention in the beginning, and the agreement with the trust, even though outlawed, had brought them into public contumely now. There was no going back. The Guggenheims could not retire to be again the unknown Jewish millionaires they had been in 1899. They must sink or swim in the rough waters of the eastern business community.

The way out involved buying the good will of H. H. Rogers and the Lewisohn brothers, who had organized the United Metals Company to sell the products of the smelter trust. Although the Guggenheims had their own sales organization in Europe, they agreed to allow United Metals to handle the products of the combined Guggenheim-American smelter properties. This was all that Rogers and his associates really wanted. Rogers withdrew the suit, so no block remained in the way of agreement. The terms of the agreement were thrashed out in an all-day meeting in lawyer Untermyer's office. Daniel was there representing the Guggenheims. Rogers and Lewisohn represented United Metals. At the end of this day, April 8, 1901, the negotiators emerged smiling and went to Delmonico's restaurant for dinner. Later newspapermen met Daniel at the entrance to his house, where they had been waiting for him for hours, and he confirmed the agreement.

The stock was delivered to the Guggenheims, and the next day, April 9, American Smelting and Refining rose thirteen points, and kept going up. Within two months the preferred stock with its guaranteed 7 percent dividend was a blue-chip stock selling well above its par value.

A week after the agreement was reached, the stockholders met again and this time approved the actions of their board of directors. Five Guggenheim brothers—Isaac, Daniel, Murry, Solomon, and Simon—joined the board of directors of American Smelting and Refining, and Daniel became chairman of the board while Simon became treasurer.

On April 27, when the board of directors met, Daniel was also elected chairman of the executive committee and his four brothers were elected to the committee, along with E. W. Nash, president; Barton Sewell, vice-president; Dennis Sheedy, A. R. Meyer, Anton Eilers, and J. B. Grant. All six of the other members of the executive committee were old mining and smelter men. Rogers and Lewisohn, who represented the original trust organizers, were nowhere in sight, nor were Moore and Schley, the brokers. The American Smelting and Refining Company was back in the hands of the mining men. There was only one difference. The Guggenheims controlled the company because they and their allies owned more than 51 percent of the stock.

13]

AT THE moment when Daniel Guggenheim was engineering the grand financial coup that would bring all members of the family wealth beyond any previous dreams they might have had, the Guggenheim phalanx was breaking down. For those blessed with hindsight, the cause of family rupture was easy to see and easy to describe: too many sons, too far apart in ages and perspective.

The split began, as previously noted, with the decision of Daniel to expand the family activities and take in a Gentile partner, William A. Whitney. William and Benjamin objected and quit working with their brothers, although they maintained their interest in the family partnership's ventures begun before that time, and took their share of the profits from those ventures in which they had participated.

The popular myth of the Guggenheims in 1900 showed them as seven dragon slayers united as one. But even as the newspaper cartoonists embellished the myth, it proved untrue.

The age difference in the family divided the boys almost as though they came from different generations, with Isaac, Daniel, Murry, and Solomon standing on one side, and Benjamin, Simon, and William on the other. The brothers were separated by much more than age. They had grown up in two different Americas. The older brothers grew up as sons of a man who began as a peddler and was no more than a well-to-do businessman when Solomon went through his teens. The younger boys grew up as sons of one of the wealthiest men in America. The youngest son, William, was also the most spoiled of the lot, and it was William who brought about the breach in the family.

Of all the sons of Meyer Guggenheim, William seemed in his youth to be the most predictable—and yet he turned out to be the unpredictable Guggenheim, who broke with his family, broke with the business concern of the Guggenheims, and indulged in quarrels so bitter that they reached the courts and exposed the other members of the family to unfavorable publicity.

William had been born on November 6, 1868, in the Franklin Street house, during that first period when the Guggenheims had lived in respectable but modest residential areas of Philadelphia. William's birth came just a few months after Meyer's coup in the lye market, a stroke followed by their move to an upper-class residential district. William, one might say, was the one Guggenheim who grew up with a solid silver spoon in his mouth. He was a pale, slender child, very small, and he was spoiled by everyone. Soon the four older brothers were gone, married, or off in Switzerland. William's influences in youth were his mother, his older sister Jeannette, his brothers Ben, Simon, and Robert, and his two younger sisters, Rose and Cora.

Wiliam had attended kindergarten, apparently the first and only Guggenheim to do so, and then went to the Philadelphia public schools as his brothers and sisters all had before him. All the brothers, and particularly the older sons of Meyer, were father-oriented; William was his mother's boy. Perhaps the reason lay in his physique. Even as an adult he never topped five feet four inches in height. He was the baby of the family.

In school he was pampered by his first-grade teacher, a Miss May. Later, writing of himself in the third person, William said, "This, too, was part of his education; gave him his first intimation of the charm he was capable of exerting on older people."

As a student William liked elocution courses. He always would like talking and when he had a captive audience in later years, as in the smelter camp at Monterrey, he would read aloud to his employees. Twenty years after he left school he could recite *The Wreck of the Hesperus*, *Excelsior*, and *Gunga Din*, and that epic *The Seminole's Reply*. Perhaps William ought to have grown up to become an actor (he once said as much). With gamecock strut and aggressive eye, he delighted in forcing himself to be "captain" of everything. He boasted of his fighting abilities, too.

After Benjamin had gone to college, the way was paved for William and in 1885, when he was sixteen years old, he entered the University of Pennsylvania. There he was coxswain of a club crew, an orator, but not a very good student. He lived at home. For a time he attended the Wharton School of Business and Finance. In the summer of his junior year of college, as noted, he had gone out to Leadville and there had sampled the rigors of work in the mines and the delights of night life in the saloons and dance halls.

In Pueblo, in Monterrey, in Denver—no matter where Will traveled, he proved himself to be contentious and difficult, and by 1899 he had quite exhausted the patience of his brothers. That year they put him in charge of the supply department of American Smelting and Refining in New York, a job he found so dull that he decided to get out of the metals business altogether. His reason for breaking with the others was given at length in his autobiography —that he had done his share—but it does not stand up very well; the real reason was pique because he did not think his brothers accorded him the respect he should receive. The other brothers were much too busy making money to bother themselves with Will's delusions. He left M. Guggenheim's Sons with their good wishes, but without their regrets.

Ben's story was slightly different. Ben had been called back from the West in 1894 to build and supervise the plant at Perth Amboy, since he had considerable experience in smelter management, which would prove valuable in the new processes. There was considerable difficulty in the beginning in finding the right people to manage the technical affairs of smelters and refining plants, but by following Meyer's old dictum of being willing to pay any price, even an unreasonable one, for the best brains obtainable, the Guggenheims soon had the Perth Amboy refinery in successful and profitable operation. For the next five years Ben continued to supervise this aspect of the Guggenheim operations. The year 1899 came, and with it the decision to form the Guggenheim Exploration Company.

So there was more to the partnership breakup than met the eye. Mores had a great deal to do with the schism. Consider the boys for a moment: Isaac, strait-laced and solemn, who married young and devoted his life to his family; Daniel, the business whiplash of the family, who had little time for humor, who suffered from stomach troubles, who never looked at a woman other than his wife; Murry, another of the old school; Solomon, the median son, who had a fine eye for a mistress but was discreet in the best Victorian manner; Simon, born between Ben and Will, but a throwback to the old ways. And then consider Ben and Will.

Ben and Will Guggenheim had grown up in the mining camp at Leadville, the only two brothers really to spend any time there, and they had acquired a taste for fast life in the saloons and bawdy houses.

Ben had married a handsome New York girl of good family, Florette Seligman of the banking Seligmans. Almost immediately he had set about destroying his marriage by an extramarital affair. Three daughters would be born in that household, and they would grow up in an atmosphere of dissension. Isaac, Daniel, Murry, and Simon looked with considerable disfavor on quarrelsome Ben in the family meetings. They also disapproved of Ben's personal excesses, which he took little pains to conceal. He was, the family believed, as near a black sheep as existed among the Guggenheims.

The other brothers did not complain when Ben left the fold. On January 2, 1900, Ben, Florette, their daughters, little Benita, little Marguerite (later to be called Peggy), and Uncle Will sailed for Europe. Forty-eight hours later they rushed back home on receipt of a cable saying that Barbara was dying. Her last illness, acute diabetes, brought the Guggenheim brothers together again around the hearth on 77th Street, but the reunion did not heal the breach. The families were growing away from one another more and more, the divisions being into age groups, with the daughters, who were no longer Guggenheims, moving away from the Guggenheim boys.

When Barbara died in March, Rose Guggenheim Loeb suffered a nervous breakdown. They called it nervous prostration. Later that year she became ill and was operated on for some serious ailment, which was kept very secret within the family. The Loebs went to Europe for several months, and this separation marked the beginning of another gradual withdrawal of one segment of the family.

Ben and his family took their trip to Europe, too, and with them the trip meant the family cord was broken forever. Ben took up residence in Paris that year and became the European émigré of the family. He acquired a French marquise as mistress, and settled down to the European life without an apparent care in the world.

When Will and the Ben Guggenheim family sailed for Europe in January, 1900, and were recalled to attend the last illness of the boys' mother, William was undoubtedly the most seriously affected of all the Guggenheims. For three days after Barbara's death he kept to his room in the house on 77th Street and refused to see anyone, even other members of the family. "In his bitter sorrow," wrote the third person autobiographer later, "he felt all foundations swept away and his soul lost."

Will abandoned his plans to return to Europe that year and instead he loafed about New York. He joined the Pennsylvania Society and the University of Pennsylvania Club of New York. He went to many unimportant meetings, and made many speeches, but after his speeches usually only he could remember what he had been talking about. What else he did during that year remains a family secret, except for one unfortunate matter that could not be kept secret: He appeared in Hoboken, New Jersey, on November 30, 1900, with a marriage license and there married Grace Brown Herbert, a Gentile divorcée from California.

William knew there would be trouble about the marriage. He told Grace that it was bound to come, because she was a Gentile, but he assured her that in time he could straighten it out and placate his father. Grace lived at the Waldorf-Astoria Hotel and William kept living at home. He was afraid to tell Meyer about his marriage, but eventually he did tell Daniel, and Daniel erupted just as Meyer would have done.

Daniel insisted on a meeting with Grace Brown Herbert Guggenheim, and it was arranged. January 2, 1901. Daniel told Will be was an incompetent fool and ordered him to stay away from the meeting and to pack; he was being sent to Europe. His ship would sail two days later.

Daniel counseled with Samuel Untermyer, the Guggenheim lawyer, before seeing William's wife. Then in his finest executive manner, Daniel told Grace she must go to North Dakota where it was easy to get a divorce. She would be taken care of handsomely, he said, after she had divorced William.

Grace said she did not want the Guggenheim money, she

wanted Will. Daniel said that Will was a weakling and not worth having, and she would be much better off with a slice of Guggenheim money.

Grace said no.

Daniel said that Will would go to Europe and that Grace would not get a cent unless she agreed to do as he said.

Will, like a little lamb, got on the ship and went to Europe. He and Ben and Florette went to Monte Carlo's Hotel de Paris to stay for a month, Will spending most of his time in the gambling rooms of the casino, losing money at roulette. They moved on to Cannes, where Will took up automobiling and drove the whole crowd through Italy, Switzerland, Belgium, and Holland. They were arrested in Switzerland for frightening the horse of a vegetable vendor and escaped jail only by paying for the wares. Their chauffeur-mechanic, who rode in the boot most of the time, was smashed in the face by a Hollander who objected to noisy horseless carriages. They were arrested there because they had no license to take "this abomination" on the roads. They went to Paris, where Will got rid of his car and struck up a liaison with a French baroness. He carried on this affair in a series of meetings at the Bois de Vincennes, at the Maison Lafitte, in expensive private dining rooms in exclusive restaurants, and finally in a sojourn at Pau and another at Biarritz.

William's affair was interrupted when he received a cable from the New York lawyers saying that Grace had moved to Chicago and had finally given in. She would consent to a Chicago divorce. Will came home and went to Chicago. The divorce was granted on March 20, 1901, and Grace received a settlement of $150,000. Will went back to his baroness, by way of New York, Florida, and Nassau. By Christmas time Grace was enough recovered from her heartbreak to marry a young Frenchman, but Will was thoroughly alienated from all his brothers except Ben.

There was the end of the homogeneous, close-knit family, although the image persisted for nearly twenty years.

14]

IN 1901, five Guggenheims were active in the mining affairs of the family. These five were also members of the executive committee of American Smelting and Refining. Meyer was retired and not very well. Daniel was now the business head of the family, at forty-five. He was shrewd, personable, and strong-minded. Isaac, two years older, was content to allow his younger brother the leadership. Murry, forty-three, was the salesman. He had built the organization in America and abroad that had so annoyed H. H. Rogers and the Lewisohns when it competed with their United Metals sales company. Solomon was a field man who knew his mines and mining men. He had managed the Mexico operation successfully from the start. Simon was the ore buyer, and he had developed a nose for mining properties. There were five, not seven brothers, active in the firm, but the five deserved the reputation given the seven, because they did function as a team.

When for all practical purposes Ben and Will left the family partnership it became a much more cohesive organization, with each member assigned his special duties in the firm. When the stockholders of American Smelting and Refining approved the purchase of the Guggenheim properties, these brothers joined the board of directors and five days later the brothers took over the executive committee.

After a few rapid changes in office location, the Guggenheims and their captive corporation took offices at 165 Broadway; ASARCO occupying the seventeenth and the Guggenheims the eighteenth floor. Daniel had a private office on the seventeenth floor, but it was connected by a private stairway up to the office on the eighteenth floor where Isaac, Murry, Solomon, and Simon all maintained desks.

On one side of the Guggenheim suite were the various clerks and typists and bookkeepers. On another side, flanked by a long comfortable waiting room which contained mineralogical exhibits from Guggenheim properties, was the big room that the brothers used as an office. Each morning the brothers came to the office, sat at their desks, and did their work or read the morning newspaper. Led by Isaac or Murry they would go down to Dan's office at eleven o'clock for a daily conference. At these conferences, the publicity-shy Murry was nearly always a leavening force, bringing the other brothers sharply back to reality when necessary, or, with a wry remark, breaking up a heated argument that threatened to become acrimonious.

In these executive sessions the brothers decided the affairs of American Smelting and Refining, the affairs of Guggenex, and the affairs of the Guggenheims that did not concern either of their companies. (Later this office plan was duplicated when ASARCO and the Guggenheims moved to 120 Broadway.)

By 1902 the Guggenheims' position in the world had been completely reversed from that of a little over half a century before in Switzerland. Then old Simon Guggenheim and his son Meyer had made obeisance and touched their caps when in the presence of Gentile folk. Now the Guggenheims were feudal lords of the industrial world, and their employees adopted a form of feudal address for them. They became known as Mr. Dan, Mr. Isaac, Mr. Murry, Mr. Sol, and Mr. Simon, titles used elsewhere only by personal servants to the rich and wellborn.

Beginning in 1902, the affairs of American Smelting and Refining prospered remarkably. Those figures bandied about during the stock fight were no more accurate than the Guggenheim figures had been; profits for 1901 had been $3,800,000. In 1902, they rose a million dollars, and in 1903, the profits of American Smelting and Refining went up nearly three million dollars more, to $7,500,000. The key in all this was Guggenheim expansion. In 1902, a new lead refinery was built near Salt Lake City and new equipment was added to smelters in Colorado, Mexico, and the Perth Amboy refinery. As financial leader, Daniel turned his attention to the reduction of American Smelting and Refining's fixed or bonded debts and brought them down sharply. He also reduced the amounts outstanding in loans from banks by three million dollars. The purpose was the usual Guggenheim purpose, to reduce the company's liabilities to any outside parties and thus assure control of the business in bad times as well as good.

Daniel Guggenheim also brought a new point of view to American Smelting and Refining, although it did not take effect immediately. He held that in order to maintain its profits and to expand, American Smelting and Refining must acquire mines and become a mining company as well as a smelting company. This point of view was totally foreign to the other members of the board of directors. In 1899 and 1900 such arguments had been made by others to President Nash and the smelter men who sat on the board, but they had countered by saying that they were smelter men and should not go into competition with the mining men from whom they bought their products.

The Guggenheims encountered this attitude in 1901 when they took over control of the company. Control was not exactly the same as outright ownership. Not all the stock was in the hands of the Guggenheims, and today's allies in the industrial world had an unpleasant way of turning up as tomorrow's enemies. So although they maintained control of ASARCO, the Guggenheims played with a light hand. Daniel suggested expansion in mining; the other members of the board offered negative arguments; so Daniel sought another way to bring this about.

Although United Metals had a contract with American Smelting and Refining as sales agent, with a commission of 1 percent on all metal sold, in 1902 Daniel appointed Henry Wagner, who had gone earlier to Huanchaca for the Guggenheims, as head of a Guggenheim London office and in a few months Wagner moved there, to open an establishment that would sell 30,000,000 ounces of silver a year in the world market. In order to be sure that the company would always have plenty of metal to sell, Daniel now turned to Guggenheim Exploration Company as the instrument to find and purchase mining properties. (Eventually the Guggenheim sales company would supplant United Metals as the ASARCO sales agent.)

Just before Christmas, in 1902, a promoter came to New York to see the Guggenheims. He had an option, he said, on a mine called the Esperanza, next to the famous El Oro gold mine of Mexico, located nine thousand feet above sea level. The Guggenheims, through subordinates, began negotiating for the mine but nothing came of the negotiations. The man wanted the moon—a million dollars. The Guggenheims smiled and said no. The promoter stamped out of the Guggenheim offices, very angry, because he had come a long way to talk unsuccessfully.

In January, 1903, a famous mining engineer by the name of John Hays Hammond became associated with the Guggenheims. Hammond was a swashbuckling adventurer, a Horatio Alger and G. A. Henty figure rolled into one. He had been associated with Cecil John Rhodes, the man who gained control of South Africa's diamond mining industry. Hammond had worked in the gold fields of South Africa, earned hundreds of thousands of dollars for himself in commissions on his findings, and had nearly been hanged by the Boer government of South Africa for participation in an insurrection against that government. These were the days when Richard Harding Davis was the ultimate in heroism to Americans, and Hammond was considered to be just such a dashing, romantic character. He was quite capable of marching out onto the desert or the veldt with a handful of porters and his guns to protect him, of living in dirt and danger for months at a time. He was equally at home in a suite at the Waldorf-Astoria, drinking champagne and discussing million-dollar ventures with the capitalists of America.

Indeed it was at just such a session that Hammond's relationship with the Guggenheims was born. Hammond did not come to seek out the Guggenheims—he was leery of a family corporation with a handful of bosses. He came to see William Whitney in his marble palace at 68th Street and Fifth Avenue, and during their conversation over brandy and cigars it was agreed that Whitney would put up money and Hammond would explore the world for mineral wealth. It would be a partnership for two years, and then they would settle up their affairs.

When Daniel Guggenheim learned that William Whitney was thinking about going into an independent mining venture, he was not pleased. He had undergone severe criticism within the family for letting Whitney into Guggenex, and he believed that Whitney owed a primary loyalty, as far as mining was concerned, to throw all his resources into that basket. He said as much. Whitney was an easy-going man and he did not particularly want to argue, so he persuaded Hammond to talk to Daniel Guggenheim. Thus an uneasy partnership was formed, with the ebullient, confident Hammond agreeing to work exclusively with Guggenex. The agreement called for a salary of a *quarter of a million dollars a year* for John Hays Hammond, plus a 25 percent interest in all mining properties he found that were acquired by Guggenex. Up to that point, it was the largest salary ever paid any man anywhere in the world, and when the penny press learned of it, John Hays Hammond was the figure of the hour, and the Guggenheims were depicted thereafter as mysterious Croesus-like men who had so much money they simply threw it away.

There were good reasons for the high salary as far as the Guggenheims were concerned. Hammond was more concerned with living like a millionaire than being one. He traveled by private railroad car when he went to visit mining properties, and he stayed at the best hotels when they were available. His expenses were high—it cost money to be a public character. As for the Guggenheims, they agreed that it was best to give Hammond a huge salary and then he would not hold out his discoveries, if there were valuable ones. And with Hammond it had been a history of valuable finds. The potential prizes were worth the risk. So it proved: In his first year Hammond made a million and a quarter dollars in salary and commissions, which meant that the Guggenheims made at least four million dollars from his services.

One reason for the Guggenheim success in the mining and metals businesses was Meyer's old practice, and it had nothing to do with the technology of mining or smelting. The Guggenheims always hired the best man in the business and let him have his head. It was for them the key to industrial empire, and no secret at all, but in Hammond's case a move that took courage.

Until now the Guggenheims had operated on the sound policy of purchasing the best producing mines wherever they could find them, and then hoping that the production continued. Sometimes it did. Sometimes it did not. They sank $10,000,000 into one set of

Mexican mines and got very little out of it. They sank $200,000 into another Mexican mine and took $5,000,000 out of it. It was simply a matter of judgment and luck.

Had Hammond produced nothing at all for the Guggenheims in the first year or two of his contract, he would have been worth the money it cost them. Based on his coming in as general manager, Daniel and Whitney increased the capitalization of Guggenex by eleven million dollars. The family, after all, needed capital with which to work, and much of that had been sacrificed in the deal that gave them control of American Smelting and Refining. This increase in capitalization followed closely on the Sunday newspaper magazine stories about the fabulous Mr. Hammond and the fabulous Messrs. Guggenheim, and there was no trouble at all in floating the stock. The more stock that was issued the higher the price went, jumping as high as $325 a share from the issued price of $100.

John Hays Hammond was worth every cent it cost the Guggenheims to keep him in their employment.

In 1902, Hammond began a thorough examination of the Guggenheim mining portfolio and sent his young assistant, Alfred Chester Beatty, out into the field to survey the mines and perhaps to discover some new properties. Beatty was twenty-nine years old, a graduate of the Columbia University School of Mines, and was receiving the impressive salary of $27,000 a year. His example showed Americans what even a young man could do if he had the right breaks.

Shortly after the Guggenheims had begun their association with John Hays Hammond, the mining engineer lost his temper when called to one of a series of meetings at which the report on a mining property was read. In Hammond's defense it must be said that in this period, as they felt their way, the Guggenheim brothers were given to much meeting and to endless discussion of the mining business. Hammond was earning at least a quarter of a million dollars a year and felt that he was worth every penny of it, and that his time should not be wasted on trivial matters.

On this particular day, the brothers had spent many minutes listening to a long, detailed letter of alibi from a mine manager whose property was not doing as well as had been expected. Hammond lost his temper when the reading was finished and demanded that the meeting be ended right then. The total investment in the mine just discussed, he said, would only pay his salary for about a month. He ought to be out and doing and not sitting around the offices waiting for Daniel to call him to a meeting. It was agreed then that Guggenex meetings would be held only monthly.

Shortly afterward, Hammond returned to New York from Missouri where he had been looking over some valuable lead properties. He brought in his maps and statistics and began to make a long report. Daniel leaned back in his chair and looked gloomily at the ceiling. Isaac walked over to the window and looked down at New York. Simon, fortunately, was in Colorado looking at better scenery. Murry picked up the newspaper and began to read. Then the question of the value of the property was raised. How much was it worth? someone asked Hammond. "About a million dollars," Hammond replied.

Murry looked up over his newspaper. If that was all the mine was worth, why didn't Hammond take care of it himself instead of wasting so much valuable time? Murry's humor was appreciated, and the tension between the brothers and their expensive mining engineer was broken.

Those two meetings symbolized something else about the Guggenheims that was an important factor in their success. They learned quickly. Hammond showed them how unimportant it was to worry about small details if they had adequate managers, and within a few weeks they had made arrangements so they did not have to worry about details—or Isaac worried about them silently and brought them to the attention of the others only when a serious matter was discovered among the unimportant.

15]

IN THE spring of 1902, John Hays Hammond moved into his private railroad car and set out for a personal examination of the Guggenheim properties. He went first to Colorado. He parked the railroad car on a siding at Colorado Springs and drove over the mountain to Cripple Creek. He came back and headed south for Mexico City. There Hammond dined with President Díaz, and a few days later set out for the Esperanza mine for which the Guggenheims had negotiated earlier. He liked what he saw. He came back to New York to recommend to Daniel Guggenheim that they buy the mine quickly for two million dollars. (He had carried out some delicate negotiations to secure an option at that figure.) Daniel Guggenheim, busy with other matters, nearly lost his chance at this mine and nearly lost his mining engineer that day. Hammond came bursting into his office with news of the great coup, and Guggenheim picked up papers and said he was too busy to talk about it. Hammond went to Whitney and they agreed to take up the mine separately if Guggenex did not want it. But when Daniel learned this, he said Guggenex did want the mine, and they bought. For a two-million-dollar investment they received six million dollars in profits before they were finished.

In two years John Hays Hammond and his assistants covered every corner of the globe that would interest the Guggenheims and American Smelting and Refining. Basically their operations were concerned with North and South America, for it was here that the great silver and lead mines lay. Silver and lead were the ores under consideration; President Nash of American Smelting and Refining firmly refused to discuss expansion into other types of smelting.

The Guggenheims, under Daniel, were not nearly so obdurate in their reasoning. They already were in the copper business in a small way in Mexico and Daniel sensed that copper was the coming metal.

In those two years of far-flung research, Hammond had amassed a vast store of information about the mining districts of the world, and it was a matter for discussion and concern that the silver and lead business could not be in the future what they had been in the past. Naturally, Daniel's bright eye and active mind began surveying other possibilities.

Daniel was urged on in this endeavor by certain problems that were developing within American Smelting and Refining. Not all the stockholders of ASARCO were happy with Guggenheim management. They recalled all too clearly the day (it was only four years before) when they had been independent operators. In 1904, these malcontents began to grumble that the Guggenheims were using American Smelting and Refining for selfish purposes. They said the Guggenheims, as the executive committee of American Smelting and Refining, made special deals with the Guggenheims as owners of lead and silver mines and that the deals invariably favored the mine-owner Guggenheims at the expense of the corporation.

Outside the trust, there still existed a group of independent smelters on Puget Sound in Washington, which were the natural marketplaces for the ore of the Coeur d'Alene mining district of Idaho. Away from the coast, the American rail system did not connect the Southwest with the Northwest United States, and it was very difficult to ship ore from Coeur d'Alene to Colorado, as the Guggenheims had learned in the early days of the smelter trust. It was very simple to ship it across any of three or four lines to the Seattle region. At this point, with the diminishing lead ores of the North American continent, the Coeur d'Alene properties and the northwestern smelters loomed very large as a threat to the well-being of the smelter trust.

The answer was to buy out the independent operators, and Daniel Guggenheim knew that it did not make too much difference how much American Smelting and Refining paid, because in acquiring these properties the trust became a monopoly. In another way, however, it made a great deal of difference how much was paid, because the ASARCO stockholders were restless, and the capital structure of the company was already monstrously high after two enormous excursions in stock watering. It would take some years for the company to absorb this arbitrary declaration of value. Now was not the time to float a new stock issue or to become heavily indebted in bonds.

Daniel sought the advice of Jacob Schiff of Kuhn, Loeb and Company, the brokerage house. From their discussions came a shrewd analysis of the Guggenheim position and a plan of action. The success of Guggenex on the world market showed how highly the Guggenheim name was held in financial circles everywhere. Nearly everyone believed that what the Guggenheims touched turned to silver.

A stock flotation based on the Guggenheim mining properties would give the Guggenheims needed capital for investment in new industries. It would also put them in the dangerous position of being subject to corporate controls. However, this represented only a temporary danger, because the purpose of all this discussion was to find new money so that the Guggenheim brothers, as an independent partnership, could go into new fields. The Guggenheims had invested nearly all their cash in gaining control of American Smelting and Refining and they had not recovered their cash strength. The creation of a new Guggenheim company would salve some old wounds, too.

Daniel and Jacob Schiff traveled to London to see Sir Ernest Cassel, who was already involved in Guggenex in a minor way. Sir Ernest was the banker of the British mineral world and he floated loans for many countries strong in mineral resources.

When they met at the British banker's house in Grosvenor Square, the three developed a scheme that would give the Guggenheims a new stock company, which would be hitched to American Smelting and Refining, with voting control still in Guggenheim hands, and with the means to buy from the firm of M. Guggenheim's Sons the lead and silver mines that the smelting company's inside critics now said should be in ASARCO's hands. (Many minds had been changed inside ASARCO as a result of Guggenheim successes.)

From this meeting came the formation of American Smelters Securities, a new corporation capitalized at $77,000,000. Much of the stock was sold in Europe. There were three classes of stock: Preferred A, which paid 6 percent, Preferred B, which paid 5 percent, and common, which held voting power as long as it paid dividends. The majority of the common was held by American Smelting and Refining. Guggenex held part of the Preferred B, just as a hedge against some unforeseen difficulties, and the rest was sold off. The Guggenheims then sold most of Guggenex's mines to American Smelters Securities for $22,000,000, giving Guggenex capital with which to go out and find new properties, and eliminating the complaints of the American Smelting and Refining stockholders that the Guggenheims had special deals for their mines with ASARCO.

Now, without increasing the $100,000,000 capitalization of American Smelting and Refining, the Guggenheims had added $25,000,000 or $30,000,000 to the ASARCO coffers in cash, plus $20,000,000 in this new stock which was held by ASARCO. Because this last sum was common stock, it ensured control of the new company as long as profits continued.

The Guggenheims controlled American Smelting and Refining, and through that company they controlled American Smelters Securities, and through M. Guggenheim's Sons they controlled Guggenex. It was a growingly elaborate structure created to support an ever heavier load of debt. That was how Daniel had gotten around the objections of the old smelter men about expansion.

With new capital in hand, the Guggenheims set out to create a smelters' monopoly, and in this effort they were now entirely supported by the other members of the board of directors of ASARCO, because such had been the aim of the company in the beginning; it was simply not very well executed for the first five years.

By and large, the Guggenheim boys had accomplished enough to warm the heart of old Meyer.

After Barbara's death in 1900, Meyer was feeling very much alone. He had continued to live in the house on West 77th Street, with William, until Will disgraced himself and broke with the family. Meyer then helped set up son-in-law Albert Loeb as a broker and he maintained a small office in Loeb's suite where he often came to lunch and to examine his investments.

The Guggenheims had become more prominent than before in New York Jewish society, first with Meyer's gift of $200,000 to Mt. Sinai Hospital for the establishment of a new wing for paying patients. Meyer also gave $60,000 to the Philadelphia Jewish Hospital in 1901, adding to many other charitable donations he had made to public institutions in the city that had harbored him in his younger days and where he had established the family fortune.

Meyer was not well. He suffered from prostate trouble and other diseases of the aged. He seldom went driving in the park these days, and when he did go, his coachman took charge, and Meyer simply rode in the carriage. He spent the cold winters in the warmth of Florida, but the cold was in his bones. The high point of these last years came on his seventy-fifth birthday in 1903, when he was taken to Isaac's house and there was greeted by nine children, seventeen grandchildren, and a host of in-laws. There was a grand party that night, with a skit about Wall Street written by one son-in-law and acted out by the children, parodies of popular songs, recitations and other performances by the family in honor of the patriarch. At the end of the family's histrionics an orchestra presented a musicale and then there was dancing for all the family in Isaac's ballroom.

In 1904 Meyer was sued by a woman who said she had been his mistress for twenty-five years. The lady wanted $100,000 for breach of promise—quite a tribute to a seventy-six-year-old man. Meyer denied everything and offered a ten-thousand-dollar reward for any proof that he had ever been seen with this woman. That same year he had an operation, his third, and he refused to go to a hospital or have an anesthetic. He did not make a good recovery from the operation and in the winter of 1905 he was taken to Palm Beach, to the Royal Poinciana Hotel. His condition grew worse and he was moved to a cottage at Lake Worth. The reports coming to New York indicated that he was weakening, and finally Dr. Edwin Sternberger, his physician then, was sent from New York by special train, but it was too late to do anything to save the old man. He died on March 15, 1905, at the age of seventy-seven.

Meyer had not been a religious man, but he had given generously to the Temple Emanu-el in New York, as he had done in Philadelphia. The Guggenheims were among the first families of American Jewry, and the death of the patriarch was a matter of interest to the entire Jewish community in America. Meyer's story represented the hope of every Jewish merchant in every hamlet in every state in the Union. The Kuhns and the Schiffs and the Seligmans and the Strauses and all the others so prominent among the American Jewish families came to the funeral at the Temple, and so did scores of Gentiles who were employed by his sons or who were associated with them in their worldwide enterprises. It was a grand and impressive funeral on Fifth Avenue, and it symbolized, as nothing else could, just how far the little Jewish peddler had come in a half-century by crossing the ocean to escape the land of pogroms.

At the end of the services, after the big organ had played Chopin's funeral march, the body was taken in a cortege to the family mausoleum at Salem Fields, Jamaica, Long Island and Meyer Guggenheim was laid in his coffin beside Barbara.

The Guggenheim will revealed that he left a personal fortune of only $2,000,000, part of it in American Smelting and Refining stock, part in other stocks, and part in bonds. The will did not show that he had created seven multimillionaires. His three daughters shared the bulk of the fortune, each receiving about $500,000 in trust. Other bequests were made to friends and servants, and to Mt. Sinai, to the Jewish Hospital of Philadelphia, to the Montefiore Home for Chronic Invalids, and to other charities in New York and Philadelphia.

In the death tributes paid to Meyer by the newspapers, by religious leaders, Jewish, Protestant, and Catholic, and by businessmen, it was said that he had never shown himself to be anything less than perfectly honest, that he had never taken advantage of a soul, and that he had achieved his wealth and started his sons on the path to wealth by fair dealing, hard work, and honest effort. The praise was fulsome, for it was not yet the time when millionaires were excoriated except by the anarchists, socialists, and syndicalists.

As a memorial to Meyer's background and the place of birth of the idea that begat the Guggenheim fortune, the boys caused a home for the aged to be built in Lengnau in Switzerland. That was one memorial to Meyer; an equally fitting one was made by the boys in the business field that year.

Daniel called a young financier named Bernard Baruch into his office one day in 1905 and suggested that he try to buy two smelters, one at Tacoma and the other at Selby, Washington. Baruch was the son of Meyer Guggenheim's family doctor in New York, and the Guggenheim boys had known Bernard since he was a child. In fact, many years before, Daniel had offered Bernard a job as an ore buyer in Mexico, but young Baruch had decided to stay in New York and make his way in the financial world.

Fortunately for Baruch and the Guggenheims, the control of the Tacoma smelter, and much of the stock of the Selby smelter, was held by an elderly financier in New York City named Darius Mills. Baruch approached him and asked for an option on the stock. Mills refused but said he would sell out at a good profit if the other stockholders were agreed. Baruch then went West and made himself agreeable to William R. Rust, head of the Tacoma smelter. While Baruch was in the West, Daniel heard a rumor that the Rockefellers (probably egged on by H. H. Rogers) were thinking about acquiring these smelters as the basis for a foray into the smelting industry. Daniel told Baruch to acquire the Tacoma and Selby stock at any price. So he did. He paid $5,500,000 for Tacoma stock, when the assets were around $500,000. It was the same story at Selby. Yet for American Smelting and Refining it was a good investment at the price, because the monopoly was now secure. Baruch's fee for the effort was $1,100,000. So millionaires are made.

In the summer of 1905, after the two western smelters were added to the American Smelting and Refining Company, the price of the stock rose steadily until it reached $120 a share for the common stock. In five years the Guggenheims had doubled the stock market value of the securities, and had created a fortune for themselves which must have been in excess of $100,000,000 on paper. (Their holdings in American Smelting and Refining alone were in excess of $50,000,000 at that time. Besides ASARCO, they held the control of Guggenex, which rose as high as $325 a share, although par was $100. If they held more than half of Guggenex's 170,000 shares at that figure, the value was 27,000,000. Besides this, M.

Guggenheim's Sons held other investments worth untold millions of dollars.)

The Guggenheim brothers had created this huge fortune by manipulation and shrewd investment. Although they had expanded and extended themselves in 1905, their position and that of their companies had never been better. American Smelting and Refining had earned $7,500,000 in the first full year of Guggenheim management. In the second year the company earned $7,905,000. In the third Guggenheim year, 1905, when all these complex transactions were carried out, American Smelting and Refining earned $8,890,-000, which meant that it earned nearly 9 percent on the investment of $100,000,000. Stock watering could be simply a question of declaring a value and then proving that it was so. What better memorial to Meyer Guggenheim's prescience could the boys have created? There was a fitting end to the first chapter of the story of the Guggenheims and the American dream.

16]

IN 1906 Daniel Guggenheim and his brothers were the most important men in mining in the entire world, and because of this fact opportunities for fortune that would have shaken less powerful men were handled with scarcely a flurry in the heavily carpeted, high-ceilinged offices of M. Guggenheim's Sons and downstairs around the conference table in Daniel's private office.

One such opportunity came to the Guggenheims early in 1906. Leopold II, King of the Belgians, wished to organize a company to develop the rubber and gold resources of the area around the Kasai River, in the Congo. Leopold, busy with his pretty French mistress, learned that Thomas Fortune Ryan was in Europe, and he summoned the American capitalist to the royal presence because Ryan knew something about rubber exploitation. Ryan came to Brussels and talked about exploitation of natural resources. The question of metals came up, and naturally Ryan thought of Daniel Guggenheim. Who else in 1906? The Guggenheims and their exploits were now favorite material for the Sunday tabloids and no week passed but speculative stories (most of them excessively inaccurate) appeared about them in the American press.

This opportunity was none of the affair of American Smelting and Refining, it was the business of Guggenex. Alfred Chester Beatty, protégé of John Hays Hammond, was sent to Brussels to discuss mineral exploitation.

From these discussions came the formation of the Société Internationale Forestière et Minière du Congo, sometimes called Forminière. King Leopold retained a 25 percent interest in this company for himself, 25 percent of it was retained by the Belgian

151]

government, and 50 percent was taken by Ryan and the Guggenheims, who put up, altogether, less than two million dollars for capital. For their share, the Guggenheims were to have *all* rights to mineral exploitation in the Congo except some areas already assigned to another company. The Guggenheims and Ryan then formed two exploitation companies, each participating in both: the American Congo Company, which would exploit minerals; and the Intercontinental Rubber Company, which would exploit other commodities. Ryan, of course, took the lead in the latter and the Guggenheims in the former. Beatty became vice-president of American Congo and supervised the exploratory activities. They found some gold, and millions of dollars worth of diamonds. The diamonds extended across the Congo border into Portuguese Angola, and soon the Guggenheim company had a concession there as well. Before, one could say that whatever the Guggenheims touched turned to silver. After 1906, it could be said that whatever they touched turned to diamonds, both literally and figuratively.

American Congo was never more than a minor Guggenheim interest, no matter how profitable. While young Beatty was prospecting in the Congo, Daniel and the Guggenheim brothers were strengthening American Smelting and Refining. The smelter company owned United Lead, which was the marketing agency for that mineral, but it was not the most important agency. That honor belonged to an independent firm called National Lead Company. In 1906 Bernard Baruch was again brought into Guggenheim operations to help float the Intercontinental Rubber Company. At the same time he was working very quietly to obtain control of National Lead for the Guggenheims. After much consideration and planning, the actual purchase was carried out in one single day in a no less public place than the floor of the New York Stock Exchange. Baruch used a broker named Harry Content, and early in the day Content began buying National Lead. Before the day was over he had traded 116,000 shares, which represented 80 percent of the outstanding shares of the company, and the Guggenheims had control. The operation was a wonder of Wall Street, because in all this activity so little attention had been attracted to the transactions that the price had not risen more than $8 a share from the $56 at which it began with the opening gong.

This year American Smelting and Refining moved to cement its monopoly control of smelting, by first making a long-term contract with a Rockefeller subsidiary which was the last holdout of any importance, and then buying the majority interest in this subsidiary, which was called Federal Mining and Smelting.

While young Beatty was traveling in Europe and Africa that year, the chief engineer of Guggenex was concerned with mining properties in the northern section of the Western Hemisphere, an area that had received scant attention in spite of Alaska's Klondike gold rush of 1896. A mining promoter named William Boyce Thompson was promoting the sale of a stock called Nipissing Mines Company. If one wanted to call attention to a mining region or a mining property, one began negotiations with the Guggenheims. Even being seen going into the Guggenheim office was worth a few points on the mining exchanges of the West.

So fast had come their rise to fame as well as fortune, that the Guggenheims did not realize how important they were in the public eye. Events of the next few months were certainly to prove that point.

In the spring of 1906 Thompson began promoting his mining stock, with reasonable success. By the end of May the stock had risen two or three points from the $3.45 at which he had placed the stock on the market. There was talk that this was the greatest find in silver since the discovery at Cripple Creek. The vein uncovered ran from a width of six inches to two feet and extended for six hundred feet. How deep it was, nobody knew.

With all the talk among mining men about Nipissing, Guggenex engineer Hammond decided to make a trip to Ontario, to the town of Cobalt where the strike was located. Promoter Thompson did everything he could to facilitate matters. Hammond had his private car and his private chef and his wine steward, Thompson employed a press agent and took along all the New York reporters whose newspapers would send them. They traveled north from Ontario toward Hudson's Bay, and finally came to Cobalt. Hammond looked at the strip of silver, nodded wisely, and came back to New York City beaming with enthusiasm. The stock of Nipissing Mines jumped to $25 a share, based on no more information than that.

In November, Hammond recommended the mine and Guggenex contracted with Thompson for 400,000 shares of Nipissing stock, taking 100,000 shares and paying $2,500,000, with the remainder to be purchased at a later date. On the basis of the Guggenheim purchase, the Nipissing stock continued to rise, to nearly $40 a share.

The date for the Guggenheims to exercise their option on the additional stock in the Nipissing mine was December 1, 1906. As that date approached one of Hammond's assistants reported secretly that he had dug down and found the silver vein petered out twenty feet below the surface. Hammond informed the Guggenheims, upset because he had staked his reputation on the value of this mine and now it was proving to be a dud.

On the last day of November, Daniel Guggenheim questioned the validity of title to Thompson's mine. Thompson said it was perfectly valid, guaranteed by the Canadian government. Daniel said he was doubtful, and arranged to see Thompson at Samuel Untermyer's office at ten o'clock on the morning of December 1.

Thompson showed up at ten o'clock, but was told to wait, because Untermyer was in conference. Thompson was sure that he was in conference with Daniel Guggenheim, and it was true. Thompson waited an hour, then panicked and rushed to a telephone to order the sale of 80,000 shares of Nipissing that he held. For some reason, he felt, the Guggenheims were not going to exercise their option, and he wanted to get out before the crash came.

Thompson sold on the weekend before the market closed. The crash came on the following Monday. That day the Guggenheims announced that they were not exercising the option because Thompson had refused a thirty-day extension for title examination. That day 200,000 shares of Nipissing were sold and the price plummeted back to $5 a share. Not only that disaster came to the mining community and its investors, but as Nipissing fell, so did all mining stocks. Public confidence was never at a lower ebb, and the whipping boys were the Guggenheims. Daniel and the others were shocked. They announced that they would guarantee to reimburse all the investors in Guggenex who had bought Nipissing through the Guggenex connection. But they could not guarantee reimbursement to the thousands who had simply followed the Guggenheim lead, saying that what was good enough for the "Guggies" was good enough for them. The public, of course, had been gulled by its own greed, as the stock-buying public was to be gulled a dozen times more in the next quarter-century. There was nothing for the public to do about it except to take out its rage against the prominent men who had aroused all the interest. The Guggenheims fell from their pedestal of public esteem and never again quite managed to climb back so high. The *Wall Street Journal* and other publications accused the Guggenheims of being party to a massive speculation which depended on public gullibility for its success. The Guggenheims, they said, had cleared out of Nipissing without losing money.

The charge was harsh, and it was not a very fair charge, given the Guggenheims' record. They had worked some very fast shuffles of assets and liabilities and profits, to be sure, but these had all been done to people playing in their own league. If the Guggenheims did use Nipissing to play bulls and bears with the stock market and make a few million dollars, they paid heavily for a small profit, considering their assets, for they lost much in public confidence. Further, the Nipissing scandal was quite outside the normal range of Guggenheim operations, and to cap it, Hammond's organization had been wrong, but not in the beginning when he vested his faith in Nipissing. The misinformation came when Hammond's man said the vein had died out. It had done no such thing, but had been pinched, and had then come out again some few feet below to blossom forth with more rich silver. A syndicate took over Nipissing from the frightened Thompson, and eventually the mine paid out nearly $30,000,000 in silver.

The Nipissing crash marked an end to one phase of mining investment in the United States, but even the Guggenheims did not realize that the public outcry against them represented more than a passing phase. Later, in the matter of Yukon gold, they were to learn the true facts, to their sorrow.

The second five years of the new twentieth century were busy and important years for the Guggenheims in the mining and smelting business. John Hays Hammond was scouring the earth. Young Beatty was working in the Yukon, trying to put together a great handful of mining claims left over from the past and harness them under a stream of fresh water (to use new hydraulic mining techniques and recover millions in gold that had been left awaste by the old hand methods).

The important matter to the Guggenheims in the early 1900's, however, was the development of an entirely new industry, brought about by new methods and new needs in the American economy. In 1900, when Benjamin Guggenheim was making a trip around the West to look into mining properties, he had been offered an interest in a dry brown mountain at the head of Bingham Canyon in Utah. He had asked what it was and what was in it, and had been told that this hill was a copper mountain. When he had asked how high the copper content went, and was told that it was only 2 percent of the total rock, he lost interest, because in 1900 the methods of mining and smelting indicated that at 2 percent recovery this would not be an economical proposition, even if the Guggenheims in the United States had any reason to become involved in copper. So Ben Guggenheim let the matter of Copper Mountain rest at that.

The copper mountain sat and waited. Colonel Enos A. Wall recognized it for what it was and staked claims. He sold a quarter-interest in his mine, or latent mine, to a sea captain named Joseph R. De Lamar. But the assay again showed the copper ran 2 percent, and if every inch of that mountain showed 2 percent, there was still no way to mine the copper and make it pay.

A mining engineer from Missouri named Daniel C. Jackling came to Copper Mountain and tried to work out a method of mining. He did not succeed before the money put up by De Lamar ran out, and the wily captain refused to put up more. Jackling went off then to work for Spencer Penrose and Charles W. MacNeill in their silver mines at Cripple Creek. Jackling told them what must be done in Utah, although he was not quite sure how it would work out in detail. There were at least five million tons of 2 percent ore in that mountain, he said. It must be mined by the open-pit method used by the iron ore miners of the Mesabi Range and the miners of Manchuria.

Spencer Penrose and Charles MacNeill listened carefully. They were not sure how the copper would be mined either, but they paid

Wall $385,000 for a 55 percent interest in his mine and bought out the De Lamar interest for $125,000. In 1903, they formed the Utah Copper Company. Two years later Jackling and his mining crews went to work, using an entirely new technique as far as hardrock miners were concerned: They were scooping up the earth with steam shovels.

When the Guggenheims learned what was happening in this Utah canyon, they sent John Hays Hammond to look over the operation. Hammond returned to New York and reported that even a 2 percent ore base of copper would be immensely profitable if it were mined in this manner.

The Guggenheims discovered that Penrose and MacNeill needed money, for theirs was an expensive mining operation. Guggenex would take over, Daniel Guggenheim said, under certain conditions. John Hays Hammond was to be made managing director of the company. Guggenex would take a 25 percent interest for $1,500,000, using half that money to retire some notes floated in the previous year, and half to build a concentrating mill. In 1906 this proposal was accepted and the Guggenheims entered the business.

The Guggenheims were quite willing to take a minority interest because at the same time they negotiated a very favorable contract between Utah Copper and American Smelting and Refining. Utah Copper agreed that for twenty years American Smelting and Refining would have all its ore. Critics of American Smelting said that this contract made Utah Copper the vassal of American Smelting and Refining. There must have been some truth in the charge, because usually a minority interest holder is not able to install his own man as chief of management, and in this case the Guggenheim man became managing director.

Guggenex then underwrote an issue of $3,000,000 in bonds and ASARCO bought stock in Utah Copper. With the money thus raised, Utah Copper was able to build the Magna copper mill, which became the longest mill in America, with 575 flotation tanks used to separate the copper ore from the inert materials and other minerals. This was the beginning of the mining of porphyry copper in America, as opposed to the old system of finding copper veins that flowed through rock like gold or silver veins. It was also a development that assisted greatly in the industrialization of the United States.

It is not always easy to tell whether the abundance of materials made possible rapid industrialization in America or the will to industrialize and the demand of an expanding economy caused Americans to find ways to do things better. In the case of the American copper industry, however, the story is quite clear. Ben Guggenheim had laughed off the concept of Copper Mountain because one of his engineers told him that the tailings piles at the Butte mills ran a higher percentage of copper than that mountain. At the time, around 1900, that statement was true because the refining techniques of the day were so inefficient. (Since that time those tailings piles have been re-refined and the copper recovered.) Not long after Ben Guggenheim's refusal, the General Electric Company was told about the porphyry copper in Utah and sent men to investigate. General Electric's interest was obvious, yet General Electric, too, passed up Copper Mountain.

To make the new system work, it took the enthusiasm and drive of Daniel Jackling. He had been an assistant professor of chemistry and metallurgy at the Missouri School of Mines before he opted for the vigorous life of mining engineer. Jackling was a rare type, and his knowledge and drive brought about the experiments that proved the value of Copper Mountain. This drive, Spencer Penrose's acuity and bravery, and the broad knowledge of John Hays Hammond were combined with the financial strength and judgment of the Guggenheims to create a new industry. In later years, John Hays Hammond would claim that the development of the electrical and automotive industries were possible *because* the copper was made available. Speaking of the radio, the automobile, general electrification, and the airplane, Hammond said: "All these and many minor but highly significant developments were made possible only by free use of electricity and it, in turn, could come about only with assured large supply of copper. It was thus that the development of the Porphyries gave, not merely the actual supply, but the assurance in advance that it would be forthcoming and at a reasonable price."

The Guggenheims were deeply involved in the copper business, and they were known as members of the group called The Copper Kings. A new name became important in the Guggenheim organization, and that was the name of Pope Yeatman, understudy to John Hays Hammond, and a specialist in copper.

The Guggenheims did not neglect their interests in Mexico at this time, either. They continued to look into silver propositions and other mining properties, but in a way one might say that the Guggenheim position in Mexico became defensive now that they were the most important mining organization in the country. They set up an operating committee of executives to watch over Mexican affairs. This committee consisted of three members, led by Henry Wagner, who had come back from London. In 1906 a rival firm in Mexico threatened to disturb the Guggenheims' pleasant situation in northern Mexico by erection of a new smelter which would then fight for the Monterrey smelter's business. The Guggenheims sought and received a new concession from the government of the State of Chihuahua to build a smelter and in 1907 it was built. But what a smelter! Secretly it was known in the Guggenheim organization that the smelter was not built to operate but to keep out competition. It was built of scrap from American Smelting and Refining's other smelters. When Wagner heard of the plan to build, he became worried and left Mexico for New York to argue against such economic waste. Edgar Newhouse in Colorado also opposed the obvious wastefulness. There was not enough business in and around Chihuahua to justify a good smelter, let alone a bad one. The Guggenheims listened and Daniel took their words very seriously. He argued with them, but went right ahead and built his smelter in Chihuahua and operated it at a severe loss.

The opposing smelter was never built. If any other justification were needed, Daniel might have pointed out the profit and loss statements of American Smelting and Refining to his worried employees. In 1907 ASARCO earned $11,509,000, paid $7,000,000 of that out in dividends, and added the remainder of the earnings to a surplus which had reached nearly $13,500,000. American Smelting and Refining, Daniel said, controlled the silver output of South America, Central America, British Columbia, Mexico, and the United States. If anyone added it up, he would find that the Guggenheims controlled 80 percent of the silver output of the world.

17]

THE PROFITS declared by American Smelting and Refining in the summer of 1907 marked one high point in the Guggenheim fortunes, and that high point was to be followed by the most worrisome period of Daniel Guggenheim's life as a businessman. Even while the Guggenheims appeared to be on top of the world, the ground was already receding from beneath them in several areas.

Most important of the unsettled areas was the money market, which was now the central arena for Guggenheim operations. After 1900 the Guggenheims were primarily financiers. Before that time they had been simply industrialists, but with the amalgamation of Guggenheim smelters into American Smelting and Refining and the coming of Guggenheim control to the company, all was changed. They were "money men" and the money market of 1907 had fallen even as the Guggenheim profits were being counted.

With their excursions into Canadian silver, Yukon gold, Mexican smelters, and American copper, the Guggenheims in 1907 were very heavily extended, even though their operations were profitable. The years 1905 and 1906 had been so profitable that it seemed hard to believe there could be any other way of life.

Yet, in the spring and early summer of 1907 there were certain signs in the financial world that all was not as it should be. Stock and bond issues that ought to have been snapped up by the public were lying untouched. Many important businessmen in New York City were overextended, and although this situation always caused them to become nervous in times of greatest stress, it was not an unusual condition for Wall Street.

In September a speculator by the name of F. Augustus Heinze

decided that he would make a killing in copper. Heinze was well known to everyone in Wall Street and to everyone in the mining business. In 1899, Henry H. Rogers had made his first big mark in the speculative world by organizing Amalgamated Copper Company, whose capitalization started at $75,000,000 and was run up to $155,000,000. Amalgamated had taken over Anaconda Copper, Boston and Montana Copper, Butte and Boston Consolidated Copper, and six other companies. Amalgamated stock had been sold by Thomas W. Lawson of Boston, a super-promoter who used huge newspaper advertisements to tell the public about the value of his investments.

After Amalgamated was floated with such a splash, a war developed between its promoters and other copper men, and in the middle of the fight was F. Augustus Heinze. Eventually it led to a suit between H. H. Rogers and Heinze over the Butte mines. The suit uncovered a mess as malodorous as a cesspool, in which charges of corruption of officers, bribery, and blackmail were uncovered and substantially proved against both sides. Rogers was a hard man who played in a hard school, but when he dealt with Heinze his hands were so dirtied that Solomon Guggenheim once spent an hour telling John Hays Hammond that Rogers' behavior was giving the entire metals industry a black eye.

Eventually, under John D. Ryan and Cornelius F. Kelley, most of the disputed properties were merged into Anaconda Copper Mining Company, but that was not the end of F. Augustus Heinze. He returned to New York and to further skulduggery in Wall Street.

In 1907 Heinze, Charles W. Morse, and E. R. Thomas gained control of the Mercantile Trust Company of New York. Trust companies, under a faulty New York banking law, had almost the same privileges that banks had, but few of the responsibilities. It was possible for these three men to use the funds of the trust company to play the stock market and to speculate on margin with depositors' funds.

In October, Heinze chose one of his old loves, a copper stock, with which to make a killing. The stock was United Copper. He was out to corner it. He started, on October 12, by dumping a huge number of shares on the market and causing the price to fall. Then he bought back all those shares plus all others available, causing the price to jump from 37¼ to 60 in two days. At that time, Heinze believed that he and his associates had achieved a majority control of the stock and could do what they would with the company. They called for delivery to be made on October 15 at two-thirty in the afternoon at the bank. There they would take the certificates and pay over the money.

Secretly, Heinze and his associates expected that most of the people who had sold to them were short sellers; that they would not have the stock to deliver, and that they would have to go to the market to buy it. Heinz and his associates proposed then to sell stock in United Copper at higher and higher figures, delivering so those other speculators could cover their short sales, and making profits on profits.

They had miscalculated dreadfully, and fatefully.

On the morning of October 15, 1907, the stock market opened with United Copper at 60. Heinze and his friends expected the price to go charging upward as the short sellers rushed to the marketplace to buy shares to cover themselves. After all, in two and a half hours they would have to appear at the bank and deliver those shares already sold.

Heinze looked in surprise at the figures on the board at twelve-thirty. The price hovered right around 60, and it remained there for half an hour; then instead of rising it dropped a little. There was plenty of stock, it seemed, to cover the investment. Either that or the short sellers were holding to the last mniute, confident of getting the stock at a lower price.

Two-thirty in the afternoon came and so did the stockholders, showing up at the bank to turn over their certificates and take the cash. The money began moving out of the Mercantile National Bank in huge bundles. Soon the cash supplies of the bank were exhausted and Heinze and his friends began selling United Copper just as quickly as it came in, in order to get the cash to pay for more United Copper as it came in, responding to their demand. The price dropped before 3:00 P.M. to $26 a share. Within two days it was down to $10 a share. Heinze was broke. His stockbrokers were broke. His bank was broke. Heinze appealed to the New York City Clearing House Association to keep his bank from closing by lending the Mercantile National money to tide it over.

The Clearing House insisted that Heinze and Morse and the others who were involved in the copper scheme get out of the bank, and they did. Then came another blow to Wall Street: It was learned that Charles Tracy Barney, president of the most respectable Knickerbocker Trust Company, was deeply entangled in the affairs of the notorious Mr. Heinze. The uneasiness that had struck Wall Street with the news about the Heinze speculations was compounded, and the Panic of 1907 began. The first run was on the Knickerbocker Trust Company. Barney tried everywhere to find the money to save himself. He even went calling in the middle of the night to see J. Pierpont Morgan, but Morgan disapproved of what Barney had done and would not see him. Two days later the Knickerbocker failed. Not long afterward Charles T. Barney shot himself, and so did several heavy depositors in his bank. The Panic lasted for three weeks, scores of firms failed, and when it was all over, everyone in Wall Street had somehow been affected by the chain of events. The copper market dropped, the lead market dropped, the silver market dropped. Consequently, by winter the shares of American Smelting and Refining had plummeted from $174 a share of common stock to less than $100 a share. Guggenex was not hit as badly because much of that stock was held abroad, but American Smelters Securities went tumbling, too, and as these stocks dropped so did the paper value of the Guggenheim fortune, and the ability of the Guggenheims to secure credit on their holdings.

That autumn, as the Guggenheim empire was threatened by national problems, it came under attack from an old enemy: the Rockefeller interests. H. H. Rodgers had never forgotten and never forgiven the Guggenheims for taking American Smelting and Refining away from him. In the winter of 1907 and 1908 the Rockefellers began buying American Smelting and Refining as it sat low on the board of the Stock Exchange. They did not buy in huge quantities so as to send the price up. They bought steadily, in the manner of someone seeking to establish a foothold that might lead to industrial control.

A simple bear raid would not have worried Daniel Guggenheim. In fact, one had been engineered by the Guggenheim protégé Bernard Baruch, and the Guggenheims had never whimpered about it. They did not object to anyone playing the Wall Street game by its strange heartless rules, and they sometimes played the game themselves, although they were far more interested in control than in quick profits. That is why the hackles rose on the back of Daniel Guggenheim's neck as he contemplated the activities of the Rockefellers in the winter of 1907. The Rockefellers did not look for quick stock market profits either. When they moved in on an enterprise there was only one reason for it: control.

It is worth pausing for a moment in this period of trial to examine the character and habits of the leader of the Guggenheims, Daniel, for on his shoulders rested the fate of a strong industrial empire. Just who—and what—was Daniel?

Daniel was, first of all, a determined man.

It was unthinkable to Daniel that the Guggenheims should lose control of the properties they had built. For in 1907 the Guggenheims were among the first half-dozen of American Jewish families, socially, financially, and politically.

In the 1890's the Guggenheims had moved into the first rank of Jewish families and alliance had been cemented by such marriages as that of Rose to a Loeb, Benjamin to a Seligman, and Solomon to a Rothschild.

(Daniel had begun to pay more attention to his clothes and other niceties. He began then to give heavily to a great many charities.)

In the 1890's and certainly by 1900, when they became the Smelter Kings, Daniel was the most powerful of all the Guggenheims. Daniel had taken over the leadership of the family from his father.

Daniel was retiring, socially. The various demands on him caused him to decide that he no longer wanted to live on the edge of Fifth Avenue, surrounded by Astors and Rockefellers, and he moved the family into apartments at the St. Regis Hotel. There he lived as a rich man may, surrounded by servants and sycophants.

Daniel was also the most progressive of all the Guggenheims. He examined the world around him with a shrewd eye and developed a positive philosophy toward his wealth that was quite unusual among millionaries of the nineteenth and early twentieth centuries. He began to feel—and show—a sense of responsibility to the public. In small things this feeling was matched by others. When his automobile ran down a little boy in Lafayette Street, Daniel picked the boy up and personally carried him to the hospital. He personally telephoned the boy's parents and comforted the family when they arrived. When William K. Vanderbilt ran down a pedestrian, the expenses were paid as they were in Daniel's case, but it was done through intermediaries. Daniel Guggenheim either remembered or could realize that the poor were human beings. Later he would exhibit even more unusual social philosophy.

Beginning with the turn of the century, Daniel made his name stand out more every year. The Guggenheims, under Daniel's suzerainty, became known as tough but honest people with whom one could do business, and people who would not cavil at a high price for a good commodity, service, or investment opportunity. They raised high the reputation of Jewish industrialists among their Gentile peers.

Physically, Daniel was small and he grew a bit stout, but he was too active a man to become fat. He got along well with men of many types: the bold Thomas Fortune Ryan and the troubled, conscientious Adolph Ochs of the *New York Times*. Samuel Untermyer, the powerful attorney, was Daniel's counselor and his friend.

Daniel liked to move around. He kept a hunting lodge in the Adirondacks, and he went to Europe frequently to see old sights and new ones. He believed in taking a month or so off at the end of every six months of business, and would not consider working long, arduous hours for days in a row, as did many of his merchant and business friends. Daniel understood very well that his abilities lay in shrewd assessment of possibilities and in judgment. He had gained from Meyer the faculty of seeing the obvious chance that others passed over. He had the faculty of making decisions, instant decisions if need be, as in 1890, when he and Murry had rushed off to Mexico with Edgar Newhouse to survey the possibilities of the Mexican mines and smelters at the time of the McKinley tariff difficulties. Daniel had not gone to Colorado in 1890 with any intention of traveling to Mexico. It was only when he and Murry began talking to Newhouse that he saw the possibilities. He was flexible enough to take advantage of the slightest opportunity that came his way.

Daniel was the one who projected the company into many ventures, simply by going and seeing and letting his imagination play on facts and possibilities. One day in 1906, after he had made an important commitment to enter the Yukon gold fields with dredging equipment, Daniel decided to see what he had gotten the family into. He left his Adirondack hunting lodge and went to Troy, New York. There he boarded his private car, accompanied by Engineer Beatty, picked up Solomon, and went to Seattle. They took a ship via the Inside Passage to Skagway, then went over the White Pass and into the Yukon. On the basis of his observations, he also decided to expand into Alaska. It was that simple.

Largely because of Daniel, the Guggenheims were more than fair with the people who brought them properties and worked for them. They created a number of millionaires, and scores of well-to-do families who owe their substance to some member's association with the Guggenheims. They could also be waspish, and Daniel was quick to turn against an old employee, or a member of the family if that was indicated, who violated his code of confidence. He demanded absolute honesty between the M. Guggenheim's Sons firm and those who did business with it.

The year 1907 stands out sharply in the career of Daniel Guggenheim and in the reversal of attitudes of a number of members of the Guggenheim family. Until 1907 one might say that the Guggenheims acted purely as exploitation-minded businessmen. Until that year they were relatively free from the bad publicity that comes with great wealth. In 1900, when they took on and defeated the smelter trust, mining men in Colorado, Utah, and Montana shouted huzzahs for the modern Jewish Davids who had defeated Goliath in so uncertain a contest. After 1902, as the policies of American Smelting and Refining became unmistakably Guggenheim policies, the public attitude toward the Guggenheims changed. The change came slowly and it was about five years in the making. In 1906 came the Congo exploitation contract, the Nipissing bubble, Yukon Gold, and the Alaska promotion.

When 1907 rolled around, the stage was set for a spate of anti-

Guggenheim activity that quite surprised and confused the family. It began with Alaska; their motives were questioned and eventually the concession they wished regarding coal in Alaska was denied because of the general fear that the Guggenheims were becoming too big and too powerful. On February 22, the *Juneau Daily Dispatch* said in an editorial that the Guggenheims, "having taken the State of Colorado into camp, are now preparing to annex Alaska so far as its mineral output is concerned." The newspaper warned that the brothers were buying up most of the land available for gold dredging and that they were moving into the coal and copper resources of the Copper River country. One might say, too, that the Guggenheim skill at exploitation of natural resources was a factor, as both cause and effect, in the program of conservationism that changed the face of the Republican Party in these years, bringing on the split between Roosevelt and Taft wings.

The essence of all this ferment was distilled in the Panic of 1907 in the autumn. During the Panic and after it, dozens of smelters and mines of lesser Guggenheim projects were closed down in the interests of economy. These closures coincided with general economic depression, and were followed by widespread belief that monopoly—the trusts—was bringing destruction to the nation. Morgan, Guggenheim, Rockefeller, and a score of other names famous in banking and industry became epithets, and wherever there were mining men the slogan was "Down with the Guggenheims."

So it was that the Guggenheims rose so far socially and financially by 1907, under Daniel's leadership. That article of February, 1907, in the *Juneau Daily Dispatch*, held a key to the Guggenheim rise in politics, for it was in Colorado that the Guggenheims became politicians, and, oddly enough the agent here was not Daniel, but Simon.

18]

AS LONG as he stayed away from Colorado he would be all right, the anonymous letter-writer warned United States Senator Simon Guggenheim in the spring of 1907, but if he ever came back to the state that had sent him to the United States Senate he had best beware.

Guggenheim would never get into the Denver Club or the Denver Athletic Club or any of Denver's best social organizations. Did he not remember that he was a Jew? He, Guggenheim, was not of the elite. Everyone in Colorado knew that Guggenheim was "a voluptuary and a sensualist," everyone knew that he was "like Napoleon Bonaparte," but without brains.

This anonymous writer's diatribe against Senator Simon Guggenheim was printed with a considerable amount of relish by F. G. Bonfils and H. H. Tammen, the lusty proprietors of the *Denver Post*. The *Post* did not usually print anonymous letters on the front page (unless they were threatening letters addressed to the proprietors of the newspaper), but in Guggenheim's case they made an exception. Bon and Tam, as they were known in Denver, were peculiarly ambivalent in their attitude toward Simon and the other Guggenheims. One day they would compliment the Guggenheims. The next day they would lambaste them. The *Post's* enemies claimed that the barometer of Bonfils and Tammen enthusiasm depended entirely upon how much advertising Guggenheim ventures had been doing in the *Post's* pages recently, but Bon and Tam had their own way of measuring what they thought was "good for Colorado," and that was their yardstick. In the years when the Guggenheims were providing wealth and jobs for Colorado, the *Post* praised the "Guggies." When the smelter trust began closing down Colorado smelters, neither Simon nor any other Guggenheim could secure a decent notice in the paper.

Except for Daniel Guggenheim, no other among the brothers made such an impact on the society around him as did Simon. To understand why, one must understand the man and the society in which he lived and grew: the mining society of Colorado.

Simon Guggenheim was the second of the twins, born in 1867 in Philadelphia. He and his brother Robert were raised in luxury. When they were youngsters Robert fell while riding a horse and died a few days later, of peritonitis caused by a ruptured appendix. Like his brothers before him, Simon attended the Philadelphia public schools. Older brother Benjamin and younger brother William would both attend American universities, but Simon pleaded with his father that he had no head for book learning, and Meyer settled for a season in business college for this son. The business college career finished at Philadelphia's Pierce Business School, Simon petitioned for a year in Europe and that favor, too, was granted. Simon went to Spain to learn the language and something about minerals.

Simon arrived in Spain in 1888 and remained there for two years. In 1890 he came home to New York to stay for a time with his mother and father in the house on West 77th Street. In a meeting of the brothers in the partners' room, then at 71 Broadway, it was decided that Simon should join the other younger brothers in the West. His position would be commensurate with his abilities: He would become ore buyer in the Southwest because his knowledge of Spanish language and culture gave him an advantage over ordinary buyers. South of the Arkansas River, which runs through Pueblo, the orientation of the Southwest tended to be Spanish (as it is yet), and the brothers had become aware of the need to cultivate the Spanish-Americans.

For a short time Simon worked out of Pueblo. In 1894 he and Ben moved to offices in the Equitable Building in Denver, and lived in the luxurious Brown Palace Hotel, built in the shape of a flatiron, with all outside rooms and in the center a huge inner court seven stories high for a hotel lobby. In these years Ben and Simon and Will moved frequently in and out of Denver. During part of that time Ben managed the Philadelphia smelter's business from Denver, and Simon held the title of secretary-treasurer. In 1896, Will joined them as vice-president, and all three Guggenheims took a house at 1277 Logan Street. That arrangement did not work too well, because their personal habits and their traveling interfered with normal household routines. The next year Simon was promoted to vice-president and manager of the smelter when Benjamin went to Perth Amboy to establish the refinery.

In 1898 William left Denver and Simon remained the sole Guggenheim representative there. For the next ten years he would manage the Guggenheim interests in the West almost alone.

Shortly after he arrived in Denver, Simon became friendly with Otto Mears (the builder of the Silverton Railroad and several other western lines). Mears was active in Republican Party politics in Colorado, and almost on arrival Simon made a decision that brought him to the attention of political leaders. It came late in the autumn of 1893, a disastrous year in the history of Colorado.

After the failure of Baring Brothers in England, and the Panic of '93, the results of the McKinley tariff struck home and foreign sales of American goods declined. Most important to the mining states and particularly at that moment to Colorado was the repeal of the Sherman Silver Purchase Act by Congress, in November. Once the requirement to purchase silver was removed, government purchases fell. One by one, the mines of Leadville and the other mining districts shut down. The miners came flocking to Denver, the poor ones to hang around the downtown saloons and the stockyards, or to seek jobs in the smelters, and the rich mine owners to sit in the lobby of the Brown Palace Hotel and gaze at the onyx walls, cursing their luck and buttonholing smelter men and politicians.

Later that autumn, the smelter men called a meeting at the Brown Palace to discuss the salvation of their industry. Simon, who was twenty-six years old, came to represent the Guggenheim brothers.

After much discussion, Edward Holden, C. B. Kountze, Dennis Sheedy, James Grant, and other smelter owners agreed that the plight of the mining industry must be called to the attention of the administration in Washington.

They said the few mines that were open could not be counted on to supply ore for long. Further, if the miners did supply ore, once it was processed the smelters could not sell it. The thing to do, the smelter men argued, was to close down the smelters and wait for better times. No one mentioned the three thousand smelter workers who would be thrown out of work if this plan carried.

Simon listened. He said nothing, as befitted an Eastern tenderfoot, and a Jewish one at that. Finally someone in the room asked what the Guggenheims would do.

"Gentlemen," Simon said, "the rest of you can do as you like. Our smelters will not close down."

The Guggenheims earned the dislike of the western smelter men that day and Simon was the symbol of the operators' enmity.

Simon also became a hero to the miners, however, for it soon became known that he alone had stood for keeping the mines open. Following that meeting, the Guggenheims could take their pick of western ores, and Simon was mentioned as a potential candidate for high office.

In the 1890's Simon Guggenheim was a short, slender man with a black mustache and a round, soft chin. Later he was called a sensualist by his enemies. He liked good food and good wines and had grown used to the Continental manner of living during his days in Spain. He was a quiet man, and so these characteristics were not apparent to most acquaintances. It was just as well. Denver was a rough, tough town and the miners and cattle men took their pleasure where they found it. The saloons and dancehalls of Larimer Street were open as long as anyone cared to go into them. Gunshots were heard from time to time in the streets as high-spirited young men kicked up their heels. The card games in the gambling halls were played for stakes of $100 and more to begin with and sometimes soared far higher. In the sedate paneled card-rooms of the red stone Denver Club on Seventeenth Street, nobody ever revealed what the limits were—if any. Around the tables of that club more fortunes were made and lost, more politicians were bought and sold, more greed was exhibited, than anywhere else in the state; and it was here that Simon Guggenheim's virtues and vices were debated. Usually the men of Seventeenth Street counted themselves against Simon Guggenheim because he was an easterner, a Jew, and represented interests they could not control. The men of Seventeenth Street, except for their peculiar attitude toward silver and gold, would all be in the conservative Republican camp.

On the other side of the Republican Party—and even crossing party lines—were the young mavericks, led by Otto Mears, Horton Pope, the Pueblo town boss, and Dick Broad, of Golden, which was not only a mining town but could lay claim to culture too. In the spring of 1896 these men began to talk about Simon Guggenheim as a candidate for lieutenant governor on the Silver Republican ticket. They talked right up until the time of the convention, when it was discovered that Simon was only twenty-nine years old, and thus too young to hold the office.

Simon was unhappy that he had not secured the honor. The lieutenant governorship was not much more than an honor, unless the governor happened to die or be kidnapped by unfriendly Indians while in Wyoming or elsewhere outside the state. The office was elective every two years, too. Still, Simon would have liked to hold that office, if only to prove to his older brothers that he was becoming someone out in the West.

". . . Extended business relations and the experience of previous years lead me to believe that I might have rendered my state good service had the people of Colorado reposed in me their confidence," he wrote Campaign Manager Broad, in a letter which was widely published in the Colorado press. A number of editors suggested that the age limitation might well have been forgotten in Simon's case. Simon read his press clippings and believed them. The fever of politics entered his blood and only one medicine could cure it—election to office.

The year in which Simon was put up and then withdrawn as a candidate for lieutenant governor was the year in which William Jennings Bryan captured the Democratic nomination and the imagination of the West with his famous "Cross of Gold" speech at the Democratic National Convention in Chicago. It was also the year in which Republican Senator Henry Teller bolted his party to form the Silver Republicans, which had headquarters in Senator Teller's Colorado.

Two years later there was no national election, but the Colorado state election issues were entirely national. The basic issue was the same as it had been in 1896, the insistence of the mining interests that the government use more silver and thus prop up the economy of a Colorado which depended heavily on mining.

In 1898 the Republican Party of Colorado was split in two. On one wing was the regular Republican Party of President McKinley, led in Colorado by Senator Edward Oliver Wolcott. The other wing consisted of the Silver Republican following of Senator Teller. There were also Democrats, Bryan Democrats, and Cleveland Democrats (as different as night and day), and Populists, all split on the silver issue.

In the election of 1896, no matter what the brothers at home in New York had done (and all were loyal Republicans), Simon had put money behind the Bryan campaign, as befitted a mining man in Colorado.

When 1898 came around, Simon actively sought the nomination as candidate for governor. But whose candidate for governor was he? Senator Wolcott was trying to pull the Silver Republican support back into the regular G.O.P. camp. Senator Teller was trying to be sure that this did not occur. Teller favored a union of the Silver Democrats, Silver Republicans, and all other silver men in sight. Wolcott, who would be up for reelection by the legislature in 1901, was very much interested in being chosen again, and to win meant that he must control the election of 1898 and the election of 1900. Simon's friend, Dick Broad, and Simon's secretary, D. C. Webber, were both eager to see Simon in the governor's job. They were also eager to keep their friend Senator Wolcott happy. There were so many meetings between Simon and his men and the Wolcott supporters that Senator Teller began to talk about them.

As Senator Teller became more nervous he also became eager for action. In Denver, in July, the Senator and other Silver Republican leaders decided that their convention would be held in Colorado Springs in September. Charles Sprague, a Colorado Springs newspaperman who was privy to the silverites' affairs, telegraphed manager S. N. Nye of the Colorado Springs Opera House to reserve it for the convention.

Meanwhile the Guggenheim supporters had been encouraged by the regular Republican organization. Simon must have realized that the silver movement was doomed to failure. (The fact that by

1898 the family fortunes no longer depended on the American silver market or American production, had something to do with his attitude.) Not long after Mr. Sprague had made his reservation, who should appear in Colorado Springs but Simon Guggenheim and Dick Broad, to walk briskly into the Opera House. Dick Broad put down $100 for rental of the theater for the days of the Silver Republican convention. They intended to hold a Republican convention, too. Mr. Nye believed he was speaking to Senator Teller's friends and took their money.

Soon, along came the Silver Republicans' Mr. Sprague and Opera House manager Nye told him all that occurred. Mr. Sprague said that Guggenheim and Broad intended to seize control of the silver men's convention hall, pack it with Wolcott men, and nominate "Guggy" for governor. Mr. Nye was horrified. He fingered Mr. Broad's check with loathing and dispatched it back to him. He accepted Mr. Sprague's check for $225 in behalf of the silver men. A Mr. J. C. Plumb, of the silver contingent, was called upon as official lessee of the building for September 6 through September 9.

In 1898, Colorado Springs was the center of Colorado's Silver Republicans. Just over Cheyenne Mountain lay Cripple Creek and Victor, and across a few passes was Leadville. The millionaire mining men kept their diggings in the mountains, sent their ores to the smelters on the plains, and played in Denver, but they lived in Colorado Springs, surrounded by beautiful scenery and the cheap labor of easterners who had come to the mountains—many expecting to die of consumption.

It was essential, if the Silver Republicans were to control the state Republican convention, that they first win a resounding victory in the El Paso County convention, which was to be held in Colorado Springs just before the state convention. At the El Paso County Republican convention, a straight silver meeting, A. M. Stevenson of the Republican State Central Committee warned that unless his brethren guarded the Opera House day and night, the Guggenheim men would seize control. So strong was the silver feeling in the El Paso County meeting that no one believed Simon Guggenheim could be opposed to the silver men. Stevenson was cheered but otherwise ignored. He pleaded until finally he con-

vinced half of his constituents late on the night of September 6.
They mounted an armed guard at the Colorado Springs Opera
House.

Word of the intention of the silverites to guard the Opera
House sifted back to Denver, and two days later when the Guggen-
heim and Wolcott men came to Colorado Springs to pack the
Opera House they brought gunmen with them.

The Guggenheim men marched on the Opera House. The
Teller men defended it behind locked doors. The Guggenheim
men shouted that the doors must be opened, whereupon shots rang
out, at both the front and side doors. Bullets began ricocheting off
the sidewalks, and the windows fell out as the glass was shattered.
A gentleman named Harris, one of the attacking party, was so unfortunate as to step into the way of a bullet, and soon he died from
the results of his error. The silver men kept possession of the building, but Sheriff Boynton of El Paso County decided it was time for
the activity to end, and soon both parties were evacuated beyond
shooting distance of one another. The silver men went to court and
sought injunctions against the Guggenheim men, and the Guggenheim men went to court and sought injunctions against the silver
men.

Meanwhile, since both sides had come to hold meetings, they
did so, in separate quarters. The Guggenheim men were unable to
hold the Wolcott men, because the latter were badly shaken by the
bloodshed they had just witnessed. Furthermore, Simon learned
that even though he was willing to pay the Harris family for the
loss of the breadwinner, he was not to be the gubernatorial candidate. He was told that a former sheriff of Arapahoe County had
received the accolade from Wolcott because of his vote-pulling
ability. The sheriff came shyly to Simon and offered him the lieutenant governorship if he would play ball, but Simon demurred.
Lieutenant governorships were quite all right for twenty-nine-year-
old Guggenheims to consider, but not for thirty-one-year-old Guggenheims. Simon was outraged. He had paid good money for this
nomination; $70,000, said old Democratic Senator Thomas Patter-
son in the *Rocky Mountain News*. The *News* reported Simon's
wrathful speech to the convention thus:

I want you men who are opposing to understand that you are down
here on my money. I am supporting you, paying your board, paying you
cash. I want you to understand that I must be nominated for governor.
I want you to understand that I have preserved a list showing the name
of every person to whom I have paid a dollar, and what it was paid for.
If I am not nominated I will publish the list. And I want you to understand that if you nominate another man that I will spend $300,000 to
defeat him.

So Simon was nominated in Colorado Springs by one section of
the Republican Party of El Paso County. Senator Teller charged
that Simon was "by the free and improper use of money endeavoring to secure the possession of the high office of governor of the
state."

The Teller Silver Republicans nominated their own man for
governor, and then both factions tried to take over the state convention of the regular Republicans when they met shortly afterward in Denver. Neither side succeeded, and suddenly Simon
discovered that the votes which had been purchased for him by his
managers were not worth very much. At the Denver convention
Senator Wolcott double-crossed Simon *and* the Arapahoe sheriff,
and nominated his own brother Henry for the governorship. The
Republican leaders agreed enthusiastically. These were the same
men who had conspired to keep Simon out of the Denver Club
when he applied for membership (but that, of course, was because
he was a *Jew*).

In the fall, as the election neared, Simon grew discouraged, and
so did his backers, Mr. Broad, and Mr. I. N. (Ike) Stevens of the
Denver *Republican*, who fancied himself as a king-maker and was
out to elect Simon to office.

Brother William Guggenheim arrived on the scene as Simon was
puzzling about what he ought to do next. William set out to campaign for his brother, and Simon caught the train for New York to
confer with Meyer and his older brothers. There, while in Denver
Will schemed and tried to arouse Colorado to support his brother,
the Guggenheims decided that Simon would be wise to run for office only on a straight Republican ticket, and since he had lost that
nomination, he had best retire from the race. He had the support

of former governor Waite and the Civic Federation, a forerunner of the League of Women Voters. He might have been elected as an independent candidate. But Meyer, Dan, and the others said no. So, no it was.

Simon came back to Colorado. On October 7 he wrote a letter to the newspapers, withdrawing his candidacy for governor, and throwing whatever support he actually had to Charles S. Thomas, the Democratic candidate and candidate of the Populists and Silver Republicans. (Thomas was elected.)

Simon's disappointment in politics was quickly forgotten that year, because on November 24 he married Miss Olga Hirsh, daughter of a wealthy New York real estate man, and they sailed away across the Pacific for a honeymoon in Japan. Five months later they returned to Denver and a suite of four rooms in the Brown Palace Hotel, decorated in the Empire fashion, with walls and furnishings of light green. This was to be a temporary home for Simon and Olga. In a few months they would move into a house owned by Otto Mears at Colfax and Washington Streets, and they would live there until they could move into the large house Simon was building on Sherman Street.

When Simon and his bride returned to Denver to make the "mile high city" their home, Simon was pleased to learn that all the insults of the past were forgotten. It was March, 1899, and the newspapers greeted him respectfully, even fawningly, as he and Olga stepped off the train and took a cab to the Brown Palace. Editor Patterson of the *Rocky Mountain News* had earlier referred to Simon as one of the "wizards of the boodle." Senator Teller had called him "nothing but a walking bank account." The Denver *Republican* had insulted him, in spite of the fact that a *Republican* staff man was one of his managers. H. H. Tammen of the *Denver Post* told William that the *Post* would not support Simon, and the *Post* had referred to him most unflatteringly as "Guggy."

Those comments had been made in the autumn of 1898, but in March, 1899, the name Guggenheim was no longer an epithet in Colorado. What had happened to cause the change? The Guggenheims had refused for their own reasons to join the smelter trust, and Simon had all the credit for this attitude. Colorado millionaire J. B. Grant was an ASARCO man. Anton Eilers was another. So were D. H. Moffatt and Dennis Sheedy. In 1899, they seemed to threaten the very existence of the miners with their trust.

By standing away from the trust, the Guggenheims created a fine reputation in Colorado. The Denver *Republican* referred on March 19 to Simon as the "wealthy, generous philanthropist" who was "idealized by the poor boys of the city." It was recalled that Simon had presented a thousand poor boys of Denver with turkey dinners on his wedding day, even though he was in New York. The Reverend Mr. Uzzell, Denver's "fighting parson," was the instrument through whom the arrangements for the feast had been made. Now, five months later, the newspapers were filled with praise for the generosity. They also recalled that Simon had given five hundred suits of clothing to poor boys of the city a few years earlier.

Simon was no longer referred to as "Guggy," but was given the respect to which a millionaire philanthropist was considered to be entitled, even by Editor Patterson in the *News*. It was quite a change.

19]

IN THE early 1900's the Guggenheim popularity in Colorado increased steadily as the family fought the American Smelting and Refining Company. When the Guggenheims forced the smelter trust to buy them out and then took control of the trust, the initial reaction in Colorado was that all would be well for the country because the Guggenheims would somehow recreate a healthy metals economy.

Such was not to come to pass; there was no chance of it. Soon the brief spurt of popularity ended, and the name Guggenheim became anathema to the miners and their families once again, particularly as the smelter trust reexamined its organization and began closing down the less productive smelters.

Simon and Olga Guggenheim set out to charm the people of Colorado. They did much good in Denver and the rest of the state but they were never accepted by Denver society, which had been created by a tight little group of former miners, former storekeepers, tinhorn gamblers, politicians, bartenders, and ladies of the evening. Yet the Guggenheims were not alone, nor were they snubbed solely because they were Jews. F. G. Bonfils, the mustachioed Corsican dandy who ran the *Denver Post*, was also snubbed by Denver society although he had more power than half the people who voted to blackball him in the exclusive clubs. (Bonfils could not get into the Denver Country Club so he and a group of friends started their own golf and country club in Lakewood, a western suburb of the city.)

Simon and Olga entertained the mine operators, people of the business world, and friends from the East who came to see the quaint city of Denver. Privately, the ladies of high society, who envied the Guggenheims their wealth, sniffed that the Guggenheim house on Sherman Street was garish and flamboyant. It had a rich green drawing room (which the Guggenheims called the parlor) with green velvet tapestry on the walls and imported heavy green carpet on the floor. The large fireplace was guarded on each side by a carved lion. The woodwork was teak and the room was filled with mirrors in silver frames.

The music room and library were paneled in teak. There were many pieces of sculpture, many carvings, and many paintings in the house, but in spite of its richness and luxury it was a comfortable house, having the look of being lived in.

As soon as he came home from his honeymoon, Simon had begun preparing for the political career he wanted. He became a strong contributor to the war chests of the Republican party. He built Guggenheim Hall at the Colorado School of Mines in Golden for $100,000.

He built the Home Economics building at the state college in Greeley. He built the law buildings at the University of Colorado in Boulder. He gave to the National Jewish Hospital in Denver, $30,000 for its construction, and many thousands later for other purposes. He gave $1000 to the university at Boulder for the Simon Guggenheim collection of minerals. He gave $1000 for the Simon Guggenheim biology collection.

In 1902, when Simon was traveling the length and breadth of the Rockies seeking ores for the Guggenheim furnaces and scouting mines for M. Guggenheim's Sons, the Colorado political picture changed. Populism ended in Colorado with the election of James Peabody as governor. Senator Teller was up for his sixth term as United States Senator that year, but his defection from Republican ranks in 1896 had cost him dearly, and only because his friends guarded the ballot box in the state capital building was his seat preserved. Teller went back to Washington for another six years. Simon, having missed the governorship four years earlier, now decided to abandon that ambition in order to seek the United States Senate seat occupied by editor Patterson of the *Rocky Mountain News*, who had won election in 1901 over Wolcott.

Simon began, in 1902, laying plans for an event more than four years away.

It would not be quite fair to say that Simon's political efforts represented personal ambition. Part of his effort was in behalf of the smelter trust. The miners' union and other workers' groups had managed to secure an eight-hour-day law in Colorado. The smelter men refused to obey the law, and the union had struck the smelters. When the fight broke into open warfare in Cripple Creek, the militia was called out.

During this struggle Simon was politically active on the side of ownership. He formed an alliance with W. G. "Boss" Evans, head of the Denver Street Railway System. The *Miners Magazine* charged that Guggenheim and Evans went into league with the Colorado Fuel and Iron Company to buy the votes of legislators for prices ranging from $2500 to $5000. (Vote-buying in Colorado was an old charge. The newspapers printed the stories and then the people forgot about them.)

In 1902, Simon's objective, since he wanted to become senator, was control of the Colorado state election to be held two years later. To achieve this control he must control the State Senate, half of whose members who would be voting for U.S. Senator in 1907 would be elected in 1904; the others would be elected in 1906. Simon and his supporters set out to find men who would "do the right thing at the right time." They were willing to pay expenses for running for the State Senate, and to do anything else necessary to elect these men.

On June 7, 1904, Simon opened a political office in the Majestic Building in Denver. Senator Patterson, target of all this maneuvering, fought back. He brought charges that Guggenheim, the Denver utilities, the railroads, and mine owners were putting up $40,000 to nominate Governor Peabody, known as a servant of "the interests," and another quarter of a million to get him elected. Peabody was then to pack the court with more "corporation men."

Simon let his attorneys handle this and kept his eyes glued on the legislative races. He was not at all dissatisfied with what occurred. It is said that he distributed $50,000 in twelve key senatorial races (and also that he kept the amounts and the names of the men concerned written down in his books).

For two years he spent money and worked at politics. By 1906, Simon had become the financial "angel" of the Republican party in Colorado. John F. Vivian, secretary of the Republican State Central Committee, found that he could count on Simon any time money was needed for a Republican purpose. Vivian became state chairman, and Simon helped him even more. So blatant did the Republican milking of the Guggenheim moneybags become that when the Democrats met in convention in 1906 they made a specific charge in their platform:

"We directly charge that the Republican Party has entered into a compact under which the sovereign power of the legislature of this state to elect a United States Senator is delegated to the executive committee of the American Smelting and Refining Company."

One day Vivian met Morton Alexander, a successful, but not wealthy, farmer from the Denver suburb of Arvada. Vivian told Alexander he could elect him as a Republican for the State Senate. Alexander said he did not know anything about politics, and was not very well known among the people. "To hell with the people," said political manager Vivian.

Vivian encountered Alexander later and told him he was as good as elected. Alexander protested that he did not have any money to spend on a political campaign. Vivian told him not to worry, he would take care of that.

Alexander was elected, along with a very heavy majority of Republicans in both houses of the legislature. The election over, Chairman Vivian of the Republican State Central Committee got down to his real purpose. He called a meeting of the Republican caucus on the afternoon of December 31, 1906, at two o'clock in the afternoon, to select the senatorial candidate of the Republican Party in the election that would be held early the next year. All but Alexander and a handful of other senators agreed when told that Simon Guggenheim was to be their man.

There was some complaint and several stirring speeches were made against *Guggenheimism* and the dictatorship of the corporations, but then the roll was called and all but a handful of Republican senators voted for Simon Guggenheim to become the next United States Senator from Colorado. Democrats and others said what Ellis Meredith later wrote in the magazine *The Arena:* "Colorado will be represented in the United States Senate for six years by a man who could not have carried any single precinct in the state by popular vote."

Years later, when Americans were debating the rights and wrongs of the system under which United States Senators were elected, the election of Simon Guggenheim to the United States Senate from Colorado (and that of Leland Stanford to the Senate from California) were held up as terrible examples of the corruption that could occur when rich men set out to buy seats in Congress. In the case of Stanford the critics were wrong; he had made no attempt to buy the legislature. In the case of Simon Guggenheim they were quite right. Simon made no bones about it. "I merely conducted political campaigns as they are conducted these days," he said.

Senator Patterson, who had been defeated, had this to say of Simon: "He has dealt only with a cabal of party managers. He has gone after the senatorship as he would go about the purchase of a desirable piece of property. . . ."

Simon admitted as much. He said, "The money I have contributed has helped to elect these men and naturally they feel under obligation to vote for me. It is done all over the United States today. I do not consider that it is wrong and neither do I think that it can in any sense be called bribery."

One Democratic senator in the Colorado legislature suggested that Simon be honored by a medal struck to commemorate the occasion of his election, a medal showing Simon sitting with his foot on the neck of a prostrate miner "with a pick in hand and with an appropriate background of smokeless mills and abandoned mines; the whole relieved by a broad border of dollar marks."

On January 15, the day that his election was made official by the Republicans in the Senate (68 Republicans voting for him, 27 Democrats voting for their candidate, and 4 Republicans voting for another candidate), Simon made a little speech of acceptance, noting that he had divested himself of all his stock in American Smelting and Refining and all his other business interests. He was "free and untrammeled," he said. He supported President Roosevelt and his policies. "I favor all legislation adopted by Congress to correct industrial evils and abuses and will support and suggest further measures that experience and wisdom may demonstrate as necessary."

William Jennings Bryan, once recipient of large sums of Guggenheim money, summed up the general opinion of the Democrats:

"As a horrible example, Mr. Guggenheim may prove a useful member of the U.S. Senate; as a representative of the people of Colorado he will be a failure from the beginning."

Later, after the victory had been assured in the state capitol building, a public reception was staged at the Guggenheim campaign headquarters in the Brown Palace Hotel, with champagne punch and cigars for all comers.

That is the story of how Simon Guggenheim, son of an immigrant peddler, became a member of the most exclusive club in America, the Senate of the United States—very much a part of the American dream.

20]

ON JANUARY 25, 1907, the Simon Guggenheims closed up the house on Sherman Street in Denver and boarded their private railroad car, hooked to the back of a Rock Island railroad train. They went to Chicago, and then to New York, and finally to Washington, where the Senator would take his seat among other men honored for their huge fortunes and political machinations. Coloradoans celebrated Simon's departure with a huge outcry against the system that had permitted his election, and a few days after he left the state, the state House of Representatives, which was not dominated by Guggenheim money, sent a memorandum to Congress calling for the direct election of United States Senators by the people.

Simon could not have been less fortunate in his timing in taking public office. Had he selected the period in which the family would be most subjected to contumely, he would have chosen the time between the spring of 1907 and the spring of 1913. These were exactly the years in which he served in the United States Senate.

The Panic of 1907 had brought a depression that affected all the nation. American Smelting and Refining had seen its markets drop away, and it had closed down several of its smelters in Colorado. The closing of each smelter might mean the closing of a score of mines whose resources were too limited for the owners to seek a new market. That is exactly what happened in Colorado and Utah, and soon towns and villages became deserted, left as awesome monuments to pitiful human failure for the eyes of a future generation. The Guggenheim name, once spoken with affection in Colorado, now became an epithet. The State Attorney General filed an action to bar the American Smelting and Refining Company as a trust. In other states of the West the Guggenheims found themselves cast in the role of oppressors of the people. The Guggenheim fortunes were in very real danger in this winter of 1907 and it would take heroic measures to pull their resources together without a major loss. They had issued second mortgage bonds on American Smelting and Refining properties, bonds which must be paid and whose interest must be met promptly, for second mortgage holders are far more restless than ordinary bondholders or stockholders. The Rockefellers, who had bought a sizable bloc of American Smelting and Refining, would insist that the dividends be paid or that the preferred stock take the place of the common for voting control. Thus the control of American Smelting and Refining might be lost to the enemy interests.

Conditions were worrisome enough that the word got out of the Guggenheim offices. Bernard Baruch appeared one day in Daniel's office with a check for $500,000, which he offered the Guggenheims as a loan. Daniel took it gratefully.

At this time, in the winter of 1908, Daniel and the other Guggenheim brothers involved themselves in the least tasteful of all their enterprises. For the first time in the Guggenheim career they set out to promote a stock in order to make money out of stock promotion. It was a practice in which the Rockefellers had engaged often enough, and so had many other speculators. It was, however, quite outside the Guggenheim tradition to depend on outsiders to supply the money to bail them out of trouble. The Guggenheims manipulated but they had always stood above the market. Now they were descending into the pit. There was only one reason for this descent: They needed the money.

Daniel called in William B. Thompson, the promoter of Nipissing Silver, to manage the sale of a new stock by Guggenex. American Smelting and Refining was not involved in this promotion, for it was a Guggenheim affair and it was designed to maintain Guggenheim control of ASARCO, not to endanger it further.

Daniel, his attorneys, and Thompson talked about gold mining investment, and Daniel took the advice offered, that no longer was there any market for $100 par shares in gold mining ventures. Too many Americans had been stung with mining shares in the years since 1900, too many rooms were decorated ruefully with wallpaper made of useless gilt-edged mining stocks. The Guggenheims organized a company called Yukon Gold, which was to be a subsidiary of Guggenex. It would be capitalized at 5,000,000 shares with a stated value of $5 per share. This automatically took the company out of the New York Stock Exchange bracket, and put it into the sphere of the cheaper New York Curb Exchange. The disadvantage of this was a loss of prestige to a family like the Guggenheims; the advantage was in the working conditions of the Curb Exchange and the fact that an appeal to buyers could now be made on a level quite different from any the Guggenheims had ever before made, to a public that was not usually in the stock purchase business.

The $25,000,000 capitalization of Yukon Gold was based on several factors. In 1905 when Alfred Chester Beatty had gone to Bonanza Creek to visit the site of the hopeful venture, he had cabled back a glowing report in which he suggested that a million dollars a year in gold could be taken out of the area by proper hydraulic mining. The Guggenheims had already invested a million dollars in roads, supplies, and sixty-two miles of flume to carry the waters of the Tombstone River to the Bonanza works. They were building a hydroelectric plant and damming the Bonanza to create a water supply.

Late in the winter of 1908, 3,500,000 shares of Yukon Gold stock were issued, the rest to remain authorized but unissued for the moment, and of these, 700,000 shares were placed on the market with the very definite implication that the public was being let in on a good thing by the generous Guggenheims, who really did not need the money at all.

Thomas Lawson, the creator of full-page newspaper advertisements for stock promotions, was employed by Thompson to manage the campaign for Yukon Gold. He was given $100,000 for advertising and promotion. He called the program Thomas W. Lawson's Fair Finance, and he dedicated parts of the advertisements to messages purportedly addressed to President Theodore Roosevelt and other notables, proving that the promotion was on the up and up. He claimed that the gold mine stock had the safety and value of a government bond. He made other wild claims. He printed a portion of a confidential report from Beatty to Daniel

Guggenheim which hopefully predicted a net profit of $36,000,000 from the Yukon goldfields.

At the end of March, after all the hypodermics of enthusiasm that could be administered via newspaper advertising, Yukon Gold was thrown onto the Curb market, and in the first few hours of trading a brisk market was established. Lawson said all 700,000 shares had been sold. Others said that about half the shares had been sold, at prices that began at $5 and ended at $6.50 per share. Obviously the Guggenheim name had created a market, but it was not a rushing bonanza market.

Many questions were asked in the next few days about the Guggenheim participation in what seemed to be a very tawdry scheme. Daniel had gone to Europe, but Solomon assured the public that the Guggenheims were behind this promotion and that they intended to remain behind it, and that they had every faith in Yukon Gold.

To a certain extent this information calmed the fears in the marketplace, but it is questionable whether the Guggenheim statement did more to allay fears, or to assure the public that the Guggenheims had descended very low in financial matters.

Yukon Gold descended lower. Within a week there was no market at all for the stock, and the *Wall Street Journal* said sardonically that "at one moment on Tuesday the celebrated Yukon crowd consisted of a boy with a sandwich board and two brokers busily quoting the stock to one another."

Yukon dropped to 4½, which meant the Guggenheims began to lose on the proposition if they were selling stock from the original portfolio. The Guggenheim brothers quarreled with Lawson when he began linking Yukon Gold in advertisements with American Smelting and Refining, trying to bolster the gold venture. It was rumored that the Guggenheims had wrecked the market themselves by throwing some of their 2,800,000 issued shares up for sale when the stock was above $5 a share. The Guggenheims said the charge was untrue; that the Guggenheims had never unloaded Yukon Gold stock.

Yukon Gold, unfortunately, never did live up to the optimistic prospectus. Finally, it was consolidated with the Alaska holdings, and in 1915, when the war made it more sensible to concentrate on copper, gold operations were discontinued. Solomon, who had taken over as head of Yukon Gold, remained a bull on the possibilities of the Yukon and persuaded his brothers to go back into operation again in the 1920's, but nothing came of it. Finally the machinery was moved to Southeast Asia, as the Guggenheims became involved in the mining and sale of tin.

21]

THE YUKON Gold promotion was not exactly a failure but it certainly was not successful; it did not supply any great amounts of cash for the Guggenheims nor did it even support the new expenditures that had to be made to mine Yukon gold by modern dredging. The Guggenheims went ahead on a sharply reduced scale, but Yukon never developed as an important Guggenheim property. The importance of Yukon in the affairs of the Guggenheims was that their need for cash to pursue the venture, and something they discovered in the process, persuaded them to sell large amounts of American Smelting and Refining Company stock. This selling was accomplished in 1908 and 1909. When it was finished the Guggenheims no longer owned control of American Smelting and Refining, but outside a very small circle, this change in Guggenheim business philosophy was unknown.

In selling off majority control of ASARCO, the Guggenheims were following advice from their lawyers and bankers that was popular at that time and remained popular for the next half-century. This theory held that it was neither necessary nor possible for individuals or a family to retain actual majority ownership of a large enterprise. Control could be as easily maintained by splitting the stock up into small lots and selling to a broad segment of the public. Beginning with the Vanderbilts, this belief was disproved time after time, but many American capitalists still believed it in 1908. The principle was put into practice by J. Pierpont Morgan to suit the convenience of William Henry Vanderbilt, who wanted to safeguard his fortune by selling large blocks of New York Central Railroad stock, yet maintain control of the railroad with a minority interest. Morgan showed Vanderbilt how it could be done. He proceeded to show hundreds of other capitalists how they could do the same, and among the men who learned the Morgan lesson were the Guggenheims.

Earlier the Guggenheims had bought control of Federal Mining and Smelting, which controlled half of the Idaho production of lead and silver, but John D. Rockefeller, Sr., had kept a large interest in the company. In 1908, the Guggenheims began to negotiate to get the Rockefellers out of Federal and, on behalf of ASARCO, out of the the smelting business altogether. But the major Guggenheim interest had moved away from ASARCO.

In 1906 when John Hays Hammond had gone to the Yukon with Daniel to look over the properties, they began to think in terms of Alaska and its potentials. Daniel formed a financial syndicate that included Jacob Schiff and J. Pierpont Morgan's bank to exploit Alaskan resources. The Guggenheims, through American Smelting and Refining, had two smelters in the Pacific Northwest and it was important to keep them supplied with ores, but there was much more to the adventure than the profits of two smelters. The lure was first copper. Then it became *all Alaska*.

It seemed that everyone had discovered Alaska copper at the same time, and that is why the rivalry was so intense. Daniel Guggenheim had come by his interests legally, and in as clean a manner as anyone could have expected, and it was hard for the Guggenheims to understand why they were berated. Daniel had signed an option in the summer of 1907 to buy a half-interest in the coal claims of Clarence Cunningham at Katalla. He had agreed to pay $250,000 for that option. This act created a struggle that went to Congress and involved the Guggenheims on a personal level. But basically what the Guggenheims were really concerned about in Alaska was the copper hidden near Kennecott glacier, 195 miles from the sea on the top of one range of the Wrangell Mountains.

Their concern went back to Yukon gold. While Beatty and Hammond were looking over Yukon property in the summer of 1906, Hammond sent Pope Yeatman, the Guggenex copper man, to visit a claim found by prospectors Jack Smith and Clarence Warner above Kennecott Creek. A graduate of Columbia Univer-

sity's Mining Engineering School named Stephen Birch had heard
of these claims and had taken an option, with which he rushed to
the Guggenheims. Soon it was learned that Smith and Warner
were part of an eleven-man team of prospectors and that with all
the various interests assigned by grubstake and silent partnership,
there were thirty-two men involved in the claim. The matter went
to the courts, and the Guggenheims sat on the option, unwilling to
spend any money until the legal questions of title had been established.

Daniel's dream of 1906 then led to what the wags and cynics of
Wall Street called "the Second Purchase of Alaska." The Guggenheims and Morgan planned a $20,000,000 railroad to reach two
hundred miles inland from the Alaskan coast to tap rich ores of
copper, which were supposed to hold as high as 70 percent pure
metal. They bought canneries. They bought steamship lines. They
began to buy coal fields and tried to buy others. They bought and
bought and attempted to make of Alaska a virtual colony of the
syndicate.

In Alaska the syndicate was hated and feared by the independent people, and it was referred to sneeringly as the Morganheim
operation.

The effort came at the height of J. Pierpont Morgan's power,
but at the time he, along with all bankers and all major corporations, was being surveyed sharply and distrustfully by press, government, and public. The years 1906 to 1910, when much of this Alaskan planning was being done and many of the acquisitions were
made, were years of growing Federal control and cognizance of the
incursions made by big business on what should be public lands. In
1906 the Hepburn Act had been passed, to strengthen the Interstate Commerce Commission. That same year the Pure Food and
Drug Act and the Meat Inspection Act were passed as result of the
cries of the Muckrakers in the press and magazines of the nation.
In 1908 came the White House Conservation Conference, and
later that year a National Conservation Commission was established, with Gifford Pinchot as its head. One of the prime reasons
for the calling of this conference was the attention focused on the
Guggenheim-Morgan invasion of Alaska. Since the beginning of

1907, the Alaskan newspapers had complained that the Guggenheim-Morgan trust was taking over the territory, seeking to buy or control every major resource and industry.

Violence occurred in the late summer of 1907 when a crew of men building the independent Alaska Home Railway crossed an abandoned right of way at the entrance to the Copper River Country, which was owned and leased by the Alaska Syndicate. In the clash between rival armed forces one Home Railway man was killed and half a dozen were wounded.

Alaska in 1907 was the Colorado of Meyer Guggenheim's day in the 1880's. The bloom was off the individual effort. No man with a grubstake could go into Alaska copper, because he could not build a twenty-million-dollar railroad or bring in a half-million dollars worth of mining machinery. After several false starts the syndicate began building its railroad from Cordova, and again here was Leadville. The men who rushed to make their fortunes in the mines found themselves working on the railroad, earning $3 a day and paying $2.50 for board and lodging.

The building of the Copper River and Northwestern Railroad is a part of the almost unbelievable saga of Alaska. It was suggested, in all its misery and glory, by this brief tale told by Harvey O'Connor. The leading figure in the building of the railroad was a tough railroad man by the name of Mike Heney:

As soon as Mike Heney got his roadbed over the hill from Cordova, he was on the marshy Copper River delta, as treacherous a bog as man ever tried to cross. In the winter it was ice, slush and muck; in the spring and summer there were floods and muck; at all times, muck, muck, muck everwhere, so deep that tens of thousands of piles and millions of cubic yards of moraine had to be placed across the thirty miles of delta until the road confronted the twin glaciers, Miles and Childs. One presented a solid face of ice four miles wide and three hundred feet high. A bridge, 1,150 feet long, costing $1,500,000, was needed between the two glaciers. Who shall calculate the cost in human misery that winter when gangs of men, their faces stung by winds roaring down from the Chugach Mountains, their hands and feet numbed by cold that descended to sixty below zero, drove thousands of piles through seven feet of ice and forty feet of moraine for temporary supports for the bridge spans. Two spans had been swung on to permanent supports by the end of April. These piers were sunk sixty feet into the river bed, solid concrete eighty-six feet around and sheathed with heavy steel rails to withstand the glacier bergs that would hurtle against them in the Copper River's twelve-mile current.

From sunrise till midnight the crews worked completing the third and last span in a race with the ice which would begin to move almost any day. Suddenly the flood came, heaving up the seven-foot crust of ice and forcing it against the wooden falsework which supported the third span. By dusk that falsework had been moved fifteen inches out of place. All night long men worked with steam lines thawing the ice around the piles while other crews rigged tackle which moved the four hundred and fifty feet of falsework back to its normal position. An hour after the span had been moved from the falsework and attached to the permanent piers, the ice broke. Great masses were hurled against the falsework, which swayed and fell. Even the pile drivers were lost in the river's wild rush, but the engineers and crew were happy—the great glacier bridge was in place. A year had been gained by the margin of one hour!

So the construction went, seemingly at a snail's pace, no matter how many hundreds of men worked how many thousands of hours. Yet, at last it was completed, and the final spike, a copper one whose ore had been hewed from the Kennecott Mountain, was driven into place. The mining could start here in the beginning of 1911.

The mine was built; it thrust its black tendrils into the sides of the mountain, and bunkhouses and assay shacks reared their wood and tarpaper sides along the creek below. Those buildings on the side of the mountain were fixed into the rock with cables so they would not slide down the steep, ever-moving rock. When the first trainload of ore was sent out, it assayed 75 percent pure copper, a product entirely different from the ore of Utah's Copper Mountain. The Guggenheims had become foremost among the Copper Kings. The Washington smelters could be enlarged and would be assured of work for many years to come as could be seen in the first ship's cargo of copper that left for Tacoma: it was valued at a half-million dollars.

When the values became known, the Guggenheims came under serious public scrutiny for their part in the Alaska expansion and the matter became the subject of bitter dispute in the press and in Congress. In that affair, Senator Simon Guggenheim introduced his most ignoble attempt at legislation. During the struggle between Secretary Ballinger of the Interior Department, who favored Guggenheim exploitation of Alaska, and Gifford Pinchot of the Forest Service, who opposed it, Senator Simon introduced a joint resolution into Congress that would have brought about an investigation of the Forest Service and would have crippled Pinchot by reducing his budget by $500,000.

The Guggenheims had gone north in 1906 with the thought of a multiple development. If they built a railroad which cost $20,000,000, as they did from the coast to Copper River's Kennecott Mountain, they might expect this investment to be played against a number of properties. In partnership with the Morgan banking firm, the Guggenheims' Alaska syndicate had purchased the Northwestern Steamship Company, Northwestern Fisheries, and the Alaska Steamship Company. They had located huge coal reserves which they proposed to exploit, and they planned to go into other mineral search and development. All these plans had been blown sky-high by a series of arguments, laws, legal decisions, and Congressional investigations.

In 1910 came a number of anti-trust decisions in the courts, which caused the Guggenheims to slow their development. Worse, in 1910 came the public squabble between Ballinger, Secretary of the Interior, appointed by President Taft, and Pinchot, conservationist director of the United States Forest Service, appointed by President Theodore Roosevelt. The squabble had begun in 1909, with dismissal of a field agent of the Interior Department, named James A. Glavis, who became involved in an argument over Wyoming lands. Under the Roosevelt administration, Secretary of the Interior James Garfield had withdrawn these lands from the possibility of sale. They were possible sites for future dams, and the Roosevelt conservation policy said that they must be retained for the use of all the people.

When William Howard Taft came to office, he and Secretary Ballinger doubted if this was legal, and Taft, who always wanted to be a Supreme Court Justice rather than President, regarded the legality of the matter as more important than public policy. Ballinger put the lands back into the general system known as "public entry" which made them available to private power companies for purchase. Glavis protested and was fired by order of President Taft. He retaliated by writing an article for *Collier's* magazine in November, 1909, in which he charged that Ballinger was selling out the public's interests in American lands. Specifically Glavis said that Ballinger had helped the Guggenheims seize control of vast coal reserves in Alaska.

Pinchot criticized Ballinger publicly. President Taft upheld Ballinger and fired Pinchot. Roosevelt, in Africa on safari, learned about the firing and broke with Taft. The Republican Party came apart at the seams and the nation's emotions were so much aroused over the questions of public policy that the Guggenheims found it wise to back away from the Alaska adventure. Ballinger, after all, had been commissioner of lands when the Guggenheim purchase of the questionable claims was presented. When the claims were rejected in 1908 by the Roosevelt administration, Ballinger had resigned as commissioner and had become lobbyist for the Alaska Syndicate.

The resulting Congressional investigations exposed to full public view a problem that was not to be settled then, a problem that would still bedevil the nation more than half a century later: How were the public lands to be used, and who was to have the privilege of exploiting them?

At issue specifically was a field that might yield sixty million tons of coal and a profit estimated by Gifford Pinchot to be $25,000,000. At issue also was the growth of Alaska.

Secretary Ballinger had said that the riches of Alaska could only be exploited by someone as wealthy as the Guggenheim-Morgan Alaska Syndicate. Gifford Pinchot said these natural resources must be kept in store for all the people. He and the other conservationists held this principle to be inviolable. In Alaska and everywhere else men lined up on one side or the other. Those who saw jobs and profits in Alaska for themselves defended Ballinger and the Guggenheims. Those who either hoped to profit themselves through exploitation or who stood on the principle of conservation said the Guggenheims were robbing the till of the American people and that Ballinger was helping them. In later years Henry Ford would join the critics of the Guggenheims, saying that no man had a right to exploit for private profit the riches that lay below the surface of the earth.

One interesting point taken by Gifford Pinchot was that Guggenheim-Morgan money was tying up Alaska's resources and preventing its development. Fifty years later when Alaska's development was stirring, it was easier to see that once the Guggenheim-Morgan interests lost their enthusiasm for the project, and stopped with Kennecott, the development of Alaska also stopped for many years.

The Guggenheims and Morgan had never had as much bad publicity as they received in the Alaska affair, with the Guggenheims bearing the brunt of it. The *Denver Post*, for example, had been after the Guggenheims for years, ever since they began closing smelters in Colorado after 1909.

"The Guggenheims have Alaska in their grasp," wrote the editorialist for Bonfils and Tammen, "and as a result labor is starving, trading places are closing, and industrial conditions are chaotic."

The *New York Times* took the opposite position: "The Guggenheims were willing to spend millions for the development of our distant and much-neglected province of Alaska," wrote the editorialist for Adolph Ochs, friend of the Guggenheims, "but the government would not have it. It would not permit them to carry on large-scale coal mining or to build railroads. . . . If Washington continues to turn out bills and laws according to its present policy and present temper, American capital will presently shun industrial investments. . . ."

The Guggenheims were puzzled and unhappy about bad publicity. The Morgan bankers did not like it one bit better. George Perkins, the Morgan partner who had engineered the Alaska Syndicate with the Guggenheims, reported at the outbreak of World War I that Kennecott could never pay out the $20,000,000 cost of the railroad on its capitalization. In earlier years that would not have worried anyone, but once the emphasis was taken away from Alaska, marvelous and profitable as Kennecott would be, bailing out the investment seemed important to the bankers.

22]

IN COMPARISON to the other members of the United States Senate, Simon was very much the undistinguished senator. Yet he was not a bad senator. One might say that he represented the family's interests when he voted sturdily for the maintenance of high import duties on foreign metals and metal products, but actually these were Colorado's interests as much as Guggenheims'. By 1907 the Guggenheims were deeply involved in various foreign enterprises, and a heavy duty on the price of lead, for example, placed their Mexican lead in a disadvantageous position.

It made no difference, however, how Simon comported himself. The rebellion against Guggenheimism erupted almost immediately after his election. No scandal about Guggenheim's election was too great to be aired in the press. One story reported that Simon had never been a legal resident of the state, that he had so declared in a federal court suit. (The story was not true; the basis for it went back to the early days when Meyer had a canny habit of getting suits against the Guggenheims shifted to federal court by saying that the Guggenheims were residents of Pennsylvania.)

By the summer of 1908 much of the press was very critical of Simon and all the other Guggenheims. Senator Patterson would never forgive or forget. He never failed to mention Simon as the "Senator of the smelter trust." Even the Pueblo *Chieftain* lost taste for the Guggenheims when the Philadelphia smelter was torn down in 1907. The Colorado Springs *Gazette* called Simon a "dollar-sign Senator."

In Colorado, in August, 1908, a move was begun to oust John Vivian, the faithful Guggenheim political lieutenant, in order to take control of the Republican organization in Denver away from the Guggenheim interests. The Colorado Supreme Court was petitioned to unseat all those Denver leaders who were declared Guggenheim men on the grounds of corrupt practices.

One of Simon's problems in 1908 was that enemy agents had infiltrated his own organization. Guy LaCoste, a prominent Denver Republican and Simon's sworn enemy, seemed able to secure copies of the correspondence that passed between Simon and his friends. On September 14 of that year LaCoste handed a reporter from the *Denver Post* a copy of the Guggenheim slate of candidates that Simon had given his political supporters *before* they met at the Brown Palace Hotel at ten-thirty. The *Post*, an afternoon newspaper, had received the list in time for that day's editions. The story seemed most ominous. Actually Simon was simply functioning as a political boss—one of hundreds of such political bosses in the United States. Simon was correct in the winter of 1907, when he defended his winning of his Senate seat by saying he did nothing that others were not doing. Simon accepted the system and really did not believe that he was doing anything wrong, while the most successful political bosses knew quite well that theirs was a system of skulduggery, that it could thrive only in secrecy, and that the electorate must be kept from knowing how affairs were managed lest the reformers secure permanent reforms.

When Guy LaCoste gave the *Denver Post* a copy of the typewritten instructions to delegates to the Denver Republican Convention, the anger of the public was aroused. The *Post*'s Mr. Bonfils and Mr. Tammen pointed out that in the past two months Simon had ousted the entire Republican County Committee of Denver—246 men and women—and replaced this organization by his own slate, and had then persuaded the state convention to ratify his decision. The *Denver Post* said that Colorado must have a direct primary election law, which would take the control of political affairs out of the hands of the state party conventions. Simon, in his simplicity, said he opposed such a plan. Simon knew how elections were managed because he had been taught by professionals in a hard school, and they had proved to him the success of their system by securing his election.

If one is to understand the campaign of vituperation against the

Guggenheims and its heights of fury, one must realize that it came simultaneously with the basic struggle over natural resources.

"Senator Guggenheim bought his seat. It took him seven years to do it but he persevered and succeeded," said the *Denver Post* on October 1, 1908. "Then he decided to buy Colorado. . . . Is Colorado for sale? Do the people want government by Guggenheim? . . . The debasement is inconceivable."

The following day the *Post* answered the question it had posed: "There shall not be government by Guggenheim." The implication was that Bonfils and Tammen would protect "the people" from this insufferable evil. The *Post* rose up to champion the people against *Guggenheimism*. This action was the best thing that could have happened to Simon. When the *Post* came out absolutely against Guggenheim, all the other Denver newspapers stopped to give thoughtful reconsideration to their position. The *Post* had suddenly become the most successful newspaper in Denver. Bonfils and Tammen, with their Sells-Floto circus, cheap coal pool, and free Christmas dinners for tiny tots, had captured the imagination of Colorado as no other newspaper had ever managed to do. The *Rocky Mountain News*, a far more respectable organ, employed Damon Runyon, Eugene Fields, and other stars to back up the formidable Editor Patterson, but the *Post* had such men as Lord Ogilvy, noble son of a real British peer, as farm editor, and General Frank Hall as mining editor, both intelligent men and characters in their own rights.

Every day Bonfils' and Tammen's editorial writer fulminated against Simon Guggenheim. Every day the opposition of other newspapers was diluted. One day Senator Patterson pointed out that the *Post*'s race prejudice was under cover, not overt. Patterson, whose newspaper circulation was suffering, could not bring himself to join the *Post*. Soon other Denver newspapers were championing Senator Guggenheim against the *Post*.

The *Post*, now having a whipping boy all its own, redoubled its attacks on the senator.

Simon came out in favor of the use of voting machines to speed elections. When the *Post* editors learned of this attitude they erupted in righteous anger. Guggenheim, they said, was trying to force the use of voting machines in order to confuse the regular

Republicans and assure continuation of his own control. "Guggenheim Plotting to Rob Voters of Ballots" said the *Post* headline.

The *Post* was not content to attack Simon on his record in politics. "How the Smelter Trust Gouges Producers of Ore," read a huge headline above a story written by mining editor Hall on October 9, 1908.

American Smelting and Refining had just announced a dividend which amounted to $4,625,000. General Hall explained that while the miners of Colorado were starving in their shacks, the smelter trust, since 1899, had paid dividends of $43,000,000. He indicated that nearly all of this sum had gone into the pockets of the Guggenheims or for corruption of the people of Colorado.

General Hall went out to interview mine owners. He found one owner who said he had sent twenty-one tons of ore to an ASARCO smelter. The smelter deducted nine hundred pounds for moisture content, charged $1 a ton for sampling, $16.77 for freight, $5 a ton for smelting. The assay value of the ore, established by an independent assay office before he sent it to the smelter, was $173. This mine owner received $21.95, or just a little more than $1 per ton for mining the ore. Here, said the *Post*, was proof of Meyer Guggenheim's belief that there was no point in owning a mine unless you owned your own smelter.

This exposure of smelter gouging so appealed to Bonfils and Tammen that they told General Hall to keep it up. "Trust Greed Sucks Blood of Mines," said the *Post* headline two days later. The article discussed rebates and the fact that the competition in ore-buying by smelters had been almost totally eliminated. The mine-owners of Colorado did business with American Smelting and Refining on its terms or they closed their mines.

The *Post*'s blaring campaign came at a time when the Guggenheim men were locked in combat with other Republicans over the composition of the election slate for that year. So much furor had been raised when the Guggenheim ticket was revealed to the public that there was to be a primary election among Republicans, before the general election. Perhaps influenced by the *Post*'s noisy campaign, perhaps not, the courts decided that an anti-Guggenheim slate of candidates would appear on the ballot of the primary, and so would a Businessmen's ticket.

Simon was not the cause of the Guggenheims' bad publicity, nor was the criticism entirely due to anything the Guggenheims did. It was a matter of the times. Harold Loeb, son of Rose Guggenheim Loeb, described the general feeling about the Guggenheims around 1910 in his autobiographical study, *The Way It Was*. He was writing of the days at Princeton:

The Ballinger-Pinchot controversy was much in the news; both Roger [Straus] and I strongly supported Pinchot, who was attempting to keep certain resources for the American people. Neither of us went behind the conservationist's slogans to consider how natural resources should be exploited.

One afternoon while strolling along the road to Lawrenceville to indulge in "jiggers" (the precursor to the ice-cream sundae), Roger was talking about Pinchot's valiant crusade against the despoilers. Suddenly he stopped and stood looking at me. "Did you know," he asked with the intensity he could so readily summon, "that the Guggenheims are trying to steal Alaska?"

I did not. Conditioned to hear the worst about the family, I merely shrugged my shoulders. After a sidelong glance to see how I was reacting, Roger continued walking and talking. He told me that my uncles were building a railroad to bring coal and ore out of their Kennecott mine. At the same time they were trying to gobble up all the other Alaskan resources; mines, forests, fisheries. . . . Pinchot was against it, Roger was against it, I decided I was against it, too.

That was the attitude of some of young America toward the Guggenheims, but it was not universal.

Harry Guggenheim, for example, cousin to Harold and later brother-in-law to Roger Straus, grew up with no knowledge of this attitude toward the Guggenheims. He lived in the protected environs of 54th Street and later at the St. Regis Hotel. Winters were spent in private schools in New York, summers at the family house in New Jersey. Horseback riding and tennis and other sports dominated Harry's life as a child. He spent his youth at dancing school, and later, at parties with girls, at coming-out parties, and at all the festivities of upper-class New York.

Harry went away in 1907 to Yale's Sheffield Scientific School. Still he learned nothing of the public hatred of his family. After one term he quit school and went to the smelter at Aguascalientes to begin working at the bottom of the heap. In 1910 he married Helen Rosenberg, daughter of a New York industrialist, and that same year he was persuaded that he needed an education. Harry returned to his studies, this time at Cambridge University's Pembroke College, where he undertook the study of politics, economics, and government. In college Harry obtained a bachelor's degree, a tennis blue, and high office as president of the college tennis club, and came home without a thought in the world that the Guggenheims might be regarded as oppressors of the American people. His generation of Guggenheims was not much concerned with the American dream.

23]

IN THE period between 1906 and 1912 the words Guggenheim and copper seemed to be almost synonymous. William Braden, once an American Smelting and Refining employee, had gone to Chile in 1904 and had taken option on the Rancagua copper mines. He had brought machinery in by oxcart, and then had gone to Barton Sewell, an official of American Smelting and Refining, to offer a private proposition. Sewell had not been able to persuade the company to finance the purchase, so the proposition was taken to Guggenex. Daniel and his brothers bought a substantial interest in the property, the mine was rechristened the Braden mine, and soon it had its own smelter and refinery in Chile.

The Guggenheims' gradual movement out of American Smelting and Refining ownership seemed to have some strong reasoning behind it, for the opportunities had swung back the other way to the mines instead of the smelters. To be sure, the solid base of ASARCO was valuable and still essential to the Guggenheims in the pursuit of their exploration of the world for mines. The mines themselves were again of primary importance, as they had been to Meyer Guggenheim in the beginning. The combination of mining and smelting interests was very powerful, but Daniel and his four brothers could sense a growing nationalist feeling in the rest of the world, which did not welcome the infusion of American capital with American control and the export of natural resources to America for American profit. Pedro Alvarado, the silver king of Mexico, for example, had in 1903 offered John Hays Hammond first $25,000,000 and then $35,000,000 for the Guggenheim properties in Mexico. Elsewhere in Mexico there were rumblings of government discontent.

In 1906, the Guggenheims had secured an important interest in Nevada Consolidated Copper Company, and they began to improve the property. They built a railroad to connect the Southern Pacific Railroad with the mines, 130 miles away from the line in the Steptoe Valley of eastern Nevada. Soon they controlled 650,000 shares of the 1,200,000 shares of the stock through Guggenex. As 1907 arrived, this stock was valued at $13,000,000, and although it fell by half in the Panic of 1907 it began coming back the next year. The Guggenheims also bought the majority interest in the Cumberland-Ely Copper Company, which had been organized by putting together claims near the ore grounds of Nevada Consolidated. A new smelter was built by American Smelting and Refining in Baltimore—and the basis for the construction was a contract that the Guggenheims gave American Smelting and Refining from the Nevada Consolidated Company. This variety of operation, using the carrot in front of the nose of the ASARCO donkey, obviously could keep the Guggenheims in managerial control of American Smelting and Refining as long as they could produce new properties to add profits to the smelting company.

In 1908, as the country was still shaking from the effects of the Panic of 1907, the Guggenheims and John Hays Hammond parted company. There were several reasons for the split. The Guggenheim reputation had been injured by the Hammond Nipissing decision, Hammond's reputation had suffered by the Guggenheims' foray into high-pressure mining promotion with Yukon Gold. But the real reason for the parting of company was more basic: Hammond was costing the Guggenheims $250,000 a year and they no longer needed him. Their method of operation had changed completely since that original contract was signed. Observers of the mining scene sometimes said the Guggenheims had sacrificed all the public good will they once enjoyed by the changes they had wrought in their methods of operation. Perhaps this charge was correct, for the Guggenheims were now under much pressure and had become very unpopular among mining engineers, mine workers, and smelter workers. The section of the public that concerned itself with the misdeeds of the mighty capitalists was much concerned with the Guggenheims; the left-wing political leaders who were developing the Socialist movement and the labor movement found them to be among their favorite whipping boys, even though the Guggenheims were simply doing as their peers were doing, operating their companies for private profit. One reason they were particularly hated was that they learned so fast. From their bankers and lawyers they had learned all the new tricks, many of them invented by J. Pierpont Morgan—including that of capitalizing a company so that the bonds bore the capital investment, and the stock was used by the owners and manipulators to milk the corporations of gains.

Nevada Consolidated and neighboring Cumberland-Ely Copper were merged and the new Utah Copper Company issued new securities, which were bought up in the expanding metals market. The Guggenheims made arrangements with Penrose, MacNeill, and other copper men to handle the output of Ray Consolidated Copper and Chino Copper. By 1910, Utah Copper Company had swallowed up the Boston Consolidated Copper Company and the Utah Company's capitalization was boosted from $6,000,000 to $25,000,000. The Guggenheims had stepped into Utah Copper to hold a quarter-interest in the beginning. In 1910, when the merger with Nevada and Boston came about, they held about a third of the stock.

What had happened to the Guggenheims in the past ten years since they took control of American Smelting and Refining? They had traded control of this $100,000,000 company, and outright ownership of more than half of it, for smaller shares of a great number of enterprises. They maintained control of American Smelting and Refining because their interests were so broad, and there was Guggenheim money in nearly every firm that supplied ore to the smelting company. They were spread much more thinly than Meyer would have liked, but these were new times and new conditions.

The wealth of the Guggenheims was now much celebrated in America, so much so that it stimulated Grace Brown Herbert Guggenheim Wahl to seek another share of it for having given up William with so slight a struggle.

Grace and her new husband, the Frenchman Roger Wahl, had

gone with the first slice of Guggenheim wealth to Europe, South America, then to Mexico and the Orient. In three years the $150,-000 she had been given in settlement was all gone, and when the money ran out so did Frenchman Wahl. He had the marriage annulled.

In 1904, William had dutifully married Aimee Lillian Steinberger, a friend of his sisters, Rose and Cora, and baby William, Jr., had been born.

Now along came Grace to claim that William, Jr., was illegitimate because her marriage to William had been dissolved under duress. She began with some private importunations to William.

"I would take the time to read this if I were you . . ." she wrote, and went on from there.

William did not know what to do, but Daniel did. He told Grace to go away and stop bothering the family; that she would not get another penny. Grace was willing to settle now for another $250,000 (an indication of how the Guggenheim fortunes had increased). On October 31, 1908, Grace's new lawyer, William Seabury, filed a suit for annulment of the Chicago divorce and the struggle began.

The struggle lasted for five years. On July 16, 1913, it was ended by a disgusted Chicago judge who called for an investigation of everyone—Grace, Guggenheims, and attorneys—who had participated in the original divorce. It had been a fraud from beginning to end, he said, but Grace's morals were so bad and her involvement so complete that she had no cause for action.

At one point, Daniel had offered Grace a settlement of $78,000, but she, sensing victory, had spurned the offer. Now she got nothing and disappeared from the story of the Guggenheims.

After Grace left him, Will had taken up automobiling and bought a pair of French Panhard automobiles. For a time he thought to rival William Kissam Vanderbilt, Jr., the leading society automobilist, but he never did. Marriage to Aimee seemed to settle him down—at least he no longer flaunted his extramarital affairs and he paid some attention to business. In 1907 he claimed to be the largest single stockholder in American Smelting and Refining, and perhaps this was true, but it was not true for long. He divorced himself totally after 1901 from all the business affairs of the Guggenheims and participated in no further ventures of the brothers, then settled down to a quiet life. He gave to good causes and he occupied his time with trivial affairs. One of these was the Pennsylvania Society, whose purpose was to "cultivate social intercourse among its members, and to promote their best interests; to collect historical material relating to the State of Pennsylvania; and to keep alive its memory."

Senator Simon Guggenheim's popularity in Colorado hit an all-time low in 1908 and 1909 when the Philadelphia and Durango smelters were closed down. He began to make a comeback two years later. Teddy Roosevelt came to Colorado and a cowboy breakfast was held for him. Among those who appeared to honor the President was cowboy Senator Simon Guggenheim, who had tried to destroy the President's policy on natural resources, and cowboy Governor John Shafroth, who had tried to destroy his public lands policy.

The next year even Bonfils and Tammen made their peace with "Guggy" because the Senator announced in 1911 that he would not seek another term.

"He has been a loyal supporter of President Taft and a faithful worker for the interests of Colorado," said the editors of the *Post*, with a fine generous forgetfulness. "Simon Guggenheim is a most lovable, high class gentleman, a man full of fine impulses, of great charity, great breadth of vision, broad sympathies and a loyal friend."

One would almost think that Simon was giving up his Senate seat for a *Post* candidate, but such was not the case. Bonfils and Tammen were simply overcome by Simon's decision to let them run the state without his further interference.

Having decided in 1911 that the way of life of politics was really not for him, Simon settled down to represent Colorado as an industrious, if not distinguished, Senator. Even his most critical appraisers decided that he was not a hard-shell Tory. He favored liberal projects such as the creation of the Children's Bureau and in time Simon even came to favor direct election of United States Senators.

Just before Simon left the Senate, the Denver *Republican* assessed his career. Simon Guggenheim had secured the passage of fifty special pension bills for Colorado veterans and widows of veterans whose service dated back to the Civil War. He had secured an increased appropriation of $400,000 for the federal building to be built in Denver and $25,000 for one in Greeley; $10,000 for Glenwood Springs, $10,000 for Monte Vista.

Simon had secured an appropriation of $25,000 for a fish culture station to be established by the federal government in Colorado.

He had secured an additional judge for the United States District Court in Colorado. He had introduced and pushed through special bills for any number of citizens, such as the heirs of a Post Office inspector, and of a mint employee who was injured and could not return to duty at the Denver mint.

Simon had introduced a law to raise the homestead size to 320 acres, another that would turn over a quarter of the money from national forest income to the states for roads and schools, and another for a botanical and agricultural research station to be established near Denver. He had secured the cession of certain lands near Denver which were in the Rocky Mountain National Park holdings, so that Denver could have its own mountain park system. He had secured an additional appropriation for Mesa Verde, the new national park.

As a member of the Senate Committee on Military Affairs, he had participated in the making of a bill that would appropriate $94,000,000 for the support of the United States Army. In 1912, he had gone to Europe to study the postal systems of Germany, France, and England. He had come home, then, to introduce a measure to cut the homesteader's occupancy from five to three years (a part of the Borah Act). He had handled three hundred cases of land contests by citizens and other problems between the people of his state and the Department of Interior in this last session of Congress. He had interceded for Colorado citizens in Mexico, and had interceded with the Treasury in numerous tax cases. His office had checked the status of 1000 pension applications. He had secured special aid for the Jicarilla Indians.

He had also publicized his adopted state, praising Colorado scenery. He was one of the first tourist promoters, urging establishment of spas like that of Carlsbad. He had secured the planting of 7,000,000 trout in Colorado waters. He had urged federal surveys of the Denver Basin east and north of the city for a reserve of oil and coal which his geologists suspected lay there. He had urged a soil cultivation program when soil conservation was in its infancy.

In other words, Simon Guggenheim had been a faithful representative and servant of Colorado. It seemed odd to many that, in spite of the diminished hatred and opposition in Colorado, Senator Simon Guggenheim decided not to seek reelection. Olga Guggenheim loved Washington and she entertained there so often and so successfully that she became one of the city's most prominent hostesses. Simon had become chairman of the Committee on the Philippines—a committee very close to the heart of President Taft, who had served as United States Commissioner to the Philippines —so his star was rising.

As the time for his retirement approached, Simon explained the reason for his position to President Taft, who wanted him to run again. He must go back to business, he said, because his brothers needed him. Daniel sought relief from his daily responsibilities with American Smelting and Refining.

In the spring of 1913 Simon closed his Washington mansion and prepared to leave the National Capital. He was to become chairman of the board of American Smelting and Refining, which meant he must live in New York. He had spent twenty-two years in Colorado or representing Colorado in Washington, and so with a tinge of regret he left both Colorado and politics. Secretly he hoped to move ASARCO headquarters to Denver.

Simon was not a strong man, but he was not a venal man. In many ways he was the most enlightened of the Guggenheims, and he knew the problems of the West. In 1913, however, Simon Guggenheim left the West. His house on Sherman Street was kept up until the early 1920's; then, finally balked in his plans to move ASARCO to Denver, he closed the house. The last Guggenheim left Colorado.

24]

___

IT WOULD be impossible for any outsider to list all the transactions and negotiations in which the Guggenheims were involved after 1910. Like any family of financiers, they were constantly on the move, trading this property for that one, always amalgamating and changing the basis of their fortune.

They retained three basic instruments for this purpose. First of these was M. Guggenheim's Sons, which would continue as the personal partnership of the brothers for a few more years. Through this company they owned their personal holdings, such as ASARCO stock, Yukon stock, Nevada Consolidated, and other companies. Second was Guggenheim Exploration Company, in which others had interests. Guggenex was the company that went after bonanza mines. The Guggenheims held control of Guggenex through M. Guggenheim's Sons. The third instrument was American Smelting and Refining Company, in which they no longer held much stock, but maintained personal control by keeping tight reins on the management of the company.

By 1910, Isaac was semiretired. Simon was in public life and therefore found it necessary to resign all his business interests. By 1910 William had broken with his family over personal matters and was traveling in his own direction, quite alone. Benjamin was involved in his personal investments, friendly with his family, but independent since the argument over establishment of the Guggenex Company.

From Paris, with occasional sojourns in New York, Benjamin dabbled in business enterprises of his own. One of these was International Steam Pump, which seemed to be a very successful affair.

The breach in business affairs did not mean that Ben Guggenheim cut himself off from his family. He was delighted to see his brothers and their wives, and he continued in close touch with the Guggenheim affairs. He simply ceased to be a participating member of the new ventures of the partnership. If other Guggenheims came to see him in Paris, or at his New York home, first on East 69th Street, later on East 72nd Street, he was happy to entertain them. The house on 72nd Street was a measure of the quiet elegance of the Guggenheims. A visitor passed through the big front door into a small vestibule, then through one glass door, another one, and into a marble foyer complete with fountain and stuffed eagle which Benjamin had shot (illegally) at his summer camp in the Adirondacks. A marble staircase ascended, and behind it stood an elevator. Upstairs was the reception floor, with a conservatory, drawing room, dining room, and a reception room in which hung a tapestry of Alexander the Great entering a conquered city in triumph. Here Florette Guggenheim sat and poured tea every week for what her children were to call the "haute Jewish bourgeoisie."

The parlor was furnished in the fashion of *Louis Seize*, except that along with the mirrors and tapestries Ben had added a touch or two of his own. One was a huge, mangy bearskin rug. The bear's mouth stood open, revealing an artificial cavity of an alarming red shade, but the tongue sometimes came loose and fell out, which upset Florette, and the teeth were forever being put back in, having been extracted by the three little girls.

Benjamin spent his days attending to his affairs, business and personal, and often came home late at night. Florette gave many parties for her relatives, one of whom was addicted to charcoal-eating (which turned his teeth black), one of whom gave fur coats to chorus girls, and one of whom later drowned himself in a New York City reservoir after trying unsuccessfully to murder his wife with a golf club.

One of Benjamin's trials was that his rich wife's rich relatives considered him to be beneath her, and they had the disconcerting habit of saying so publicly. The strange collection of Seligman relatives, plus Florette's determined grasp on Jewish society, would have been enough to sour a man of the mildest character. Ben was driven to other women, while Florette seemed not to care at all. Daughter Peggy called her father "fascinating and handsome," but all realized that he was very unhappy, with Florette traveling to Europe every summer to visit "hundreds of French and English Seligmans."

By 1911, Benjamin and Florette had become man and wife in name only, and Benjamin had deserted his French marquise for a new mistress, a young blonde singer. He was then expanding International Steam Pump (which built the elevators for the Eiffel Tower) and his business kept him in Paris most of the year. Ben was in Paris for most of 1911 and until April, 1912, when he booked passage back to America on the White Star Liner *Titanic*, which was making its maiden voyage to the United States. He had engaged passage on an earlier vessel but a strike of stokers had postponed the sailing, so he had decided to take the new *Titanic* instead.

On April 9, 1912, one of Ben's nephews, Harry, son of Daniel, met his uncle on the street in Paris. Although Ben was leaving for New York the next day he took the youngster to lunch and talked to him about life for most of the afternoon. The next day Ben took the train to Cherbourg, and that evening of April 10 boarded the *Titanic*.

Benjamin was not traveling alone—that was not his fashion. Aboard with him were his secretary Victor Giglio and the young blonde singer. The *Titanic* sailed on the evening of April 10 from Cherbourg, her captain determined to make a world's record for the crossing of the Atlantic. Aboard the ship on this maiden voyage was a select group: Bruce Ismay, president of the steamship line, was there; Isadore Straus of the Macy's family was aboard; as were J. B. Thayer of the Philadelphia Thayers, and John Jacob Astor.

The captain of the ship was so interested in a record on this voyage that he did not see the iceberg that sliced open his ship's bottom on the night of April 14. A few minutes after the accident, the *Titanic* listed heavily and it was apparent that she would sink. There were ships within call but none that could arrive in time to save all the passengers. There were not enough life jackets for all, and not enough places in the boats for more than a quarter of the 2100 people aboard.

After the ship had struck the iceberg, John Johnson, room steward, awakened Guggenheim and Giglio and told them to get dressed. They put on life preservers that he handed them. Ben said his life preserver hurt his back, and so he took it off. Johnson said it was time to go but Ben said he wanted to pick up a few belongings and would meet him on deck. Johnson went on deck and helped women and children into the boats. Later—much later—the steward said he saw Ben and Giglio, both dressed in evening clothes, both without life jackets. Steward Johnson asked what they were doing, and where their jackets were, and was told that they had given them to women. Ben and his secretary said they intended to go down with the ship.

Johnson lost sight of the two men but then he saw them later. Ben was walking along deck, helping women into the life boats. "Women and children first," he shouted, as he saw some men try to push women aside and jump into the boats themselves.

There was one last moment and a last conversation as Steward Johnson was ordered into one of the boats to man an oar, and Ben gave Johnson a message for Florette.

"Tell her that I played the game straight to the end and that no woman was left on board this ship because Ben Guggenheim was a coward," he said.

The lifeboat was swung out and over the side, and Johnson did not see Ben Guggenheim again.

Within an hour after the collision, the *Titanic* went to the bottom of the sea, carrying 1517 men and women.

In New York, the Guggenheims knew that Ben was supposed to be aboard the *Titanic*, but they were not sure he had actually sailed. Daniel wired the *Carpathia*, which had picked up most of the survivors a few hours after the sinking. Was Ben Guggenheim aboard? he asked. "No," the captain replied. This information was transmitted to the children of Ben Guggenheim, but for some reason Florette was not told, and she was kept in ignorance of the fate of her husband for many hours. Finally, when the *Carpathia* docked, Steward Johnson went to the St. Regis. He was introduced to Florette, and he told his tale. That same day, the youngsters of the Daniel Guggenheim family had gone down to meet the survivors and there they had met Ben's mistress, who had been put into one of the boats. Perhaps that was the answer to the disappearance of Ben Guggenheim's life jacket.

25]

IN THOSE last few prewar years, Daniel was still the kingpin and he would remain so for the rest of his life. Murry and Sol were his able right and left hands, never arguing against Daniel's leadership, never criticizing publicly anything that he undertook or committed the family to do. M. Guggenheim's Sons was as solid a partnership as ever existed after a life of a dozen years.

By 1914 one might also say that the Guggenheims achieved the pinnacle of social success, through marriage. The summer of 1913 was a busy time for the New York Guggenheims. Gladys, Daniel's daughter, had become engaged in July, much against her mother's wishes, but only because Gladys was seventeen years old.

Gladys's fiancé was eminently suitable by any standards. He was Roger Straus, Harold Loeb's old friend. He was attending Princeton at the time and would graduate the following year. Marriage of a Guggenheim and a Straus would cement wealth and social position, for Roger's father was twice Ambassador to Turkey and served Theodore Roosevelt as Secretary of Commerce, while Daniel's name was the most important in the Jewish world of business.

Gladys, who was at Rosemary Hall that year, dutifully promised that they would wait a suitable amount of time. She was supposed to go to Bryn Mawr that autumn.

But Bryn Mawr never saw Gladys Guggenheim, for by fall she and Roger were so much in love they decided to be married in the winter.

They were married at the St. Regis Hotel in the ballroom by Dr. Silverman, Rabbi of Temple Emanu-el, and took a brief honeymoon in Asheville, North Carolina, where George Washington

Vanderbilt was building a resort. But the honeymoon was quickly cut short because the impatient father of the bride wanted the groom to begin learning the business of the American Smelting and Refining Company. Roger Straus hurried home with his bride and went to work in the company's personnel department.

In a way, Gladys Guggenheim represented the power and position that the Guggenheims secured during the first decade and a half of the twentieth century. Then the Guggenheims became *the* most powerful Jewish family in America, and second only to the Rothschilds as most powerful in the world. The hatred lavished on them was proof enough of power—they were the declared enemies of the International Workers of the World, and the most prominent of those enemies, because the I.W.W. was always strong in the mining camps and smelters. But the Guggenheim power and prestige could be measured in another manner, and so it was in 1913, when Gladys became engaged to marry Roger W. Straus. If the Guggenheims, latecomers that they were, married with the powerful and patrician Strauses, then they had indeed arrived in the New World. On Sunday, January 11, 1914, Adolph Ochs' *New York Times* so indicated in a headline that extended across a full page of the society section: "Guggenheim-Straus Marriage Unites Noted Families."

"There is much in common with the Strauses and the Guggenheims," said the *Times*, "their high conceptions of family life and public service. To become good citizens as well as good husbands and fathers are their ideals. These ideals are rooted in the rich soil of race. The gigantic undertakings of the Guggenheims recall the Rothschilds; there is the same audacity and the strong bonds of fraternal affection.

"The same parallel may be made in the case of Nathan, Isidor and Oscar S. Straus . . . There is the stuff out of which may be woven gorgeous romance in the unique history of the Guggenheims and Strauses—the wedding of their two children in a happy and striking climax in their life symphony."

The *Times* society writer may have been carried away by her own prose in this description of the Guggenheim-Straus marriage, but the wedding was a symbol of the growth in strength and power of the Jewish community in the United States, a change that had

come about in less than a score of years. It would be improper to
say that Jews were held down in America until the twentieth century. A Jew served high in the councils of the Confederacy, there
were Jewish members of Congress and important Jewish businessmen, but the fact remained that the Jews were not powerful in
nineteenth-century America and were sometimes detested. They
were denied admission to hotels (even in the middle of the twentieth century, Jews were not encouraged at some of the "finest" resort hotels in America). There were a hundred forms of discrimination against them, but the discrimination dropped sharply as the
Jews gained in economic power, and when the Guggenheims and
the Strauses and the Ochses faced the world they need fear no
man.

In another way, Gladys Guggenheim Straus represented change
and social position for the Guggenheims. She and her mother became extremely active in New York civic affairs, beginning in the
second decade of the twentieth century.

The beginning of the second decade was a time of social ferment
and the Guggenheim interests were certain to be affected by it.
The social legislation enacted by the states included laws relating
to wages and hours, to child labor and equality of women in employment, to safety and health in factories, mines, and smelters. In
this period Theodore Roosevelt was organizing the Progressives to
break away from the Republican Party over the questions of national resources and the control of those who were coming to be
known as "the malefactors of great wealth." In the mining and
smelting areas of the nation no family was more cursed than the
Guggenheims. They were held personally responsible for the conduct of the enterprises they controlled and generally for every evil
inherent in mining. Unions had organized in Colorado and the
other states and territories in which the Guggenheims held interests. The unions were quick to organize in the mines and smelters
because of the vast difference in economic conditions between the
men who worked the earth and the owners. When the ore was
taken away to smelters and refineries, it was treated by other working men who were no better off than the miners and their families.
They all worked for the owners who earned millions without lifting
their fingers. The miners and the smelter workers worked hard and

sometimes they died hard, and for what? To make the owners rich? Small wonder, if any, that these men became embittered and turned radical and revolutionary in their thinking. It was to be so, even until the middle of the twentieth century when the Mine, Mill and Smelter Workers Union would be one of the most radical unions in America.

After long and bloody strikes in Colorado and other states of the West, the miners and smelter men of the Western Federation of Miners joined the new International Workers of the World, which had been formed in 1903 by Socialist Eugene Debs and Daniel DeLeon of the Socialist Labor Party. The I.W.W.—Wobblies, they were called—was the most militant labor organization ever formed in the United States. It was dedicated to meeting violence with violence. The history of the labor movement in America indicates very clearly that the original violence came from the side of the employers. When there were strikes, the employers hired strikebreakers. A number of special agencies advertised their services as strikebreakers. They employed thugs and plug-uglies who were expert at wielding clubs and blackjacks and were not afraid of using guns if it seemed necessary. The Guggenheims used these strikebreakers as did almost all industrialists. Of course, Daniel did not pick up the telephone and call the strikebreaking agencies; he had managers to do that; yet the Guggenheims had to accept the responsibility for their dealings with labor, along with the other industrialists. American Smelting and Refining was built on exploitation—the exploitation of natural resources for the benefit of a few, and the exploitation of labor. The Guggenheims did not invent either idea. There is no indication that they sat up late at night thinking of new ways to wring sweat from the workers and profit from the ground. They simply followed the accepted paths of capitalism in America. Meyer Guggenheim came to the United States and found a social system that he understood very well. Dog had eaten dog in Europe. Dog ate dog in America. The difference was that in America the breed did not count; any mongrel could grow strong. In America, a man, Jew or Gentile, made his own way according to luck and ability. Meyer and his sons can scarcely be faulted for not setting out alone to change the system in their youthful days. Meyer would never try to change it. He was single-minded, seeking fortune for himself and for his family, and having found it he retired from the scene, satisfied. The others, the boys, would seek fortune and double it and redouble it, and then, leading nearly all other Americans, they would recognize a debt to the country wherein they had become so very rich, and would try in their own ways to pay that debt. In that sense the Guggenheims would be among the best-behaved of American millionaire families.

But to expect them to clasp the unwashed miner to their family bosom was expecting too much. When the American miners proved fractious, the Guggenheim managers hired foreign labor, Japanese and Greeks and Bulgars, straight off the boats. In 1912 came a strike that was met viciously by the importation of hired thugs and gunmen to the copper mines in Utah. The six thousand workers there shut down the mine. The union then shut down Nevada Consolidated with its 3500 men. Solomon Guggenheim came out from the East to investigate, but he did nothing to stop the importation of strikebreakers.

The Guggenheims received the blame for the strike of 1912, and there was a good deal of blame to take. This was the year of the Bull Moose, the year in which the Progressive forces of the Republican movement were demanding strong conservation measures, the year in which the idealist college president-politician Woodrow Wilson would bring out old ideas about the rights of men and dust them off again. The Democrats would win the election with him on a platform that called for strong measures of conservation, a corrupt-practices act, and the abolition of monopolies. The new President Wilson was on record as demanding the dissolution of trusts because, he said, they were inimical to the existence of free competition.

The Democratic platform of 1912 might have been written to put the Guggenheims out of business, as their business was conducted in that year. When Roosevelt and Wilson and all other politicians talked about conservation of natural resources, they damned the Guggenheim movement into Alaska. They damned the Guggenheim smelters trust. They damned the Guggenheims for purchasing legislators. It was charged that the Guggenheims bought Senate seats and employed legislators as other men buy theater tickets or hire boys to cut the lawn.

Did the Guggenheims buy legislators? Perhaps they did. It was common enough practice in East and West, and if they did not try to buy them, then they were almost alone among industrialists. The legislators sold themselves very easily. It takes two to make a corrupt bargain, and the corruptibility of legislators in America cannot be laid entirely at the door of big business when the public responsibility of legislators and other officials in America operated on a sliding scale. To be sure, American government was growing more responsible at every level, and had been since the first stirrings of reform in the Garfield administration, egged along by the Arthur administration from which no one expected honesty. Government was strengthened immeasurably by the Cleveland, McKinley, Roosevelt, and Taft administrations, all of which were essentially honest. On the national political level honesty and incorruptibility were becoming prized assets. These ideas were trickling down through state houses and city governments, but corruption was still very much a part of the state and city government picture in America in 1912. Any city of the time must also admit to a paving scandal, a public transportation scandal, or some similar disgrace in which the public weal was turned to private gain.

The exploitation of the working man was nearly criminal in its completeness, particularly in the mines and smelters of America. In Pueblo, Mexican smelter workers were paid $1.50 a day, and how they managed to survive on so little money is a tribute to the tenacity of mankind. These were years in which the workers starved, and huge corporations like American Smelting and Refining paid out more in dividends to their stockholders than they did in wages to their thousands of workers. In *The Guggenheims,* Harvey O'Connor noted that as late as 1913 one man of every four who worked in an American Smelting and Refining plant suffered a disabling accident every year, a casualty rate of 25 percent!

The election of 1912 brought about basic changes in the industrial labor picture. President Wilson created a new Department of Labor. A new anti-trust law (Clayton Act) was put in the legislative works. An Industrial Relations Commission was established under Frank P. Walsh and this body took itself so seriously that it called industrialists on the carpet to testify in public investigation of labor conditions. The Guggenheims anticipated the changing

climate by creating their own industrial relations bureau, dedicated
to bringing about reforms in their industry. They talked about pension plans, housing projects, hospitalization for employees, accident compensation, incentives, and other ways of bettering the
condition of the people who worked for the Guggenheims.

Such activity did not cut seriously into the profits of the American Smelting and Refining Company. In 1914 that firm earned
nearly $12,000,000. Obviously, the exploitation of natural resources
continued to be the most highly profitable business in the world.

As times changed, the Guggenheims responded. In Mexico, beginning in 1910, the Guggenheims were subject to the same criticisms that they were receiving in the United States. The Mexicans
had the further plaint that this exploitation of men and resources
was being carried out by foreigners who drained the capital from
their land. President Porfirio Díaz was still dictator of Mexico and
it still suited his aims to have the Guggenheims control the smelting industry, so nothing was done, but the criticisms mounted—
partly because anti-Díaz politicians could mask their hatred of the
regime in criticism of the foreign capitalists.

In 1911 the Guggenheims fell on evil days in Mexico after Francisco Madero, scion of an independent smelting family, staged a
revolution against the Díaz government and won. As a smelter
man himself, he appreciated the Guggenheims' problems, but in a
few months he was dead by assassination and the revolutionary
Victoriano Huerta was in control. Strikes were staged against the
Guggenheims, and instead of taking huge profits from Mexico, in
1913 the American Smelting and Refining Company was losing
money there.

During the next few years the Guggenheims played their hand
carefully, supporting Pancho Villa in northern Mexico because he
held the power of life or death over their smelters and mines. So,
while other Americans—settlers and property owners of northern
Mexico—sought American government intervention to destroy
Villa and eventually secured the intervention of an expeditionary
force under General John J. Pershing, the Guggenheims gave Villa
comfort and he gave them, in return, freedom to run their business.

When the Wobblies came in to organize smelter workers in

Chihuahua, Villa announced to the union men that they must leave town or he would shoot them. It was a simple method of dealing with organized labor. General Carranza, who held the southern part of Mexico while Villa held the north, complained to President Wilson about "the Guggenheim interests" with all their powers of corruption. The Guggenheim interest was simple enough: They had five plants in Villa territory, all operating. They had several smelters and important mines in Carranza territory, none operating. Carranza had levied a tax on smelters which was 800 percent of the old tax established by Porfirio Díaz. The Guggenheims waited and watched and tried to keep out of trouble in Mexico.

Further south, the Guggenheims were experiencing better luck with their investments. In 1900 a Guggenheim engineer who had been sent to South America reported on the finding of a rich copper deposit halfway between the Andes Mountains and the Pacific Ocean in Chile. It was desert land, located at a place called Chuquicamata. The property could be purchased for less than $250,-000, the engineer reported. In 1900 the Guggenheims were just beginning to become interested in copper. The market for the metal was developing, and their mines in Mexico were proving most productive and profitable. Yet the Guggenheim interest was still largely in lead and silver, and Daniel did not wish to dilute the family's interest so much at that time as to become involved in management of mining where it would take months of travel back and forth. In 1900 the Guggenheim family was still trying to exert active management in Guggenheim properties. The move from industrialist to financier was occurring, but it was not complete.

The Guggenheims did not buy Chuquicamata in 1900. They did not buy it until 1910, and when the financier Guggenheim paid one hundred times as much for the property as the industrialist Guggenheims would have paid a decade earlier; but they were in a better position to pay one hundred times as much, in stock, as they had been ten years earlier. In a way the Chuquicamata adventure was a symbol of what had happened to the Guggenheims between 1900 and 1910.

What they bought in Chile was another mountain, nine thousand feet high, carrying hundreds of millions of tons of porphyry copper ore, which ran 2¼ percent copper. Again it would be an open-pit mining venture, which meant heavy machinery. This kind of mining was possible only for a syndicate or a wealthy firm, for it demanded the use of much of this expensive machinery. The Guggenheim luck held again in 1910, because the machinery was available and not far away. The builders of the Panama Canal had completed their work and the army engineers were seeking to dispose of the steam shovels, open gondolas that could be used to carry earth or ore, locomotives, and other expensive equipment that had been used to build the canal. In 1910 the Guggenheims began buying. They also ran tests on the ore and began establishing the framework of exploitation. First they formed a company called Chile Exploration Company, sometimes called Chilex and sometimes called Chile Copper, with Daniel as president of the company and Murry as vice-president. Chile Copper issued 3,800,000 shares of common stock, valued at $25 per share. A million shares of this stock, or $25,000,000 in stock, was given to Albert C. Burrage, the Boston mining engineer who had brought Chuquicamata to the Guggenheims' attention this second time. Burrage had done far more, because the Guggenheims in 1910 were deluged by offers and tips about mining properties. Burrage had offered just the kind of proposition the Guggenheims wanted these days. He had gone to Chile, bought up all the surrounding territory so that there could be no complications, and cleared the titles. Then he had offered the proposition to Daniel Guggenheim. Burrage had owned the property, but had not been in a position to exploit it. This was really only the beginning of the age of *big capital*. Huge sums were still in the hands of individuals and families and because of their unique positions in a burgeoning America, families like the Guggenheim family were doubling and redoubling their fortunes in a few years. But times would change.

Having given out $25,000,000 in stock for ownership of the property, the Guggenheims put away $70,000,000 in stock, then set about arranging the financial matters that would enable them to exploit Chuquicamata's copper ore.

Chile was a poor country, electrified only in the cities, with virtually no roads that ran where American capitalists wished them to run. The Guggenheims must do everything for themselves if they were to bring out the copper ore. They built a shipping center at the little port of Tocopilla, ninety miles away from the site of the mine, and equipped it with an oil-fired electric plant at a cost of $3,500,000. They built the lines to transmit the power to the mine. They secured concessions from the government of Chile to use fresh water for the personnel, and water from a brackish river fifty miles away for industrial purposes. They spent $12,000,000 to prepare the Chuquicamata mine for exploitation, and, instead of selling any stock, they financed it all by floating a $15,000,000 bond issue with the American public, through the brokerage firm headed by Bernard Baruch.

Soon, a town arose at the base of the mountain and work began. As the town grew and the work proved profitable, a new problem arose: William Guggenheim began to nurse a grudge against his brothers.

In the years after his defection from the Guggenheim partnership, Will had spent his time as a gentleman of leisure. In 1914 he joined the American Defense Society, an organization favorable to the Western Allies and opposed to "Pro-Germans, Socialists, Pacifists, Anti-Militarists, Anarchists, I.W.W.'s and similar organizations." Soon he was devoting his full time to this patriotic organization. He became chairman of the Vigilance Committee, the Teachers' Loyalty Committee, the Army and Navy Committee, and the Publication Committee. He attended the meetings and faithfully recorded the fact in his autobiography that he shook hands with President Theodore Roosevelt at a meeting. He was also decorated by the Italian government. He had, it seemed, achieved everything he wanted from life.

In 1910 Will and Ben had signed waivers permitting the other brothers to form the Chile Copper Company. The waivers were necessary because the brothers had not reorganized M. Guggenheim's Sons when Will and Ben withdrew from active participation in new ventures at the turn of the century. A year later—1911 —when Chile Copper proved to be extremely profitable and Will found himself with a fortune that was being diminished by expenditure and poor investment, he decided that he had been defrauded by his brothers because they had not told him they were going into a sure thing. He repudiated his waiver in 1912 and demanded that the brothers let him invest in the company, on the terms under which they had invested.

Daniel and the other brothers refused to let William enter at so late a date. For one reason, the investment package was closed and to open it again would create considerable difficulty for the original investors. For another, Will had shown no interest in the partnership affairs since he "retired" in 1900 at the age of thirty-one, with an income of $250,000 a year. Also, M. Guggenheim's Sons was in the process of dissolution, because after Ben's death in 1912 the old partnership came to an end. The attorneys were drawing papers for a new partnership when Will stepped into the middle of the proceedings with his claim. He began a suit in New York, saying that he had been hoodwinked out of $10,000,000 by his brothers because they had concealed the true nature of the Chile Copper investment from him. He had been told that millions of dollars must be sunk into the project to make it pay out. Strictly speaking, this was no more than the truth, but because they put together the firm by floating bonds, the Guggenheims had not put up any money at all.

Daniel, Isaac, Murry, Solomon, and Simon all appeared in court to contest Will's suit and testified that Will had never contributed any assets to the partnership. After 1900 he had shown no interest in the business. He had signed waiver after waiver when the plans called for investment of his own capital.

Even now, they said, Daniel had offered William a chance to come back into the partnership if he would end his "idleness and speculation." If he would go to work again, Daniel said, he would give him an interest and even lend him the money to participate in the next venture. But not in Chuquicamata. That matter was closed. Will had refused the offer, Daniel said. If he could not come into the Chile Copper venture he did not want into anything.

It came out in the testimony that the brothers *had* concealed the nature of the investment from Will. Their defense, then, was that they had no responsibility to take him into their confidence, because they were carrying out the venture as individuals, not as partners of M. Guggenheim's Sons.

It was a specious argument and if Meyer had been alive he might have harked back to his own Old Testament teaching in Switzerland for a remark about his brother's keeper. But the Guggenheims were very much annoyed with Will, who had been such a source of trouble to them for so many years.

The argument became more spirited when Will indicated that he had retired only temporarily from M. Guggenheim's Sons. He had gone into International Steam Pump with Ben, he said, and the other brothers were interested in that. In other words, he and Ben had taken them into new investment, Will said, taking the major risk upon themselves in behalf of the whole family.

Finally after Daniel and the others showed themselves to be obdurate, Will's attorneys played their last card. They said that the truth or fiction of various statements made about the Guggenheim investments could be ascertained only if the books of M. Guggenheim's Sons were brought into court as evidence. Since such an action would expose the workings of the partnership, the other brothers backed away, and settled with Will for an amount estimated to be around $5,000,000.

M. Guggenheim's Sons was reorganized after the settlement and William was given no option to join the new partnership. It was not even called M. Guggenheim's Sons in the end, for Will objected to the use of the name since he was not allowed to participate. The new firm became Guggenheim Brothers. It included Isaac, Daniel, Murry, Solomon, Simon, Harry F. Guggenheim (son of Daniel), Edmond A. Guggenheim (son of Murry), and William C. Potter, a Gentile and an outsider.

William retired to spend his time on various utopian schemes.

26]

BY 1914, when war broke out in Europe, most of the Chuquicamata development work was completed. The Guggenheims were in the fortunate position of controlling the copper output of half the world, at a time when the market for copper suddenly began to increase at an unheard-of rate. With war came the need for thousands of ships, millions of miles of wire, thousands of airplanes, and hundreds of thousands of automobiles and trucks; and every one of these products used copper, to say nothing of the millions of tons of shell casings and other military supplies to which copper was vital.

As long as World War I remained a European venture, the Guggenheims and other American industrialists were praised by the United States government and purchasers for the Western Allies for their ability to expand and meet needs that developed. The Guggenheims now owned all or part of seven important copper mining companies, whose operations ranged from South America to Alaska, all of them producing huge amounts of copper, and all profitable in terms of operating expense. Not all, however, were profitable in terms of total investment. The loser was Kennecott, the adventure in Alaska.

Urged by their bankers, the Guggenheims first tried to sell their Alaska railroad to the government as a national asset. But the government, having taken the position on principle that private capital should not exploit public domain, decided it had no interest in acquiring a railroad, no matter what principle was involved. The Guggenheims tried to persuade the Taft administration to buy.

Young J. P. Morgan, Jr., tried to persuade the Wilson administration to buy. Neither would consider the proposition.

Another new problem—at the time of the outbreak of World War I, the Guggenheims were very much concerned with what would later be called "their public image," although Freudian and industrial psychologies had not then progressed so far that they could put an easy name to their worry. So great was this new concern that after the Panic of 1907, when Daniel was interviewed by newspaper reporters in Denver he denied the responsibility he was given for social problems or for that depression. Being in Colorado, he urged the silver men to get together and force through Congress laws helpful to the silver mining interests of Colorado. That idea was appealing in Colorado, and the Guggenheims were in a position to push the laws, because 1907 was the year of what was referred to by the Alaska newspapers as the Guggenheim "purchase" —the election of Simon Guggenheim to be United States Senator from Colorado. Following Daniel's remarks, tension eased a bit for a time.

Even as he was publicly evading responsibility, Daniel Guggenheim was privately turning over in his own mind his relationship to the American society in which he lived. He was slowly coming to some conclusions that were quite unusual in a capitalist of that time. John D. Rockefeller, having braved the threats and hatreds of the people, had decided to restore to the people some of the benefits of the money he had made in exploitation of natural resources. In 1901 he had founded the Rockefeller Institute of Medical Research, and later this public-spirited private enterprise was expanded and succeeded by other Rockefeller foundations, so the idea of the very rich returning some of their gains to the public at large was not a new one. Far from it, in the 1860's, George Peabody had given away most of the fortune he acquired as an American banker in England to found housing for the English working poor, and to America to educate the newly-freed slaves, to establish museums, and to aid universities. Andrew Carnegie had given matching funds to build public libraries across the American landscape. This was the background against which Daniel Guggenheim stood as he contemplated his relationship to the society that had made him wealthy.

After success ceased to mean anything, when the millions of dollars became so many that there was no further cause for personal striving, Daniel Guggenheim relaxed a good deal. He began traveling to Europe to the spas to take the baths and the cures. He became an advocate of orderly control of the metals industry, assuming, of course, that the control be exercised by the men who owned the means of industrial production. His attitude toward trusts matched that of J. Pierpont Morgan; both saw the harmful effects of cutthroat competition in industries in which they were involved, and both believed in the beneficial effect of cooperation among industrialists. Like the elder Morgan, Daniel believed that his industries could stand the burden of many millions of dollars worth of securities.

For a number of reasons, the mining and smelting industries were the proving grounds of organized labor in America in the years between 1907 and 1914. One basic reason was that these were dangerous industries and to work in them at all a man must feel that he had a foot in Hell or Heaven. Such an attitude makes men willing to quarrel and fight for their desires, and it often leads them to zealousness on behalf of the general good, or what they see as the pot of gold at the end of the rainbow. Miners and smelter men were oppressed. If they objected to their lot, Chinese and Poles and quiet little men from the Balkans were brought in and given their jobs. The foreigners were then oppressed and paid starvation wages so that they were easy marks for union organizers of the radical left. Such organization led to strikes which crippled the metals industry in 1911, 1912, and 1913, and, after fighting the strikers with as much vigor as anyone else, eventually Daniel Guggenheim realized that he must make some concessions to the laboring men in the interests of an industrial peace that was too long in coming. It was simply bad business to have so many enemies and so much trouble. On that basis the Guggenheims set up their own bureau of labor relations to handle their affairs in American Smelting and Refining, and they began to follow the same general policies of paternalism in their other enterprises.

Daniel's basic attitudes toward the industrial society were revealed in the hearings conducted by the new United States Industrial Relations Commission that was established under the Wilson administration in 1915. When called to testify and asked about his attitude toward organization of labor, Daniel said he believed employees were completely justified in organizing, because capitalists were often arbitrary in their relationship to laboring men. Under questioning, he painted a picture of the Guggenheims not before seen in America, and summed it up with a statement that might easily have been made by an industrialist half a century later, but hardly on the eve of World War I.

There is today too great a difference between the rich man and the poor man. To remedy this is too big a job for the state or the employer to tackle single-handed. There should be a combination in this work between the Federal government, the state, the employer and the employee. The men want more comforts—more of the luxuries of life. They are entitled to them. I say this because humanity owes it to them.

The full import of this statement cannot be felt unless one considers the condition of organized labor and the attitude of American state and federal government to labor in 1914 and 1915. No child labor law yet existed in America. A Department of Labor had just then been established, and it was fumbling for delineation of its authorities and responsibilities. The injunction, the company union, and the "yellow dog contract" were perfectly accepted weapons of the industrialists against labor. Hardly any industrialists honored the right of employees to join an *independent* union. Laboring men in America, in effect, were just beginning to raise their heads and demand as rights what the industrialists chose to regard as license. Workers were winning victories. (In 1902 Mississippi had become the forty-eighth state to pass workmen's compensation laws.)

Daniel had other concepts of government and its responsibilities, which were also quite unlike those of the run-of-the-mill industrialists.

I think the State should furnish work for the men who lack employment. You may call me Socialistic, if you like, but it is a job of the United States to look after its people. Were it not for philanthropic work, there would be a revolution here. But sufficient help is not given in this case. People won't give up the money they make easily, even if they have more than they need. So the government must raise the money—raise it by taxing the estates of the rich, if you will—but the United States must raise it some way.

Were ever more prophetic or more realistic words spoken by an American millionaire about the direction of American society?

Actually, Daniel was not so much a labor philanthropist in action as he was in theory. American Smelting and Refining was an open-shop employer and union organizers were not welcome there. He was, like all rich men of good will, an anomalous character; he did not always practice what he preached. In Mexico, in Chile, and in other countries where the Guggenheims operated, they participated in the exploitation of the working classes. They did not invent that exploitation, and perhaps it was asking far too much of any industrialist to ask him to try to change the social system of another nation. The Guggenheims did not do so. They became prominent among the exploiters of labor and natural resources, so much so that a half-century later members of Guggenheim Brothers winced if an outsider used the term "exploitation" in their presence. To them and to millions of other people, "exploitation" had become a dirty word.

Until the time of World War I the newspapers were interested in Guggenheim comments on financial matters. It is an indication of the growing importance of the Guggenheims in the American scene that as of about 1914, any Guggenheim could talk on any subject and be quoted. Their prominence had suddenly given them what in the press passed for omniscience. Sol was as likely as Isaac to use this license.

At the outbreak of World War I, he was interviewed on the prospects of industry in a world suddenly badly shaken up. Everything would be all right, said Sol; the Guggenheims were going to increase their copper exploitation.

When the war began and the copper prices rose, with foreseeably great demand, it seemed a very good time to reorganize the Guggenheim copper holdings in order to appease the public and the bankers and to tidy up the ledgers. So the Guggenheims created a new Kennecott Copper Corporation, which would have 3,000,000 shares. This corporation bought up the Guggenex copper holdings. It took over the investment in Utah Copper (about 25 percent of that company's stock), the investment in Braden Copper (ownership control), the Copper River Railroad, and the other Alaska Syndicate holdings.

Actually, Guggenex was cannibalized and disbanded, with the Guggenheims, the Whitneys, Thomas Fortune Ryan, the English investors, and other investors taking out their profits and taking stock in the new Kennecott venture. Guggenex had been an extremely profitable investment for all who had been involved in it: Daniel announced that on an investment of less than $28,000,000 they had realized $97,000,000 in sixteen years. Of that, dividends of $24,000,000 had been paid. Assets of $73,000,000 were now distributed.

Soon the new Kennecott Copper Company was valued at 195,-000,000, even with its costly railroad. And within a year or so the worries of the bankers were quite forgotten. In one week, the Alaskan town of Cordova shipped out a million dollars' worth of copper ore. The supply entering Puget Sound became so great that the smelters there could not handle it and the ore had to be shipped as far as Salt Lake City for smelting and refining.

27]

BY THE beginning of World War I, Daniel felt that he was entitled to a rest. His stomach bothered him, he was not feeling well, and his semi-annual trips to Europe, his stays at Carlsbad and other spas, did not bring him permanent relief. Business worries bothered him more than they did some other executives; he found it difficult to relax. He hoped to abandon business, turn it over to the younger members of the family, and keep a kindly eye, but not a tight rein, on the world of the Guggenheims. He was disappointed, because with the coming of war in 1914 his services could not be spared. Too many decisions must be made, much must be decided quickly in which only he had the background and grasp necessary for the right decisions.

During the war years, Daniel *did* begin to spread himself personally. Long Branch had become quite unfashionable at this time, and Long Island—the near North Shore—was the area in which the millionaires kept their estates. On this Gold Coast stood the magnificent castle of Howard Gould, son of Jay, who had gone to the Riviera to take a flier in establishment of "the complete resort," including a gambling casino. In 1917, Daniel bought Hempstead House, this palace of Gould's, and began to fill it with art work and furniture treasures of his own choosing. He had paintings by the well-known Charles François Daubigny, the landscape artist of the middle nineteenth century, whose work became popular among the world's millionaires of the first few years of the twentieth. He had paintings by Homer Martin, the American landscape painter. He had paintings by Jean Baptiste Camille Corot, whose work stood the tests of time, and by Isabey, Tryon, and Jakob

Maris, whose luck was not so good. He was a patron of the world of music and the symphony. He loved flowers and became quite expert in his knowledge of the rare and exotic plants that were grown under his supervision in the conservatories at Hempstead House.

From the beginning of World War I, Daniel Guggenheim took a place of leadership in the gearing of the American industrial machine to meet the needs of its own defense and the war effort of the Western Allies. During the war, when some legislators suggested that the cost of the American war effort be paid by those who had profited most from the war (which meant the Guggenheims and other industrialists), Daniel suggested a system of war finance that was to become established in America as a basic idea of government financial philosophy. He believed that obligations assumed in times of stress should not be paid off by the current generation, but should be passed on to the future generations. His idea did not gain overwhelming success at that moment, but like many of his others it did come to pass in time.

During World War I, Daniel had an opportunity to exercise some of the theories about labor-management-government relationships that he had expounded before the Industrial Commission in 1915. He and John D. Rockefeller, Jr., met with Samuel Gompers of the American Federation of Labor, and Gompers agreed on many items of principle, including the need for a united front of labor, capital, and government to prosecute the war. There were strikes in the mines and strikes in the smelters. There was violence and killing on Guggenheim property and armed guards patrolled the perimeters of the camps of Utah Copper and Ray Consolidated in Arizona. Guggenheim biographer Harvey O'Connor said it was easy enough for the Guggenheims to be detached about the condition of their workers because they were insulated from them. "Certainly," O'Connor remarked, "it could not be said that the Guggenheims were more callous than their fellow-millionaires toward the misery which enveloped the world in the throes of war and postwar adjustment." This is true, yet the fact was never completely accepted by American society in the first half of the twentieth century, nor by the third and fourth generations of Guggenheims (some of whom grew to hate the source of the money), nor even entirely by Daniel and his brothers, who came to know a sense of shame because they had grown rich in exploitation of resources and men.

During the war years, the Daniel Guggenheim family's ladies became very active in New York civic affairs. Daniel's wife, Florence, was the first to interest herself in charities and matters outside the family. She became a director of the National League for Woman's Service—an organization to promote women's work for the war. She helped establish the Soldiers', Sailors', and Marines' club on Lexington Avenue. She sold more than four million dollars worth of Liberty Bonds. She was to go on to become a member of the board of governors of the American Woman's Association, treasurer of the Women's National Republican Club, and treasurer of the Emanu-el Sisterhood of Personal Service. Gladys would follow her in many of these activities and Florence would be active in public affairs for the rest of her life.

Of the eight sons of Meyer Guggenheim, by 1916 only six were alive and William had moved outside the bosom of the family. Among the sons there was a definite shortage of male descendants. Isaac had three daughters. Daniel had two sons and one daughter. Murry had a son and a daughter. Solomon had three daughters. Benjamin had three daughters. Simon had two sons. William had one son. Meyer's three daughters had four sons among them— Rose had three sons—but they were not Guggenheims.

Daniel's two boys were as different as night and day. Harry showed some interest in business, and decided to enter the partnership. Robert showed none, and did not. Edmond, Murry's son, entered the partnership, too. One of Simon's boys died at an early age and the other boy was ill, and William was so far out of the family councils that his son was not really considered, nor would ever be.

The new Guggenheim Brothers partnership was quite different from anything Meyer would have imagined: five Guggenheim brothers, two grandsons, and one outsider. The two young fellows, Harry at twenty-six and Edmond at twenty-eight, were turned over to William C. Potter and sent to learn the Latin American mining operations and the Latin ways. Perhaps Daniel was not so far out of the tradition of his father, after all. Meyer had gone into business with Edward R. Holden and had continued in the smelter business with him until he and his sons began to learn how to comport themselves. That partnership had then ended suddenly. Potter might be regarded then as a teacher and agent employed for a time while the boys learned the business; with the variety of Guggenheim enterprises the stiff little partnership that Meyer envisaged no longer seemed in keeping.

The first full year of the war proved to be immensely profitable for the Guggenheims and for the rest of American industry, but it was nothing compared to the next two years. Germany went marching into Belgium in that autumn of 1914, confident of quick victory. The German armies moved swiftly, and soon they reached the Marne and were within cannon sound of Paris. They had expected victory and a relatively amicable settlement with Britain, at which Germany would secure her colonial status and Britain would agree not to interfere with her.

After the first battle of the Marne the Western Allies took hope. No one on either side expected a long war. But in a year they all began to change their minds. Britain established a purchasing commission in America, headed by J. P. Morgan, Jr. The Morgan bank was their agent, and, of course, the Morgan bank knew a great deal about what the Guggenheims had and what they could do. The relationships between the House of Morgan and the Guggenheims certainly did not hurt the latter's profits in these war years.

The profits of all the Guggenheim properties were immense in 1916; that of American Smelting and Refining alone was $25,000,-000. That same year, with the liquidation of Guggenex, the Guggenheims took some $40,000,000 in capital recovered. Their estimated *dividends* from copper stocks that year were around $10,000,000.

In the spring of 1917, when the United States and Germany went to war, the American government, the American people, and American capitalists were faced with a new problem. Until this war the United States had always been a debtor nation. The Revolution, the War of 1812, and even the Mexican War did not allow for any huge profiteering. In the Civil War there was profiteering in the North and Meyer Guggenheim participated in his wholesaling and brokerage of foodstuffs and dry goods. There were flagrant cases in which the Vanderbilts and other shipowners leased leaky ships to the Union for the foray against New Orleans, taking millions of dollars in profits at the expense of a hard-pressed government. J. Pierpont Morgan, the elder, had engaged in a shoddy gold speculation during the first years of the war, profiting handsomely at the expense of his government and the gold market's losers. Meyer Guggenheim was never accused of undue profiteering; taking profits and high ones at the expense of the government was considered simply part of the business world at the time.

The Spanish-American War was so short-lived that profiteering was not really in the picture. The United States, in 1898, was still very much of a debtor nation, and the profits from many raw materials which were purchased went to people outside the country.

By 1917, the picture was much changed. France, England, Italy all were heavily extended in their war efforts and they floated loans in the United States, largely through the Morgan bank. That money went to buy lead from the American Smelting and Refining Company to be made into rifle bullets, copper from the various Guggenheim mines to be made into wires and shell casings. The Guggenheims responded by subscribing handsomely to the various war loans, European and American. They bought bonds by the millions of dollars. They declared special dividends of 1 percent in various companies to go for the work done by the Red Cross and the Salvation Army. This amounted to two and a half million dollars. Guggenheims joined the service, army and navy. Mrs. Daniel Guggenheim sold Liberty Bonds by the millions among her lady friends, and organized her chauffeur and those of her friends into an effective selling force among the workers for the rich.

The Guggenheims were good, loyal citizens in spite of their Germanic language background, and there was very little criticism of them, as there was much criticism of other Americans, Jewish and Gentile, who bore names that originated in Germany.

All that praiseworthy effort and praise for it existed on one level. On another level the Guggenheims came in for more criticism than ever before: for war profiteering.

When America entered the war one of the early moves of the Wilson administration was to create a Council of National Defense. (The council was actually created several months before the declaration of war.) The purpose, at first, was the assurance of an adequate supply of raw materials and manufactured goods to serve the war effort. Bernard Baruch became chief of the mines and metals section of this council, and later head of the War Industries Board. Guggenheim associates were in nearly every important activity in the control of the civil war effort.

In the beginning, when the government was worried about supplies, Daniel Guggenheim and other leaders of the metals industry said they could have their metal at the average price for which it sold in the years just before the war boom. The Guggenheims and John D. Ryan, head of Anaconda Copper Company, agreed to sell the government 45,000,000 pounds of copper at .167 cents per pound. It seemed a great deal when the story appeared in the newspapers, but this amount represented about 10 percent of war needs.

In discussion of this proposition fifteen years later, Guggenheim biographer Harvey O'Connor took a critical look, and charged that the Guggenheims did not lose anything even by selling copper at this price. Were they supposed to lose something? That was a question that had not before been raised in consideration of the affairs of American businessmen. During the Civil War, Americans and the government had become indignant when the government was cheated, but not about high prices. Cheating meant giving bad merchandise. Price was a matter established by the market.

The *Engineering and Mining Journal*, often most critical of the Guggenheims and their methods of finance, answered critics who argued that the copper kings ought to abnegate profits during the war. Such talk was nonsense, said the *Journal*. The essential matter was that production must be maintained at the highest levels and nothing should interfere with incentive to do this. Miners must be well paid and owners must gain high profits. The *Journal* here exhibited the old free-wheeling attitude toward capitalism that the Guggenheims accepted as a way of life.

The argument was brought up by the Administration in every quarter of the business world. Everywhere the answer was the same: government needed the goods, industry was ready to supply them, but the laws of supply and demand must govern the war effort. If industry was asked to step up its efforts it must be compensated in extra ways for the work.

In Congress there was much criticism of "profiteering" and again the Guggenheims came in for their share of charges. Soon the price of copper was fixed at .244 cents per pound by the War Industries Board. The price was high and it represented for the copper companies a doubling of their net profits after the new federal income and excess profits taxes had been levied. The action was taken with full understanding that it would mean high profits for the companies that produced copper economically. The object was to make use of every resource. The fixed prices were made high enough to insure production at a peak level, and that is what they did.

The Guggenheims complained against government, in turn. They had maintained a low capitalization on the properties they desired to control, keeping the fixed debt against first mortgage bonds, and borrowing with bond issues for money for expansion. The capital stock was used for dividends and control. During the war four of the Guggenheim copper companies, with stock at par worth $45,000,000, suddenly shot up in market value to $170,000,-000. The government's wartime taxes were figured on the basis of profits against capitalization, and not against market value. With so small a capital base, the Guggenheims paid far higher taxes on these four properties, Utah, Nevada Consolidated, Chino, and Ray, than the new Kennecott Company paid, because it had been reorganized with a capitalization of $195,000,000. All the more so since in 1917, Utah, with a capital of $16,000,000, earned $23,500,-000, while Kennecott that year earned under $16,000,000. American Smelting and Refining showed a profit of more than $25,000,-000 that year.

After M. Guggenheim's Sons was disbanded and replaced by Guggenheim Brothers, another partnership, Meyer would not have approved of the way things were going, for in this partnership outsider William Potter was a very important figure. He had been a vice-president of the Guaranty Trust Company who had grown up in the Guggenheim service in American Smelting and Refining. Potter was the Guggenheim expert on Latin America, and he came back to take charge of this most important of their interests. Everything they had done in the past year or so had pointed to the furtherance of their southern affairs. Meyer would have said, of course, that one of the boys should have been trained to deal with the Latins. In fact, two of them had been so trained, Ben and Will, and both were gone from the partnership. Ben was dead in his prime. Will's case was even more tragic as a lesson in failure of a man given every opportunity to find himself.

During World War I, Will invented Gasless Sundays. Citizens were to refrain from Sunday driving and spend the gas money for defense stamps. This plan was supported by William's American Defense Society as an important effort in winning the war. When the Defense Society announced the plan, however, the American Automobile Association objected. What about the poor boys in camp? Who was to visit them, and how? A compromise was worked out whereby the two associations agreed that automobile owners might use their cars to carry friends and relatives to "comfort the boys in camp" and a national crisis was averted. "Who is the Genius?" asked the New York *Sun.*

Will Guggenheim remained active in the American Defense Society until the armistice of November 11, 1918. Then, even as the Germans went home in defeat, the savants of the Defense Society attempted to invoke a permanent boycott against all German manufactures and farm goods. This hatred was too much even for Will. He said the Teutonic race should take an important part in the development of the world. He quit the Society and turned his attention to the International Benjamin Franklin Society and on its behalf he persuaded New York Governor Al Smith to create a National Thrift Week.

For many years thereafter Will divided his time between his house at 833 Fifth Avenue and an estate at Sands Point, Long Island, where he entertained lavishly, but was slowly forgotten by the business community.

As with William, no matter what anyone said, they must admit that in their own ways the various Guggenheims had tried to support the American war effort in 1917 and 1918.

Harry had been at work in Santiago in 1916, along with his cousin Edmond. Henry Wagner, then in charge there for the Guggenheim brothers, said that neither Harry nor Edmond seemed to have too much desire to work. "They both had entirely too much money," he wrote, but he was most harsh about Harry's brother Robert: "Robert was as different from Harry as two brothers could possibly be. He was . . . entirely irresponsible."

But in 1917, while on vacation in Florida, Harry Guggenheim decided to learn to fly an airplane. He took ten days of instruction at Lake Worth, and on his return to New York he bought a triplane flying boat, and organized a private flying club at Manhasset. In the autumn, after war was declared and men were going overseas, Harry received a commission in the Navy and began training, first at Bay Shore and then overseas at a school near Bordeaux. Later, he was sent to the Italian front, where he qualified as an Italian naval aviator, too. He served during the remainder of the war in the naval air service.

Harry's older brother, Robert, had enlisted in the Fighting 69th New York regiment, had become a major and a general's aide, and had distinguished himself in a military career as he had never distinguished himself before.

Robert Guggenheim had entered the family businesses very briefly. By the time he was twenty-four years old he was working for a construction firm outside the Guggenheim orbit. In marrying his second wife, the horsewoman Margaret Weyher of Scranton, he deserted the nominal interest of the Guggenheims in the Jewish faith and became a Catholic convert. He played with business, and with dog and horse breeding, on an estate at Babylon, Long Island. When World War I began, Robert enlisted, acquiring a love for military ways and discipline that never left him.

The war years found the other Guggenheims very busy, too. Florence continued to occupy herself with her charities. She gave the money in 1915 to buy five new ambulances for the French that year. Edmond was ill in 1916 but two years later he accepted a job as deputy police commissioner of New York City.

When the war ended, the Guggenheims were being listed by the newspapers as members of one of the world's most wealthy families, and they became more flamboyant in their gestures of public charity.

In the year after the war ended, Daniel and Murray gave a house to the New York Botanical Gardens. That same year Guggenheim Brothers donated $250,000 to Mt. Sinai Hospital, which had been one of Meyer's favorite charities. They gave money for Jewish relief, for the Hebrew Union College of Cincinnati—for a hundred worthy causes.

28]

IN 1919, on his return from a fact-finding trip to Europe, Solomon Guggenheim told the press mournfully that Europe was in terrible shape. Then he brightened. All the more reason, he said, for America to build up the domestic market that had been sacrificed to war needs during the past few years.

At the end of World War I, when markets were glutted and the specters of depression and revolution leered out across the world, Daniel Guggenheim made some suggestions for control of industrial strife. These ideas were interesting in the reliance they placed on federal government as a power to limit labor organization and—by extension—to limit business control of its own labor policy. He suggested that the federal government take control of labor relations in interstate trade, forbidding strikes until investigations had been held. He suggested the formation of a Federal Labor Commission which would control the bartering and financial responsibility of labor unions. His thinking on labor relations was fuzzier than his thinking on social problems (he failed to include any provision for labor men to sit on the government board of the Labor Commission he envisaged).

In Daniel Guggenheim's brave new world there would be federal rules for health and safety in industry, inclusion of occupational disease in workmen's compensation coverage, old age and unemployment insurance, restriction on child labor, and restriction on the labor of women. Daniel would not live to see all these ideas come into effect but they would come into effect. He would not live to see those who brought them into effect in the New Deal years called socialists and worse. His own thinking was that this was a middle-of-the-road progressive policy that would stabilize industry, encourage individual initiative and enterprise, and build up a self-respecting group of workers. He did not believe that the workers had any right to their own powerful organization. It might have been too much to expect an American industrial leader to grant labor a share of the controlling voice in industry, but he was far ahead of his time in the examination of the general social scene in the early part of the twentieth century. If the Guggenheims' own industries refused to permit outside labor organizations to share in what the brothers considered to be management prerogatives, and if the coming of strong organized labor to the Guggenheim plants was delayed until after his death and the passage of the Wagner Act, still it must be said that Daniel Guggenheim was an industrialist ahead of his time. Before his death he was to make an attempt to repay society for some of the benefits he had reaped from it, and to add a fundamental chapter to the story of the Guggenheims and the American dream, quite unconnected to his odyssey of business success.

In *Metal Magic, The Story of the American Smelting and Refining Company*, Isaac Marcossen pointed to the record of the Guggenheims in developing ASARCO between 1902 and 1918 from a firm with a gross annual income of $82,000,000 to one with a business of $390,000,000, and from profits of $2,900,000 a year to profits of $27,000,000. In 1918 American Smelting and Refining made 816 percent of the profits it earned in 1902.

In the First World War the Guggenheims achieved the pinnacle of their power and wealth to become the most powerful men in the metals industry, but one result of this success was that in 1919 and 1920 American capitalists were subjected to much criticism for profit-taking during the war. Congress investigated the aircraft industry, the metals industry, and many others covered by the War Industries Board. The metals men testified that they were public-spirited citizens who had done their best to help the war effort. Union men testified that profiteering in copper had cost the American people $350,000,000. Public servants testified that the copper men were both profiteers and public-spirited businessmen at the same time. Bernard Baruch was among these public servants and Baruch, who had run the metals controls for the government dur ing the war and was a successful capitalist himself, seems to have come closest to the mark.

And criticism was not the only postwar problem. When the First World War ended the copper industry was heavily overbuilt, as were other metals industries and, for that matter, as was American industry in general. The Guggenheims had also gone into the zinc business and since the earliest days in refining they had been in the lead business. All these metals suffered after 1918. It did not take a Ouija board or a crystal ball for the capitalists to see what was going to happen, but they were powerless to stop it. In the criticisms of the capitalists, in the halls of Congress, no one got around to mentioning how capitalists were forced to take their lumps as well as their profits in the cycles of the free enterprise system. When war ended the government insisted that the mines keep operating at peak capacity or near it, to keep labor employed, and so the mine owners had little choice in the matter. They could understand the simple economics of depression as well as anyone else, they hoped that production could be tapered off, and that surpluses of American manufactured products could be sloughed off on world markets without dislocating the American wartime economy. The idea was fine, but in execution it failed to produce the desired results, because it counted on a return to "normalcy" when only in America were conditions anything like those of the days before the war. The European social and political systems were strained and undergoing change. The European economic systems had been bled white by the war. In 1919 Africa and Asia counted only as adjuncts to the European economic systems; there were not more than a handful of independent countries on either continent and most of these were tied to the sterling or franc blocs.

The hope of American industry in 1919 was that peacetime expansion could be used to pick up the slack. For many reasons, including the preoccupation of President Wilson with international problems, the peacetime market did not expand. The rapid development of needed transportation and communications, power systems, and rural electrification might have saved the copper industry, but if the need was there the demand was not, and so for several months there was absolutely no sale of copper from the smelters into the market of manufacturers. Meanwhile, the smelters were forced to buy up all the copper ore that the mines produced, and to pay for it at prices established during the wartime boom. The wartime price of copper in America was 26 cents a pound, fixed by the War Industries Board. The prewar price of copper was about 14 cents a pound. When the sales of copper did begin again, early in 1919, the price went to 15 cents a pound, which by prewar standards was fair enough, but by wartime standards was disastrous. The smelter companies were paying the mine owners higher prices than ever and their labor costs had gone up along with all other costs.

In 1920 the big banks became leery of making loans on copper. The Federal Reserve Bank of New York refused to accept loans or drafts on copper except at 50 percent of their market value. If this situation had been allowed to continue, all these huge piles of copper would have had to be sold on the open world market, the price would have plummeted, and even as strong a company as American Smelting and Refining might have been wrecked.

The answer of the American Copper producers was to form an export company which bought up the copper in stockpiles in America and resold it outside the United States. The copper companies sold 400,000,000 pounds of copper to this association in 1920 and thus kept the market from plummeting. Simon Guggenheim was the chairman of the association, and a leading figure in this negotiation, and in the efforts of the copper men to keep the price of copper high by holding all the nation's copper reserves in this association. The copper men talked of selling copper for 23 cents a pound. These were brave words, but the price fell to around 14.5 cents and remained there, and in 1921, Solomon, who went to Europe to try to stimulate sales, came home with the picture of a ruined market.

Soon most of the copper mines in which the Guggenheims had interests were closed down and one by one the smelters began to shut or to work at a small percentage of capacity. Even solid American Smelting and Refining began to pass dividends, so serious was the crisis.

Yet the crisis must be put in focus in relation to the Guggenheims. With the end of the war, Daniel Guggenheim decided to retire. (As noted, he had hoped to retire in 1916 but the problems of war production brought him back to active management of the various concerns.) In 1919 he did retire, crisis or not, and Simon Guggenheim became president of American Smelting and Refining, assisted by Roger Straus, Daniel's son-in-law. Edgar Newhouse became chairman of the board. (Under the Guggenheim system of operations the office of president of ASARCO was more important than that of board chairman.)

The crisis was more serious, longer-lasting than anyone thought it could be. Simon was to bear the brunt of an attack on Guggenheim management of American Smelting and Refining, as a result of it. As long as the company showed huge profits, as in wartime and all other times in the past, it had been hard for enemies to make trouble within the company or in the stockholders' meetings. There were enemies, and there had been enemies since the very beginning, when Henry H. Rogers tried to smash American Smelter and Refining stock rather than let the Guggenheims have control. Many of the old smelter men, the Grants, Sheedys, Eilers, and Nashes, had objected to certain aspects of Guggenheim management in the past because they were all smelter men when the Guggenheims were selling lace and they could not forget that fact. Their children grew up in households permeated with smelter talk and smelter enmities. One of these children was Karl Eilers, son of Anton Eilers, the Pueblo smelter man, and in 1920, Karl represented the last of the old western smelter families on the board of directors of American Smelting and Refining.

In the spring of 1920, Karl Eilers was dismissed from the board of directors. One does not dismiss a director of a company; a director is elected by the stockholders and is responsible to them; yet this happened. After Simon Guggenheim became president of the company, he wrote to Karl Eilers and told him that since Karl had been so much out of sympathy with the Guggenheim administration and since he differed so radically from Simon on matters of policy, they could no longer be associated together. ". . . This letter is written that you may have the opportunity of yourself taking the initiative and tendering your resignation before the coming annual election if you so desire," Simon wrote.

Karl Eilers refused to resign. When the annual election day arrived, Simon showed the Guggenheim strength—control of the majority of the stock. Karl Eilers was ousted as a director.

More than anything that had occurred in eighteen years of Guggenheim management, this action indicated the strength of the Guggenheim control of American Smelting and Refining. But such a naked exhibition of strength was resented by many stockholders. The company's affairs were no longer so prosperous as to lull the 19,000 shareholders. Eilers stewed about his summary discharge, and in the winter of 1919–1920 he filed a suit to challenge the Guggenheim right to control the American Smelting and Refining Company. He charged that the Guggenheims maintained control in 1920 simply by *having* physical control of the Board of Directors and the offices; he said Guggenheims did not own as much stock as Eilers and his family owned.

Eilers also said he would prove that the Guggenheims had milked American Smelting and Refining for their own purposes. The Guggenheims replied that Eilers was simply a disgruntled employee, but the argument went much further than that and the stockholders sensed it.

In the washing of dirty linen the shocked stockholders of ASARCO discovered that the Guggenheims, who had once owned, with William Whitney, an absolute majority of American Smelting and Refining stock, had reduced their holdings to less than 10 percent of the total. There were 650,000 shares of American Smelting and Refining in the beginning, with $100 as value, and the capitalization was increased by $35,000,000 to a million shares, when the Guggenheim family took over in 1901. They never held absolute majority ownership by themselves, but they held close to 500,000 shares and now, in 1920, it was revealed that all the Guggenheims owned less than 50,000 shares of ASARCO stock.

The change was the result in the change in capitalistic thinking, coming from old Pierpont Morgan's belief that control could be exercised by manipulation. The Guggenheims had deserted Meyer's philosophy of ownership for the more modern way. Now the time had come to pay the price for that decision.

The court struggle of 1920 and 1921 was as unpleasant a bit of corporate infighting as has ever been revealed in the United States, for wild charges and old enmities were unearthed in every bit of evidence submitted to the court. Summing up, the most important fact to be revealed was that for many years the Guggenheim family had controlled American Smelting and Refining through the force of Daniel's character.

Knowing this fact, the Eilers group set out to unseat the Guggenheims and seize control for themselves, charging that the Guggenheims, as financiers, had milked American Smelting by letting it carry expenses and take risks in discovery and exploitation of new companies of their own or used existing family partnerships to skim off the cream for themselves.

Eilers was airing personal grievances that went back to the days of his father. This was known, and it weakened his case. The point of importance to others involved in the American Smelting and Refining struggle was that the common stock had declined in value. The market figure was the lowest it had been since the Guggenheims took over. This puzzle could be explained to the general public in terms of the depression in which America found itself in 1921, but it was not readily explainable to stockholders.

The target of the Eilers faction was the annual meeting of stockholders to be held at Jersey City on April 6, 1921. Until the day of that meeting the Guggenheims were confident of ultimate victory, but at that stockholders' meeting they learned that the opposition was stronger than they had suspected. The charges were made, Eilers speaking for his group, Solomon Guggenheim speaking for the family, and offering a Guggenheim olive branch: Eight new directors who were not employees of the company to be appointed to join the twenty employee directors. This pertinent strategic move ended the argument for the year when the Guggenheim plan was accepted by a vote of 684,526 shares for the plan to 202,479 shares against, and through the majority of employee directors the Guggenheims still controlled ASARCO.

The margin of only three to one for them worried the Guggenheims, for here in 1921 they were experiencing their first major opposition within the company, and they did not have the stock ownership to back up their control. If affairs went badly the shareholders might very easily and very quickly switch allegiances. Another worrisome development was a demand made by the Eilers group for an investigation of ASARCO's affairs.

It was agreed that a Stockholders' Committee of seven would investigate the management of the company in the months to come. Former President William H. Taft was to examine the report and make a statement about it, but when Taft was appointed Chief Justice of the United States Supreme Court during the course of the investigation, Elihu Root, statesman, jurist, diplomat, and Republican politician, was appointed to handle the report. The result of the study was a shock to the Guggenheims and to many other stockholders. The majority of four members, independent of either the Eilers or Guggenheim groups, found that there was very good reason for complaint about Guggenheim management of the company in recent years.

The investigators found that Daniel Guggenheim had exaggerated the profits of Guggenheim smelters and investments back in 1900 when the Guggenex properties were purchased by American Smelting and Refining. The majority report said that in the beginning Guggenheim management had been all that could have been desired, but that in recent years too many dividends had been paid (particularly during the war) and not enough money had been laid aside in reserves.

The Guggenheims claimed that this criticism was pure hindsight; they said American Smelting and Refining Company's position at the end of World War I was like that of nearly every American company. It was easy, from the vantage point of 1921, they said, to see what ought to have been done in December 1918.

Yet the majority report was devastating to the Guggenheims. It stated openly that the Guggenheims had used American Smelting and Refining mercilessly to strengthen their personal fortunes. The majority report said that the Guggenheims had created American Smelters Securities, which was backed by American Smelting, solely for their personal profit. The stockholders were also annoyed by the Guggenheim transfer of the sales agency for the copper properties from American Smelting to Guggenheim Brothers after the war, when the Guggenheims wanted to protect the price of copper. The Guggenheims, by putting the sales in the hands of their wholly-owned company, had taken the easy sales profits for themselves instead of putting them into American Smelting and Refining to offset production losses.

Having made all these discoveries, the majority of the committee recommended election of a board of directors that was entirely independent of Guggenheim control.

The minority report, representing the Guggenheim point of view, praised the efficient management of the Guggenheims, and pointed to the improving condition of the company in 1921. Through the plan devised by the Guggenheims, the company had liquidated its copper surpluses and had paid off its bank loans against these surpluses. An improvement in the economic affairs of Mexico was bettering the company's position there.

No two reports could have been more dissimilar. They did not seem to deal with the same company; yet there was truth in both reports. The Guggenheims had given American Smelting and Refining good management and had brought high return to the investors on their securities for many years. In twenty years the stockholders had received the equivalent of their original purchase money back plus 6 percent per year interest—and still owned the shares of a company then worth $128,000,000. This was not bad, but it was not as good as the business might have been, given the huge profits made by the company. In later years other companies would split stock and show huge growth and reserves in like situations. American Smelting and Refining had increased in value very little in twenty years, considering its opportunities. Had the Guggenheims maintained actual control of American Smelting and Refining and sunk all their profits and all their efforts into that company, the story would have been a different one. But then the Guggenheim family would not have been so rich.

Before the day of the 1922 stockholders' meeting the Guggenheims had appraised both these reports, and although they gave no credence to the majority report, they knew what it meant to them. They agreed to the election of a board where the balance of power would be held by independent members. Eighteen outsiders and ten employees of the company were seated on the board in 1922. Eilers had achieved all that he might have expected, and he did not contest the election. So only a handful of votes were cast against the proposition. The importance of the change was that now the Guggenheims would control ASARCO on the basis of future performance. In essence, their relationship to American Smelting and

Refining had changed in two years; they were still recognized as the leaders of the company, but the company was not theirs to do with as they wished, and consequently, from 1922 on, American Smelting and Refining became far less important in the affairs of the Guggenheims than it had been in the previous twenty years.

It would be easy to say that time and old age had overtaken the Guggenheims. Harvey O'Connor wrote just that in summing up the effects of the Guggenheim relinquishing of absolute control of American Smelting and Refining. That appraisal seems too simple and does not square completely with the facts. In the 1920's, the American metals market was shrinking, the profit potential was shrinking.

In addition, the Guggenheims were very much involved as international metal merchants and mining speculators outside the United States, and had abandoned many old American claims. The family was to become very much interested in nitrates, used in many compounds, from fertilizer to explosives, and in a new, untried process of extracting the valuable substance from huge fields of nitrate of soda that lay in Chile, Bolivia, and Peru. In short, they were concentrating their genius elsewhere.

A partnership in the nitrates business was developed between the Guggenheims and J. P. Morgan and Company. Isaac and Harry Guggenheim became the family experts on nitrates. Both went to London to talk about nitrates to bankers and nitrate producers there, while specialists in the Guggenheim Brothers firm continued to develop the nitrate extraction process.

In 1922, the process was as complete as it could be made without a test plant in the field, a plant that Harry Guggenheim wanted to build. The Morgan-Guggenheim partnership had invested about a quarter of a million dollars in the processes and development, but for the Guggenheims that was not a very large investment in something in which they believed.

At about this time John D. Ryan, head of Anaconda Copper Company, made a huge offer to the Guggenheims for control of their Chile Copper Company, whose major asset was the Chuquicamata mining enterprise. The offer was $35 a share, or $70,000,-000 for the controlling interest. Daniel, Isaac, Murry, Solomon, and Simon were growing old (although Simon was only 56 when this matter came up). Perhaps the brothers were simply interested in taking the huge profit that was offered to them. In any event, the brothers, the sons of Meyer, wanted to accept the Anaconda offer.

In this regard it was unfortunate that Isaac Guggenheim chose the spring of 1922 to go to England for a pleasure trip. For Isaac had definite views on the subject of copper and conservative exploitation of what the Guggenheims owned, rather than flying off in new directions.

But go he did, with his wife Carrie, to stay at the Hyde Park Hotel in London. They saw friends and made side trips around the countryside, visiting for a time with the Corlette Giorneys since Giorney was Isaac's son-in-law, second husband of daughter Helene.

Unfortunately Isaac suffered a stroke shortly after this visit, and was not available for consultation with the brothers on business affairs. He remained in England in the hopes that a long rest away from business would let him recover all his faculties, and he did recover, it seemed, for that summer he seemed very spry.

He visited Solomon's daughter Eleanor May, who had two years earlier accomplished that high aim of the daughters of American millionaire families: She had married into the British nobility. Eleanor May was a generous girl, who, when her family gave her $50,000 as an engagement present, she divided it among her favorite charities because she would not need the money. She married the Viscount Stuart of Castle Stuart, who would succeed to the Earldom on his father's death, and she had then gone to live in England and raise a family of four children.

He also visited Eleanor May's cousin Barbara Hazel, Benjamin's youngest daughter, who married Sigmond Kempner a few months after the noble wedding. Although happiness was predicted for Barbara Hazel it did not come, and she divorced her husband even as Isaac was in England.

On October 9, Isaac motored down to Southampton to meet his friend Henry V. Marsh, who had rented Warwick Castle and was coming in on the *Aquitania* to take up residence. Isaac waited long for the ship, and then he and Marsh went to the Southwestern Hotel at Southampton because it was late. That night Isaac complained of severe chest pains, and his friend was worried, but brandy seemed to relieve the pain and so no more thought was given to it.

In the morning Isaac still felt ill and rang for the chambermaid. She came and he told her he was very sick. A doctor was called, but before he arrived, Isaac was dead of a cerebral hemorrhage.

The loss of Isaac to the Guggenheims was felt on many levels. As long as the lace business had been a part of the Guggenheim interests, Isaac had continued to look after it. When the Guggenheims quit lace in 1899, Isaac was one of the incorporators of Guggenheim Exploration Company (Guggenex) and he gave the detailed operations of this company much of his time in the next few years. As noted, in 1901 Isaac had joined the board of directors of American Smelting and Refining Company, along with four of his brothers, and he became treasurer, the guardian of the company's wealth. With Isaac this responsibility weighed heavy.

In many ways Isaac was the least interesting and certainly the least adventurous of the brothers, and yet he was the brother with the strongest sense of destiny and family responsibility of all of them. His daughter Beulah married William I. Spiegelberg, and when a son was born to the young Spiegelbergs, a burning ambition was aroused in Isaac Guggenheim. Isaac persuaded Beulah and her husband to name the boy Isaac Guggenheim II, with the promise that he would become the principal heir to his grandfather's fortune. He was willing to fudge to perpetuate the Guggenheim male line.

This positive viewpoint about the family was odd in Isaac, because he was the most retiring of men, apparently not at all aggressive or dominant. To be sure, he came to live in the highest reaches of Jewish society in New York, moved to 410 Park Avenue, an impeccable address, and joined the Lotos, Criterion, and Lawyer's Clubs. Of all the brothers he was probably the most studious and the most intellectual and it was apparent that he was aware of the historical implications of changes in the business world, far more than the others.

He was a lifelong Republican, yet he was more business leader than Republican and when President Theodore Roosevelt spoke out against the trusts, and began the suit to dissolve the United States Steel Corporation, Isaac spoke publicly against this action. Otherwise he was a very shy man, and so nervous a man that midway in his career he suffered a nervous breakdown and went to Europe for many months to recover. He and his wife Carrie did everything possible to remain outside the public gaze; their social life was private and their summers were spent dodging publicity. Only on occasions, such as the Roosevelt speech and the times when the Guggenheims were in trouble (the Nipissing bubble, the Panic of 1907) did Isaac speak out, and then, strangely enough, it was Isaac who was chosen to become spokesman for the family. He came to know many of the business leaders of the country very well, for he was one of them. George Cortelyou, Secretary of the Treasury, spoke frankly to Isaac when they met. John Hays Hammond listened when Isaac spoke and so did the Morgan bankers. Meyer's principle by which the family partnership was ruled for many years was preserved in Isaac, and he insisted that brotherly opinion be unanimous before an action was taken that involved expenditure of large sums of money. He was, in that sense, the conservator of the family tradition.

That last trait is why, as far as the family was concerned, it was a disastrous blow when Isaac's counsel was lost. As a director of ASARCO and the overseer of the nitrate development he was well aware of many nuances regarding this venture, including the fact that although he and others were trying to persuade the various British nitrate producers to join in the promotion of the Guggenheim laboratory process for reduction of nitrates, the British owners were unimpressed by the potential. He knew that in nitrates the Guggenheims had a long way to go.

Daniel was the bull on nitrates. He was certain that the Guggenheims could gain control of the world nitrate market and that this would mean control of fertilizers, and above all, munitions. "Just wait," Daniel would tell his family, chuckling, "you will see that nitrates will make us rich beyond the dreams of avarice." Others might argue, but Daniel would not really listen. Convinced as he was that nitrates meant the future, he was prepared to risk all their fortunes on his judgment.

It was after Isaac had sailed to England, and after he had suffered his stroke, that the offer of $35 a share for the Chuquicamata copper mine came into the house in New York.

In 1921 Chuquicamata copper had shown a paper loss of a million dollars, but even if that loss had been real, the mine was still extremely valuable to the Guggenheims. Any conservative would have considered twice before sacrificing it, since it was known that copper would be needed in the developing technology of the twentieth century in ever greater amounts, and Chuqui copper, treated with the porphyry reduction processes that had been perfected in Utah, was known to be the finest and cheapest in the world.

The decision of the Guggenheim brothers to sell Chuquicamata copper was the most difficult decision they ever made because it involved so many imponderables. Isaac, with his sense of family responsibility, would have almost certainly sided with the younger members of the family to retain Chuquicamata copper, rather than with the older members who wished to take their profits. Isaac would have discovered the depth of the feeling of his nephews Edmond and Harry Guggenheim, and would have felt that by outvoting them, and forcing the sale against their wishes, against the Guggenheim tradition of unanimity, the Guggenheim tradition would be destroyed. It *was* the failure to observe the old principle of unanimity that caused the breakup of the family partnership for the second time in 1923, a schism that was far more destructive to the unity of the Guggenheims than the first break, created by the formation of Guggenex.

The young men of the third generation of Guggenheims, Harry, son of Daniel, and Edmond, son of Murry, quarreled with their fathers over Chuquicamata. They had been sent south to learn the copper business from the mine up. They believed in copper and they believed in Chilean copper. They did not want to sell the finest copper mine in the world, which could produce a third of a million pounds of copper a day and would be able to produce that much every day for at least a century, according to the reports of the geologists. Chuquicamata, on the basis of 1923 costs, producing at capacity with a profit of only five cents a pound, could earn a net profit of six and a half million dollars a year.

The older Guggenheims—Daniel in particular—insisted on having their way, but in the process they lost the younger members of the family. Harry Guggenheim and Edmond Guggenheim resigned from the partnership of Guggenheim Brothers and thereafter began to devote themselves to other interests. Without at the time seeming to do so, this parting marked the end of a phase of the story of the Guggenheims, and the end of their control of the metals industry.

Guggenheim Brothers retained a large block of stock in Chile Copper, but it was simply an investment with them after 1923; Anaconda was in control. Guggenheim Brothers still controlled Braden Copper in South America, and they were the biggest stockholders in Kennecott Copper, remaining so until Utah Copper, in which they had never held more than a minority share, was combined with Kennecott in 1923. Two outsiders were now admitted to the Guggenheim Brothers partnership, John K. MacGowan, a mining man who had been with the Guggenheims for many years, and Cappelen Smith, the developer of the nitrate recovery process which would be called the Guggenheim process. Thus, the Guggenheims moved away from copper and into the nitrate field.

The center of the Guggenheim activity in 1922 was shifted to South America, where the partners also became involved in the Caracoles Tin venture. This investment was not among their most successful, comparatively speaking, because they could not solve the reduction problems to beat the British tin price, and the British were the most important tin producers in the world in the 1920's and 1930's.

When Isaac died and his properties were sold, for the first time many people in America learned in what lordly splendor this quiet Guggenheim brother had spent much of his life. His residence on Park Avenue and a country house at Sands Point, Long Island, contained some $75,000 in furnishings. They were worth far more than that—or they had cost far more—but that is what they brought when sold. His Italian Renaissance estate, called Villa Carola, had a private golf course, a private yacht landing on Hempstead Harbor, and hundreds of acres of landscaped gardens and lawns. Villa Carola cost Isaac $2,000,000 to build, although it sold for $610,000 at auction.

Isaac owned other real estate and his share of the various Guggenheim Brothers investments was put at $10,000,000 after all taxes had been paid. That estimate was a very low one, made for tax purposes, and even so the estate taxes came to nearly two and a half million dollars.

Isaac's three daughters each received two million dollars from the estate; Carrie received a large sum and other properties for herself; and Isaac Guggenheim II, the grandson (né Spiegelberg), received two-thirds of Isaac's share of Caracoles Tin, a fortune in itself that might be valued at four or five million dollars. The idea, as far as Isaac was concerned, was to give the boy a chance to make something of himself, to add to the strength of Guggenheim Brothers and to keep the family name alive and growing. The young man did not see it that way. To him Caracoles Tin was not a gilt-edged investment since there was so much competition from Malayan producers and other British companies, and the proving of the tin investment as a road to fortune would mean much hard work. Five years after Isaac's death, the young man in question changed his name to William I. Spiegelberg, Jr., and was seldom heard from again in the councils of the Guggenheims.

29]

WITH THE changes of 1922 and 1923 a little more of the Guggenheims' American dream began to die.

The younger Guggenheims did not have the same attitude toward the community and natural resources that the brothers had gained from their father. Too many changes had come to American society by the 1920's for them to hold Meyer's views any longer and still be accounted public-spirited citizens.

Further, the Guggenheim family had changed greatly in the lifetimes of Meyer's sons.

Of Daniel's children, only one son, Harry, had been persuaded to follow a business career since Robert, the elder son, had no taste or ability for business. Daniel would leave each of his three children $2,000,000 in his will, sums that in no way represented the total of the Daniel Guggenheim fortune, because his foundations were already established and heavily endowed, and the residuary estate remained in the hands of Daniel's widow. There was a difference in the manner in which the moneys would be left to the three children: Robert's was put into a trust fund because Daniel knew his own children, and he knew that Robert was a playboy. The facts would have been hard to conceal: Robert had married four times, and once declared that it was his intention to become a gentleman of leisure because "every wealthy family could afford one." Robert had two sons: Daniel Guggenheim II was born in 1906 (and died in 1925), and M. Robert Guggenheim, Jr., was born in 1910. By the middle of the 1960's, this Guggenheim had given more indication of following his father's footsteps than those of his grandfather.

Daniel's second son, Harry, gave every indication of also becoming a professional "scion of the filthy rich."

Harry was divorced from his first wife and married again in the 1920's. Another child, a girl, was born of that marriage. For two years Harry and his second wife, Caroline, traveled around Europe, gathering objects of art and furnishings for the grand thirty-room house called Falaise that would be built for them at Sands Point on Long Island.

The land for their magnificent house was given to them by Daniel, and the house was built for them by him. It was a gesture of some importance: It showed the world that although the Guggenheims might disagree over business matters, father and son were the best of friends.

Murry, the third son of Meyer, and Leonie Bernheim Guggenheim had two children, Edmond and Lucille. Lucille married a Gimbel, adding another important alliance to the family, but she divorced him. Edmond, who was born in St. Gall, Switzerland, in 1888, grew up in New York City, where he resisted secondary education and quit school but did later attend Columbia University for two years. He then went to work in the Guggenheim copper fields and showed enough real interest to attend Yale's Sheffield Scientific School. For a time in his twenties he worked in an ASARCO smelter as an ordinary workman, and in the Perth Amboy refinery. Later, he went to South America with his cousin, Harry, to learn the metals business and to be placed under the supervision of trusted Guggenheim managers there. After resigning angrily from the family business enterprises and Guggenheim Brothers in the quarrel of 1923 over Chuquicamata, Edmond retired from business altogether to devote himself to gentlemanly pursuits, to marry three times, and produce one daughter.

Solomon's three daughters, Eleanor May, Gertrude, and Barbara Josephine, were all attracted to England for one reason or another, perhaps because among Sol's half dozen houses was a shooting lodge in Scotland. Eleanor had studied art in Italy before she married Arthur Viscount-Stuart. Gertrude, Solomon's second daughter, did not marry, but she moved to the England she preferred and lived there. Barbara Josephine also married an Englishman, John Robert Lawson-Johnston, an attaché of the British Embassy in Washington, but that marriage foundered quickly and both parties were married again, Barbara, to Fred Wettach, Jr., of New Jersey. She then lived in New Jersey and brought up her son by the first marriage, Peter Lawson-Johnston, and two children of the second marriage, Pamela and Michael Wettach. Of these, only Peter Lawson-Johnston was to reappear in the story of the Guggenheims.

Meyer's eldest daughter, Jeanette, fifth of the children, married Albert Gerstle and they had one daughter, Nettie, who married Samuel Knox and disappeared from the story of the family. Jeanette later died in childbirth.

Benjamin Guggenheim and Florette Seligman, of the banking family, produced three daughters: Benita, who died in 1927, Marguerite, and Barbara. Benita and Barbara married, the latter unhappily. She was divorced shortly afterward. She married again, in 1923, and two sons were born of this second marriage. A few years later, Barbara's husband asked for a divorce, and she came to America with her sons. She took both of them to a penthouse apartment, onto a roof, and a few moments later the two boys, one four years old and the other a baby, lay dead on the street sixteen stories below. The deaths were termed accidental and Barbara went to a mental institution. Later, she returned to England and married an Englishman. Marguerite would retain the name "Guggenheim," as will be seen—because she was resolute in her intent to remain an individual.

Simon Guggenheim and Olga Hirsh had two children, John Simon and George Denver. John Simon died in 1922. George Denver committed suicide in 1939 while staying at the Paramount Hotel in New York City. Thus most of Simon's fortune was left to the John Simon Foundation.

As noted, William married Aimee Steinberger after the Grace Brown Herbert affair that destroyed his relationship with the remainder of the family. Their son, William II, survived until he was thirty-nine years old in 1949. He died that year, leaving a son, William III, but this branch of the family was totally separated by that time from the other Guggenheims, and played no further role in Guggenheim mining, business, or philanthropic affairs.

Meyer's daughter Rose married Albert Loeb and they had three sons. Best known of the three (Harold, Edwin, and Willard Loeb) was Harold, who founded an economic theory and program called *Technocracy*. Harold worked for a time for the Guggenheims and considered a mining career. He turned against the family and established a radical bookstore in New York City. In Paris at the end of World War I Harold became an intimate of Ernest Hemingway and was the prototype for a character (Robert Cohn) in Hemingway's *The Sun Also Rises*. He founded *Broom*, an experimental literary magazine of the 1920's, and also wrote several books, including three novels.

Meyer's last daughter, Cora, married Louis Rothschild, and they had a son, Louis, and two daughters, Muriel and Gwendolyn. All were Rothschilds, not Guggenheims, and they were never close to the other branches of the family after the deaths of Barbara and Meyer.

The loosening of family ties in the second generation made itself felt in the divorces and wild conduct of many of the Guggenheims in the third generation. With so much money and so little discipline as most of the Guggenheims enjoyed, it is remarkable that any of them escaped becoming wastrels or simply rich men's sons and daughters. Yet several—particularly two Guggenheims—rose above the crowd. Each became successful, although in entirely different worlds. These successful Guggenheims were Harry, son of Daniel, and Marguerite (Peggy), daughter of Benjamin. About the others, there is little to be said. Some of the children of the girls became successful men, but their tradition was not the Guggenheim tradition. Twenty-four children in the second generation of Guggenheims were born in America: These were the grandchildren, staff and distaff, of old Meyer. Among the children there were fifteen divorces and annulments. (This includes some very happy first marriages, and the two sons of Simon, who died young.)

One might say that the Guggenheim record after the Guggenheim Brothers is typical of wealthy American families, and yet that is overly simple. In 1936, Harvey O'Connor declared that the curtain had dropped forever on the Guggenheim era, that the children had none of the virtues of the fathers, and that the spring had run down. More important, he said that the days in which great

American fortunes could be won and great reputations made in the field of business were gone forever.

Peggy and Harry Guggenheim both disproved O'Connor's contention. Peggy Guggenheim set out in her youth to become someone, and how well she succeeded is indicated in these pages. Harry Guggenheim, relatively late in life, set out to recapture the traditions of the Guggenheims, and how well he succeeded, or if he failed, is also indicated. One thing was certain, however, the old Guggenheim spark in the 1920's seemed very near to dying out, if the younger generation had to be depended on for the future. Only one of them, Peggy Guggenheim, showed much promise of originality in her early years, and her originality was not of the variety to bring praise from what had become an essentially conservative family.

30]

FOR A child born with a gold spoon in her mouth, Benjamin Guggenheim's daughter Marguerite, or Peggy, managed for herself a singularly unhappy childhood; "excessively unhappy; I have no pleasant memories of any kind," she was to say of it many years later. The reason must be ascribed to her sensitivity to her family, for a glance at a picture taken in 1910 when Peggy was twelve years old shows an immensely attractive girl in a big picture hat and a princess dress. Her face then was a round child's face, and she looked very much in that picture like the later child star Shirley Temple. Three years later Peggy was a young lady, shown in another photograph cuddling a black and white Pekingese. She had lost the baby face but was still very attractive with regular features marred only by a Guggenheim nose, which sat uneasily in a girl's face. Her hair that year was cut fashionably in a straight, short bob that hung just above the chin line, with bangs that reached nearly to her eyebrows.

The unhappiness, which shows not at all in the first picture and only in the set of her narrow mouth in the second, was occasioned by the frequent absences from the hearth of her father, who preferred the company of his mistresses to that of his family. As with many of the children of the rich, Peggy and her two sisters were brought up by the servants; they had an entire floor of the Benjamin Guggenheim house on East 72nd Street. The children lived the sequestered lives that the children of the rich can live; they did not go to school until they were in their teens, but were taught by private tutors. They were watched over by maids and butlers and governesses, but seldom by the family. Ben's Florette was too much the society lady to devote her time to bringing up the children. Peggy recalled that the only time in a day that she could be sure of seeing her mother was during the hour that Florette sat before the long cheval mirror in her bedroom while a maid or hairdresser brushed her hair.

Benita, who was three years older than Peggy, was her only friend. Barbara was five years younger and lived in quite a different world from her sisters. The girls adored their father but knew of his infidelities and the tension in the household; how could they help but know? Their governesses made it a point to be sure that they guessed the relationship between the Marquise de Cerutti and Benjamin, and they were forever encountering the Marquise in such places as the salons of the fashionable dressmaker Lanvin.

The girls went to Europe every year with their mother, and from headquarters in Paris they were sent on guided tours: the Louvre and the Paris churches and the historic sites. Their tutor taught them French history by taking them to Napoleon's tomb and the Bastille and later on a tour of the chateaux of the Loire valley.

The family spent every summer in Europe because Florette's connection with the international banking family of Seligman Frères gave her as much tie to France and England as to America. To understand Peggy Guggenheim, one must understand that she grew up in a protected, but an international, atmosphere. She never really learned anything about America as a child, at least not about the America outside the rich man's district of New York City.

One reason Florette preferred the Continent to the United States or to England was because there was less anti-semitism in France than in either of the two other countries in the early years of the twentieth century. The consequence was that the girls were heavily oriented toward Europe during their growing years. By 1911, for all practical purposes Florette and Benjamin were separated, Ben spending the winter in Paris, while Florette and the family lived in New York in winter.

The tragic loss of her father on the *Titanic* was followed by another kind of tragedy. After Ben's death it was discovered that much of his fortune had vanished into International Steam Pump and this company, into which he had put so much faith and so much money, went into the hands of receivers. Daniel, Sol, and the other brothers did not tell Florette all these business details, but set out to save what they could. They advanced her money until she finally learned that they were doing this from their own fortunes, and then she insisted on retrenching. With a flourish she cut her expenses, gave up her expensive New York town house and discharged most of her servants.

Peggy said that from the moment that she discovered that Benjamin had not died rich, she no longer felt like a Guggenheim. That was an important clue as to what it was to be a Guggenheim in 1913.

Benjamin had not died penniless, however, and when under Dan's suzerainty the brothers had salvaged International Steam Pump, each of the three daughters of Ben and Florette received $500,000 as their inheritance from their father, and Florette was given a much larger amount.

Jewishness was much more a part of the life of the Seligmans than of the Guggenheims, and when Peggy was finally sent to school in 1913 she attended a private day school for young Jewish girls on the west side of Central Park. In those days a girl could walk through Central Park safely, and Peggy walked alone to and from school each day. Since it was a Jewish school, Peggy's acquaintanceship in New York was almost entirely limited to the Jewish community; when there were school parties only Jewish boys came to them; when Peggy made her debut in 1916, it was at the Ritz Tent Room, before a Jewish crowd. By this time, Peggy had fallen under the influence of an ardent young woman teacher at her school who was dedicated to improvement of the world via the radical course, and Peggy's enchantment with the world of parties and young men was never more than superficial.

She did all the things that wealthy young New York girls are supposed to do; she went riding in Central Park, and to the Opera, and to the theater, and had her hair styled and took beauty treatments at Elizabeth Arden's beauty parlor. During the war she discovered young men. "I had several fiancés during the war," she said, "because we were always entertaining soldiers and sailors."

In 1919 Peggy Guggenheim came into the fortune she had inherited from her father. She was twenty-one years old and very lonely and unhappy because her only friend, sister Benita, had just married an American aviator and had left home.

Peggy's first gesture of independence was to take a trip across North America, to California, Mexico, Canada, and Chicago, where she met the parents of her latest fiancé. They rejected her as flighty and she came home more unhappy than ever. She tried plastic surgery to change the nose she disliked but encountered an incompetent doctor who made it worse. She went gambling in French Lick, Indiana, and lost a thousand of her half-million dollars. She went to work for Harold Loeb, her cousin, in his radical Sunwise Turn Bookshop in midtown Manhattan. The shop was frequented by avant-garde painters and writers and talkers, and by Peggy's relatives. Peggy's mother brought her rubbers on rainy days and her aunts brought their tape measures and bought books by the yard to fill the shelves of their libraries.

Through her friends at the bookshop Peggy met abstract painters and encountered her first abstract painting. She said she turned it around four times before deciding which end was up. (Her only pay was commissions on the sale of books.) At the Sunwise Turn Bookshop Peggy met her future husband, Eugene Lawrence Vail. After several months in the bookshop Peggy went to Europe and began rushing from one city and museum to another, trying to see every painting she had ever heard about. She was helped by associates of the Duveens, who advised her on ways to begin a serious study of art. She studied the works of Bernard Berenson but she also lived at the Crillion Hôtel in Paris and collected suitors. Her mother came to Paris and she stayed with her mother at the Plaza-Athenée Hôtel. It was there that she determined to lose her virginity to Lawrence Vail, and did so with a flourish, which she described in some detail in her first autobiography, the avant-garde *Out of This Century*, published in the 1930's. (A book known to members of the Guggenheim family as *Out of My Mind.*)

For some time Peggy reveled in the world of bohemia with Eugene Lawrence Vail. She mingled with lesbians and homosexuals; she was victimized by the artists she befriended but she did not mind; she was sure this was "living."

After they had carried on an affair for some time, Vail asked Peggy to marry him, and she did, at the *mairie* of Paris' Seizième

Arrondissement on the Avenue Henri Martin. It was a grand affair
—for a civil ceremony. The groom had invited all his friends to
come to the party, without mentioning the name of the bride. The
bride invited all her friends, a motley collection of artists and down-
at-the-heel writers. Florette, representative of Jewish high society,
was there in her furs, crying at the thought of the *mésalliance* as
much as anything else, but unable to stop it. The happy couple let
Florette sign the register, and then made her give them a champagne reception at the Plaza-Athénée.

The party lasted all night, since the marriage was more or less of
an afterthought and its "consummation" was not vital. The wedding party, which changed in personnel and character through the
night, moved on to a hotel in the Rue de Rivoli and then to the
Boeuf sur le Toit nightclub in the Rue Boissy d'Anglais.

The next day Peggy decided she really had not wanted to get
married.

The moderately happy pair went to Rome for a holiday, and
encountered cousin Harold Loeb once again. He was staying there
since he had embarked on his literary adventure with *Broom*.

Peggy did not know it then, but she had begun a life that would
keep her in Europe for the next twenty years and bound to Europe
for the rest of her life. She was, in 1922, still very much the American girl: After she became pregnant she moved to England because
she wanted to be sure that her child did not have French citizenship, since that might mean French military service if the child was
a boy. The boy was born on May 15, 1923, and was named Michael
Cedric Sindbad Vail.

Vail, a painter, sometimes styled himself King of the Bohemians,
and he led Peggy Guggenheim a merry chase. It was his habit to
celebrate the fourteenth of July—Bastille Day—by dancing in the
streets for three nights running. Peggy could not keep up with him,
she only tried, and paid for it in many ways, in health and happiness.

The little family moved frequently and was augmented almost
all the time by various nonpaying guests. They lived in Paris, and
in Normandy in a villa so old and shabby that it gave Peggy visions
of the ugly Victorian mansion her Seligman grandfather had built
in New Jersey and where she had spent miserable summers as a

child. They went to Capri where Vail got drunk, fought with his sister's lover, and was arrested by the police. He spent ten days in chains in jail and Peggy had some difficulty in having him released. It cost $1000 for the services of a good Roman lawyer named Tirelli, who threw in a trip on his yacht because he liked the crowd. It cost another $500 to have Vail's name removed from the criminal records of Capri. Peggy paid.

The young couple went to Amalfi, then to Egypt. They camped in the desert in luxury and went to Luxor. There Vail was untrue to Peggy and caught a social disease, which she said served him right, but since she was so very broad-minded a girl she stayed with him.

After a season in Egypt the lovers returned to Paris and an apartment on the Boulevard Saint-Germain on the Left Bank. It was a very respectable neighborhood (their landlord was a viscount) and they scandalized the neighbors by giving bohemian parties. Peggy was thin and vital and nervous, attractive if not beautiful, and searching desperately for some hold on life. In Palestine, which she visited briefly, then just established by the British as a "national home" for the Jews, she had some sense of belonging—yet it was accompanied by a sense of shame, because the Jews of Palestine looked upon her with distaste for marrying a Gentile.

Peggy was doing her best to become a bohemian, but she did not find it easy. She did not drink, and most of the guests at her parties drank like fish and fornicated like flies. After each party she spent hours cleaning up, using a Lysol solution; that was the popular disinfectant of the 1920's. The parties were so open and so wild that at one of them Peggy forced a relative to guard the silver for the entire evening because she did not know her guests.

Under her husband's guidance, Peggy had come to know and love Venice. In the spring of 1924 she went to that city again with her mother, her sister Benita, and her bohemian husband. All the time, of course, Peggy was a bohemian traveling in style. She had maids and cooks and all the fancy foods and drinks that one could wish. When she traveled she took a house at her destination. It was a very pleasant if wasteful life. She and her husband bought a house at a place called Le Canadel on the Côte des Maures and lived there until it came time for Peggy's second child to be born.

She went then to Switzerland, to the Beau Rivage Hôtel on the bank of Lake Geneva, for the delivery of the child—a girl. She and her husband took the baby home and tried to settle down to a peaceful existence, but that, apparently, was not possible for Peggy and her wild husband in the 1920's. They went to Paris, he insulted people and ended up in jail again. Peggy got him out, and to celebrate he took her to a brothel where they were greeted at the entrance by fifteen naked girls.

Peggy's quarrels with Lawrence were fierce and frequent, and eroding to both of them. He wrote a novel based on their life together and she took exception to parts of it, so he angrily burned the work of weeks in the stove. She opened a shop in Paris for a time and sold lampshades, apparently with some financial success, but his family, then in Paris, was outraged that she had descended into common trade so she unhappily gave up the shop.

From time to time Peggy, her husband, their son Sindbad, and their daughter Deirdre, went to America to visit Peggy's relatives, but after a few weeks they always came back to France.

Peggy met Isadora Duncan, dancer, artist, and feminist, who christened her Guggie Peggleheim.

Peggy's sister Benita died in childbirth, and she was seriously affected by the loss, so seriously that her husband was annoyed at the emotion his wife wasted on a dead relative; thus came the beginning of the end of a marriage.

Lawrence and Peggy went to Paris, quarreling more often about less important matters. They went to Toulon, where he threw her down on the pavement in the street, and then, for some reason set fire to a hundred-franc note—perhaps to show that he did not care a fig for his rich wife's money. Lawrence was arrested by the gendarmes, not for creating a disturbance, or for beating his wife, which every redblooded Frenchman had a right to do, but for destroying the product of the Bank of France.

Peggy met everyone in Europe who amounted to anything in the world of art and left-wing politics. For example, the communist Emma Goldman became her good friend and companion.

Peggy took an English lover named John Holms. By now—this was the middle of the 1920's—Peggy was drinking like a sailor, having learned all the bad habits that one could be taught in France.

She and Lawrence were still fighting physically in public places (one night he tried to tear her clothes off in a bar and on another night he threw her down the steps of his studio), and after one particularly vigorous struggle which involved Peggy's lover, she left Vail and went away with Holms and his wife. Her marriage of seven years was over.

One might say, as the family did, contemplating this *ménage à trois*, that Peggy had made a thorough mess of her life. To this point it certainly had not been conventionally successful. But there was a deep-seated reason for her behavior: like the other Guggenheims, Daniel included, Peggy was seeking some way of atoning for her possession of great wealth. In the 1920's it was most apparent that this feeling of guilt was a serious Guggenheim problem.

31]

WHEN MEYER GUGGENHEIM invested in the A.Y. and the Minnie in the 1880's, the wealth of the earth existed for anyone to find, and if a man was fortunate enough to find a vein of valuable ore, then the riches that he clasped to him were for him to enjoy for himself. There was no question about his right in the minds of any but a handful of utopians. The miner who worked for $2.50 a day pulling down the ore in Meyer Guggenheim's mine might envy Meyer his luck and curse his own circumstances, but he never basically questioned Meyer's right to stake a claim on the land, take the mineral resources, and use the profits for his own purposes. The right of the individual to exploit natural resources was retained in the American system; it continued to exist into the middle of the twentieth century, when it was last tested in the granting of off-shore oil claims by the federal government to the states. There were some Americans by that time who believed that natural resources belonged to all the people of the nation, and not to the lucky finders, but this view was not yet upheld by American law, and it was doubtful if it would be the American view, at least not for many years to come.

The beginning of conservation as a theory of social betterment in the United States came in 1887, just at the time that the Guggenheims began to get into stride in their exploitation. The first realization of the demands for conservation came in the establishment of a Division of Forestry of the Interior Department. Not long afterward Major John W. Powell's work became known. As early as 1879 Powell had surveyed the mineral and other geological resources of the Rocky Mountains. He made some recommendations about the uses of the western lands, and he became director of the United States Geological Survey. Among his recommendations was the material of the Carey Act of the 1890's, which authorized the granting of a million acres to a state government to be used for irrigation, reclamation, settlement, and cultivation.

Other moves toward conservation of resources followed. After 1909, when the National Conservation Association was formed, the Ballinger-Pinchot struggle, fought over the Guggenheim plans for Alaska, brought about an increase in awareness of the value of natural resources, and caused more Americans and more state governments to take the position that the people at large had some indefinable stake in the natural resources beneath their feet, yet the question remained very fuzzy and no particular guidelines were established. During the early 1920's in the Teapot Dome scandal, after the Secretary of the Interior opened certain government oil reserve lands to the Sinclair Refining Company, it was indicated how far the government and business could *not* go. In the huge land grants to the railroads of the nineteenth century the government had gone very, very, far, and this Teapot Dome affair represented, to some extent, a public reaction to exploitation of the public. No one could put his finger on the public's rights, but the public felt that it had certain rights, nonetheless, and this fact was growing increasingly clear.

The Guggenheim brothers were very much aware after 1907 of the criticisms leveled against them as "milkers of the earth." The criticisms did not come only from the I.W.W. and the Socialists who followed Eugene Debs; they came also from such men as Henry Ford, who went on record as saying that no man had the right to grow rich by exploiting the earth's natural resources. After the first decade of the twentieth century, other nations began to deny the right of a man or a group of men to exploit the resources for themselves. Many countries, in Latin America and in the Middle East, began to take the position that the people, through their national governments, retained the ultimate title to natural resources. The people could authorize the exploitation of the resources, but it must be done in such a manner as to reward the owners as well as the exploiters. That belief led to the establishment of Cosach (Compañía de Salitre de Chile) as a monopoly of the nitrates of Chile in the interests of the Chilean people as well as of the capitalists who could extract, treat, and sell the product. The workings of the systems of retaining public interest in resources remains quite another affair; but in Latin America the principle was established, just as it was established, against the Guggenheims' interest, in the Alaskan development in 1908 and 1909.

The Guggenheims were businessmen and as such they could not be expected to listen to the whimperings of the luckless. Yet the Guggenheims were also only one generation removed from the poorest of the poor, the lowest of the low, the most miserable of human beings, the Jews of the ghettos of Europe.

Isaac, Daniel, Murry, Solomon, and Simon all considered the problem at one time or another in their own way. Isaac, the eldest, returned part of his wealth to the public in the form of bequests to Sydenham Hospital and other favorite charities. When he died he split his fortune among his wife and three daughters, and as they died they left bequests to charities, friends, relatives, and principal heirs. Isaac's family followed the normal path of fortune, and in the course of time much of the wealth of Isaac Guggenheim returned to the people in the form of expenditures and taxes. This resolution represented the old, familiar cycle of wealth in America.

Daniel Guggenheim considered the problem in a different light, urged by different circumstances and a different point of view that was emerging among the wealthy of America in the 1920's. Daniel and Murry had enjoyed a taste of what might be called "living philanthropy" during World War I. In 1917 Edwin Franko Goldman began presenting free band concerts in Central Park and he continued this for six years although each year it was a struggle to find enough donors to meet expenses. In the summer of 1923 Goldman announced that he had two thousand donations but still ended the summer with a deficit. Daniel and Murry Guggenheim stepped in then and announced that they would meet the deficit in the interest of civic betterment and that they would defray *all* the expenses of the band concerts in the next year.

John Francis "Red Mike" Hylan, the mayor of New York City, suddenly discovered that the band concerts in the summer were, as Bandmaster Goldman put it, "the greatest gift ever made here for the cause of free music . . ." and he decided to take them over.

First he had his own name placed on the programs in big type, giving the impression that none other than Red Mike was supplying New Yorkers with free music. *The New York Times* called Red Mike dense, but this political leader who looked like a carrot-topped fireman was not dense about attracting votes. Also, he had the Hearst press behind him, saying that the Guggenheims were trying to steal Central Park just as they tried to steal Alaska.

If Mayor Hylan was really in fear for the safety of Central Park from Guggenheim exploitation, he behaved exactly as he ought to have behaved. He first covered up the Guggenheim connection like a dog covering a coveted bone, and then in June, 1924, he had his own programs printed and confiscated those of Goldman. The next year he threw the Goldman band out of Central Park altogether and began the Red Mike Hylan series of concerts, played by police, fire department, army, and industrial bands who played more loudly but not so well as the Goldman band.

Meanwhile, the Goldman-Guggenheim force had secured a foothold further north when New York University officials offered them the use of the Washington Heights campus for the band concerts. The public then had a choice: One could go further (to Washington Heights) and hear a better band, or stay closer (in Central Park) and hear an inferior one.

Red Mike should have guarded his flank. Had he assembled a really good musical group he might have carried the day and won many votes. Instead, he found himself besieged at City Hall by pickets—small tots and indulgent mothers who demanded the return of the Goldman Band to Central Park's mall. No one can say for certain that interference with the arts was the cause of Red Mike's political downfall. Suffice it to report that music lover James J. Walker, pride of the East Side, sometime song-writer, most beloved of publicists, replaced Red Mike as mayor of Gotham, and Mayor Walker calmed troubled waters by returning the Goldman band victoriously to Central Park. Perhaps two million people were pleased to hear the Goldman concerts in the park each summer thereafter. The cost to the Guggenheims was about $100,-000 a year, and from that small expenditure, in terms of their resources, they derived as much pleasure as the people did in the concerts. It is far more satisfactory to be greeted with smiles on the streets of your own home town and known as a public benefactor, than to be greeted by tight-lipped hatred and known as an exploiter of the people. The Guggenheim Memorial Concerts in Central Park, endowed by Daniel Guggenheim's money, became a permanent part of the summer life of New Yorkers after his death.

At about the same time, in the middle of the 1920's, Daniel, Murry, Solomon, and Simon all announced the establishments of tax-free foundations for the betterment of mankind.

It was not that they neglected their business affairs and other affairs and turned philanthropist-idlers. Not at all.

Take Sol as an example:

Solomon Guggenheim was one of the two most active Guggenheims in the political sphere, the other being Simon, who, as noted, actually became a United States Senator. Sol had no such ambition, but he did enjoy the give and take of politics as much as that of business. After he left the board of directors of American Smelting and Refining, Solomon kept up a pleasant fiction that he was "retired" from business. All that meant was that he was retired from holding office in business, but it also meant he had more time for frequent travel in Europe, and more time to devote to his various interests, such as his and his wife Irene's collections of paintings; to his daughters, two of whom married upper-class Englishmen; and to political and public affairs.

In 1923, when Secretary of the Treasury Andrew Mellon suggested that the income taxes which troubled the very rich should be cut down considerably, Solomon agreed with all his heart. The Guggenheims preferred to invest their money in industry, rather than put it into tax-exempt municipal and other bonds, but they could do it either way, they said. In the true spirit of the capitalistic entrepreneur, they kept capital flowing, exploiting one natural resource after another. And they did not want to be taxed for this.

In 1924 Solomon became a delegate from New York to the Republican National Convention, which nominated Calvin Coolidge for the Presidency. On November 6, after the returns were in, when Solomon was interviewed by the reporters, he rejoiced in the election. The tax matter came up again, and this time Daniel added his approval to Solomon's pleas for a tax reduction for the rich.

It made no difference which party was in power, Sol had his say about national affairs. He would talk confidently of prosperity in 1932 when Hoover, the family's favorite president, was in office. He would talk confidently about the National Recovery Act a few months after Franklin Roosevelt assumed power. In matters other than those of Wall Street, Solomon, with a twinkle in his eye, was more or less public spokesman of the family, and if the other brothers and their descendants did not always agree with him, usually they were genteel enough and cautious enough not to let it be known to the press.

Until he died at the age of eighty-eight, Sol had that twinkle in his eye and that stubborn streak running down the length of him. A story was told within the family that although he liked visiting the Crawford Notch Inn, in New Hampshire, he did not like its practice of giving guests one napkin and a napkin ring, and forcing them to use the napkin until it was truly soiled. Sol's solution to this problem was to crease and twist his napkin at every meal so that it became unrecognizable as a napkin. Thus he received clean table linens at every meal. It was the same in everything he did: Sol *would* have his own way.

Withal, Sol was true lover of life and a friend to all the family, a man who frightened none of his younger relatives (as Daniel always frightened them) and who was beloved more, perhaps, than any other Guggenheim.

Sol was as earthy as old Meyer, in a more modern way. One day, while talking over the problems of life with his nephew Harold Loeb, Sol warned the young man never to make love before breakfast.

"You might have a better offer before lunch," he said with a twinkle in his eye.

Sol often did have better offers before lunch, and he indulged himself in them, and in high life with a gaiety that earned him a reputation among members of the family as the great lover of the Guggenheims. Long after his death his niece Gladys Guggenheim Straus recalled, almost with awe, that his mistresses were the most beautiful women she ever saw.

For that was what Sol wanted out of life, gaiety and beauty, and he gave much of his time and energy in pursuit of these. Yet no one ever accused him of failing to pay as much attention to business affairs as was necessary to keep Guggenheim Brothers in motion. All the members of the partnership were called upon for hard work from time to time.

In 1922, as the Guggenheim Brothers partnership faltered over the copper sale, the older brothers established the necessary pilot plant for nitrate reduction in the Antofagasta pampa of Chile. For a year and a half the plant produced twenty tons a day of nitrate. The results of this Cecilia Pilot Plant, as they called it, were all they could wish, and they decided to go ahead with further investment.

The Guggenheims moved in several directions. They bought shares of the Anglo-Chilean Nitrate and Railway Company on the open market, 40,000 shares out of 900,000 outstanding, to give them a basis for later negotiation if they decided to buy Anglo-Chilean. They also made preparations to be represented at a public auction of a large tract of land, the Coya Norte, in the Tocopilla Pampa. This land was said to contain some five million tons of recoverable nitrate. They sent engineers out to sample the grounds. They called on the J. P. Morgan company and told the bankers that they proposed to expand several million dollars on this nitrate venture. J. P. Morgan and Company decided this was a bit risky for a banking house, and asked out. The Guggenheim Brothers paid out $345,000, which represented the Morgan participation to that date, and then owned their venture outright.

Before and after young Harry Guggenheim left the firm, serious efforts had been made to bring existing nitrate producers into a joint venture, but the Guggenheims were totally unable to accomplish this end. After the Morgan interests departed, the Guggenheims decided in 1924 to go ahead on their own, much as Meyer had decided to enter a new kind of business, first with mining and then with smelting.

As it came time for the auction of the Coya Norte land, it became apparent to the Guggenheims that they must have the Anglo-Chilean Nitrate and Railway Company, whose property was adjacent to Coya Norte since Anglo-Chilean owned three nitrate plants and had good ore reserves. The Guggenheims negotiated a sale—conditional on their acquisition of Coya Norte. They financed the purchase of Anglo-Chilean with two bond issues: a sterling bond issue of £3,600,000, which was secured by a first mortgage on the property; and a $16,500,000 United States bond issue to purchase Coya Norte and build the Guggenheim reduction plant. Coya Norte was purchased for $3,400,000. Lehman Brothers offered the bond issue in America, and soon the Guggenheims owned Anglo-Chilean and Coya Norte and were more deeply involved in nitrates.

One plant was built and in 1927 another was planned. Harry and Edmond were in this scheme, each holding about 10 percent of the new Anglo-Chilean Consolidated Nitrate Company stock.

One of the sad peculiarities of the nitrate business was that costs rose while the results were not as good as had been expected. In addition, late in the 1920's European manufacturers discovered a method of making synthetic nitrate cheaply. The price of nitrate fell and fell again. In 1927 the Guggenheims borrowed $5,000,000 to finish their reduction plant. The money was not enough, and they put in another $9,000,000 of their own money, because the bankers looked at the falling price of nitrate, the competition of synthetics, and refused to loan any more money. What the bankers wanted to see was a very strong position, preferably a monopoly, so the Guggenheims set out to acquire it.

A British company called the Lautaro Nitrate Company was the most important in Chile, controlling twenty-six plants and numerous reserves, although the twenty-six Lautaro plants used an old-fashioned process called the Shanks process for extraction of nitrate. Daniel began negotiation in New York with the representatives of the company and in the spring of 1929 the Guggenheims bought it for Anglo-Chilean, forming a Delaware corporation. Lehman Brothers handled the financing and the National City Bank floated a $32,000,000 bond issue to provide funds for construction of a Guggenheim process plant.

With this move the Guggenheims controlled Anglo-Chilean, which controlled Lautaro, and through these two, the Guggenheims were able to name the president and control the activities of the Nitrate Producers' Association of Chile. The problem that remained was to stabilize the market for natural nitrate, and this involved securing control of *all* producers. The Guggenheims evolved a plan under which this would be possible. As noted, they suggested formation of the Compañía de Salitre de Chile, sometimes called Cosach. In this the Chilean government would hold one-half of the total shares. The company would be composed of all the producers of nitrate in Chile.

To work this out the government must abolish the export tax of about $12.50 per ton of nitrate. The government would contribute government lands which contained 150,000,000 tons of nitrate. Only 6 percent income tax would be charged against the company, and in return the government would have a guaranteed revenue, and the companies involved would have half the shares of the stock.

The tempo and scope of the negotiation indicated why and how the Guggenheims were so successful in their business ventures: they went further and faster than anyone else had ever thought of going.

32]

IN THE 1920's the elder Guggenheims, sons of Meyer, were in a very great hurry, for all of them felt the heavy hand of time on their shoulders—save perhaps the ebullient Sol—and each of them, including Sol, yearned to be remembered in America as other than businessman.

Their answer was to join other millionaires in the established practice of creating foundations.

Best known of all the Guggenheim foundations is the one usually referred to in public simply as *The* Guggenheim, most people not knowing that it is called the John Simon Guggenheim Memorial Foundation, or that it is named for the son of Simon Guggenheim.

In 1905, when Simon was only beginning his campaign for the United States Senate seat, John Simon Guggenheim was born in Denver. Soon iron bars were erected outside the windows of the second floor of the big house on Sherman Street, not to keep the burglars out, but to keep John Simon in. Two years later John Simon's brother, George Denver, was born into a family then savoring the excitement of the move to Washington for six years.

John Simon Guggenheim grew up in Washington and later in New York when his father became chairman and later president of American Smelting and Refining. When he was old enough to go away to school he attended Phillips Exeter Academy in New Hampshire, and he was ready to enter Harvard College when he died after a mastoid operation.

John Simon died on April 26, 1922, and for the next two years Simon Guggenheim pondered the manner in which he might preserve the boy's memory and give some Guggenheim money back to the people. He sought the counsel of men who had been closely connected with the Rhodes scholarships of Oxford University. Soon Henry Allen Moe, a young Rhodes scholar, was chosen to run the foundation and set up a tiny office at 120 Broadway. The foundation moved to 42nd Street, then to Fifth Avenue where it remained for many years, and finally to Park Avenue.

In the beginning, the foundation tended to split its grants among writers, composers, artists, scholars and scientists. In the years after World War II, however, with the emphasis of the nation directed to science and scholarship, the foundation began to follow fashion, and the number of grants to scientists and scholars came to outstrip those to artists. By the 1960's the emphasis was entirely on the world of academic affairs; a few independent writers and musicians and artists received fellowships, but very few. In a way the change also represented another change in American society: In the 1960's there were very few independent writers and artists in America.

The first Guggenheim fellowships were awarded, fifteen of them, in 1925. Ten years later four times as many fellowships were awarded annually. Thirty years later there were thirty times as many fellowships as had been given originally, and they were less valuable in terms of purchasing power for the holder—but in nearly every case the fellowship represented only a part of the fellow's income (it was not even called income by internal revenue standards).

Originally, the Guggenheim foundation grants were made only to people in America, but in 1929 Simon gave another sum of money to make it possible to include Latin Americans, for it was embarrassing for the Guggenheims to be so intently concerned with exploitation of resources there and yet not willing to grant the needy scholars and artists of that continent any assistance. (By the 1960's the Guggenheim foundation was giving away more than a million dollars a year, which represented the income of its endowment.) Thus Simon Guggenheim began to return his share of the American dream, with interest.

Daniel and his wife established two foundations: the Daniel and Florence Guggenheim Foundation, established in 1924, and the

Daniel Guggenheim Fund for the Promotion of Aeronautics, established the same year.

The Daniel and Florence Guggenheim Foundation was begun to carry out a number of small projects to which Daniel and his wife wished to address themselves. (By 1964 it had made 300 grants to 62 organizations, helping hospitals and medical institutions in the United States, Chile, the Congo, and Palestine.) It sponsored various museum exhibits in several museums in the United States. It gave money to various educational institutions and organizations.

The Daniel and Florence Guggenheim Foundation, useful as it has been to society, was surpassed from the beginning by the Daniel Guggenheim Fund for the Promotion of Aeronautics. One might also say that the Guggenheims were the founders and perpetuators of applied practical aeronautics in the United States, and that without the Guggenheims the development of aircraft industries and flight in the United States would have languished after World War I. It was no accident that an America that could not produce an acceptable fighter or bomber aircraft during World War I was able to outproduce all other nations but Germany in quality of aircraft during World War II. The Guggenheims had more to do with this change than most Americans are likely to know.

The beginnings were small enough, but promising. In 1925, Daniel Guggenheim endowed a school of aeronautics at New York University's College of Engineering with a half-million dollars. He then made what was as close to a statement of personal policy as he was ever to make.

"I shall dedicate the rest of my life," he said, "with the active aid of my son, Harry F. Guggenheim, to the study and promotion of the science of aeronautics. I shall do this as a part of my duty to my country whose ample opportunities have ever been at my hand and whose bountiful blessings I have had the good fortune to enjoy."

Daniel was willing to endow schools of aeronautics at half a dozen American universities, but he was cautioned to proceed slowly, because the United States was not ready for schools of aeronautics in 1925. If 500 aeronautical engineers were to be turned out in one year, perhaps 50 of them could find jobs somewhere in the world, the other 450 would either have to go back to school or forget their specialty. There had been no marked improvement in design or stability or safety of aircraft since World War I. So un-promising was the aircraft industry that when he came home from World War I, Captain Eddie Rickenbacker, the leading ace of the United States, went into the automobile industry and laughed when people talked to him about airplanes.

Harry Guggenheim, World War I pilot and aviation enthusiast who had kindled his father's interest in the subject, counseled with Ivy Lee, the publicist, and they suggested that a fund be estab-lished by Daniel to promote aviation and thus secure a climate in which the industry could prosper.

Then, in 1925, began Harry's intensive period of aviation inter-est and development. Daniel put up the money for the fund for promotion of aviation. Harry did the work. He set up the offices on New York's Madison Avenue, he hired the army of publicity men and contact men, he secured and he read all the reports on aviation activity in the country. By 1925 it was probable that Harry Gug-genheim knew more about what was going on in world aviation circles than any other man in America. He sought out the pioneers of aviation, the Wrights and Glenn Curtiss and Glen Martin and Richard Byrd.

Aviation was languishing, and there was no question about it. After World War I the United States disbanded its military ma-chine. The air service of the army was reduced to a small service and the general staff's idea of air power was a half-dozen single-seater biplanes which could scout out the positions of the enemy. General Billy Mitchell, the prime military advocate of aviation, was making claims that an airplane could sink a battleship. These claims annoyed the admirals, and the admirals, who played golf at the Army and Navy Country Club with the generals, let it be known that they were annoyed. Billy Mitchell was too insistent. The entire atmosphere of Washington in the middle 1920's militated against Mitchell or anyone else who might promote aviation.

Daniel Guggenheim was more shrewd in matters of this type than his advisers; he insisted that before any big money was spent to promote aviation, the backing of the United States government be obtained, so as the agent of his father, Harry Guggenheim went to Washington in December, to see if he could stir up enthusiasm on the highest levels. He visited Dwight Morrow, an old Guggenheim business associate and friend. Morrow was president of the special Air Board which had been established by President Coolidge to dispose of the questions of air power. Harry saw Morrow in his government office and informed him that Daniel was willing to put up three million dollars for promotion of aviation if President Coolidge would back the plan by accepting the money in behalf of the government. Morrow was certain that Coolidge would accept and Coolidge did accept the money, or at least he showed that he would not interfere with the plan. His own enthusiasm was no greater than it had been for anything else. "What's the use of getting there quicker if you haven't got something better to say when you arrive?" he asked. But he did approve, and so did Secretary of Commerce Herbert Hoover. The Guggenheim effort to promote aviation was launched.

In 1926, a staff was assembled and a number of programs for promotion of the new "science" of aeronautics were begun. Daniel provided money for aviation conferences, reports on European progress in the field, experiments on new engines, work on altimeters and other instruments, and for a survey of aviation insurance. One of the most useful programs for aviators was a campaign which persuaded nearly five thousand American communities of less than 10,000 population to put up roof markings as guides to fliers.

Daniel Guggenheim, with his old prescience, saw aviation as the servant of all the people, while Harry and his friends looked upon it as a game for the bold and a new arm for the military. Daniel insisted that the emphasis be placed on commercial aviation, and a meeting of air transport companies was arranged. Nearly all the airline men insisted that the airlines business must have government subsidy. They wanted the same kinds of subsidies that shipping companies had always enjoyed. They talked in terms of a "merchant marine of the air."

Daniel did not argue. In 1926, to prove his point, he financed a model airline, Western Air Express Company, to operate over the 365 miles from San Francisco to Los Angeles, using trimotored planes. Daniel loaned this company $150,000 to buy the airplanes. Within two years the experiment proved successful, the loan was repaid, and air travel in America was beginning to grow. In 1928 some 48,000 passengers were carried by scheduled air services in the United States. Seven years later the figure would reach about a quarter of a million passenger trips.

Daniel's Fund paid the expenses of Floyd Bennett, pilot for Commander Richard F. Byrd, to travel around the United States and exhibit the trimotor plane in which they had flown over the North Pole in 1926. The Fund supported Charles A. Lindbergh when he returned from his triumphal flight to Paris, and made it possible for Lindbergh to use his influence in behalf of aviation. (Lindbergh turned down a $500,000 movie contract with William Randolph Hearst for promotion and movie-making.)

Harry took the thoroughly dazzled young Lindbergh off to his great house at Sands Point and gave him room and time to write the book about his exploits, which would be read by millions. Lindbergh was grateful because the respite gave him the opportunity of refraining from commercialization of his flight. As Harry's guest he was safe from prying eyes and unwelcome offers of quick money. In an arrangement sponsored by the United States Department of Commerce (Herbert Hoover, Secretary), Harry arranged for a 22,000 mile tour for Lindbergh, and in their frequent meetings the pair became friends. Harry liked the shy, competent flier. Lindbergh approved of the slender, engaging Harry and the work he had set out to do. Yes, work. For the first time in his career Harry was dedicating himself to a task with all the gusto that Daniel Guggenheim and his brothers had devoted in years past to the mining business. Daniel, in these last years of his life, saw and sympathized. Perhaps he remembered that the impetus that sent the Guggenheim brothers into the smelting business and out of the safety of laces had come from old Meyer. Daniel had fought against the change, unwilling to take the chance his father offered, until persuaded by the old man's stubbornness. In the 1920's, Harry was in his thirties and by any standards he was a young man and it was far from late for him to be finding his way.

In the spring of 1926 Harry had gone to Europe to examine the status of European aviation. He came home in April. In May, Richard Byrd made his successful flight across the North Pole, a great event in the story of American flight, and Harry cabled the congratulations of the Guggenheim Fund. Harry made speeches on aviation at the drop of a flying helmet. He talked about the future of commercial air travel, and predicted that soon there would be trans-Atlantic flights, carrying passengers. To some he sounded like H. G. Wells, telling tales of outer space.

He arranged for the Fund's "safe airplane" contest, and he gave, or arranged to have given, $5000 to a University of Michigan Greenland expedition in behalf of the air potential. Harry spoke everywhere, before the American Society of Mechanical Engineers, to university groups, to luncheon clubs.

In the first few weeks of 1927 Harry sailed to Brussels to serve on the League of Nations Disarmament Committee as a specialist in its studies of aviation.

From that point on Harry and Daniel were regarded as "fathers" of American aviation. When Commander Byrd made his trans-Atlantic flight, Harry was called on by the newspapers for comment. When E. L. Smith flew to Hawaii, the newspapers wanted Harry's opinions on what this meant to the future of aviation. He was consulted when the city fathers of New York wanted a site for their municipal airport. He made flights as pilot and passenger to promote safety. He, among all the Guggenheims, was first in the news in the 1920's, surpassing even his father.

Daniel supported Jimmy Doolittle, later to be famous as racing pilot and the leader of the famous B-25 raid on Tokyo during World War II. Doolittle established what was known as the Full Flight Laboratory, seeking instruments and methods of flight so safe that a pilot could take off, fly, and land an airplane without seeing the ground. The problem involved the development of a reliable altimeter, an attitudinizer or turn and bank indicator, and a directional guide which would show the pilot which way he was actually flying. None of these instruments existed; they were to be developed, largely through the Guggenheim moneys. In 1929, Jimmy Doolittle made a perfect flight in a blacked-out plane, whereupon the Guggenheim Aeronautical Fund gave the test airplane to the Army Air Corps and closed down its Full Flight Laboratory. With an expenditure of $65,000 the basic problem of flight in bad weather had been solved.

Daniel's Fund offered $100,000 as a first prize in a contest for development of safe aircraft, a prize won by the Curtiss Aircraft

Company in 1929. The Fund inaugurated an experimental weather service, developing new ways of forecasting weather changes. In two years Daniel spent $27,000 on this service, brought it to a higher degree of accuracy in forecasting than had before been possible, and turned over the plan to the federal weather bureau.

For five years the Guggenheim aeronautics fund led the way in advancement of aviation, and at the end of those five years so many improvements had been made and so high was public interest in aviation that it was apparent the Fund had done its job. It closed in January, 1930, having spent slightly more than two million dollars, and having established the Guggenheims as the prime backers in America of modern aviation.

Hundreds of thousands of dollars went to Massachusetts Institute of Technology, Stanford University, Syracuse University, the University of Michigan, the University of Washington, Georgia School of Technology, and the California Institute of Technology for establishment of centers for various aerial studies, from engineering to photography.

In all his life, Daniel Guggenheim never went up in an airplane. In his business years he was too busy to be more than vaguely aware of the development of heavier-than-air craft. By the time his son had interested him in aviation, Daniel suffered from a serious heart condition and his doctors would not let him fly. He spent much of these last few years after his retirement from the board of American Smelting and Refining in trips abroad in search of good health; relaxing in the baronial atmosphere of Hempstead House, surrounded by priceless antique furniture culled from the castles and manor houses of Europe, the walls of the rooms hung with traditional but valuable pieces of art, including some sixteenth-century Flemish tapestries; and entertaining friends on his nine-hole golf course or in his bowling alley and casino. He was a little man growing old, with the wife who would survive him by some fourteen years. Until the end, Daniel Guggenheim interested himself in his philanthropies in a very firm and businesslike manner. He gave money to synagogues, to hospitals, to New York for its botanical gardens, and to many colleges for many purposes.

With his brothers he had discovered the delights of using his money to promote human accomplishment. He was not the originator of this idea, nor was John D. Rockefeller, whose foundation is often regarded as the primary venture in the field of return of the money to the people. Leland Stanford was among the earliest of Americans to enjoy the delights of playing creator. At a time when the University of California's student body numbered only three hundred students in Berkeley, and Berkeley was all of the university, Stanford had used moneys returned by that great national experiment, the transcontinental railroad, to build the nucleus of a great *free* university, Leland Stanford Jr. University. In the East the newspapers and educators and politicians said Stanford was crazy to waste his money thus; there was no room for another university in California; Daniel Guggenheim proved that he was not crazy at all when forty years later he gave nearly two hundred thousand dollars to help Stanford's university when it had fallen on evil days because Stanford's huge fortune was not large enough to carry on the master plan unaided.

Daniel sat in his huge living room in the last days, a German shepherd named Bismarck laughing at his feet. Daniel could contemplate a busy and satisfactory life behind him. He had begun life as the second son of a Philadelphia merchant, then of moderate means. The merchant's son had become one of the richest men in all America and one of the most powerful in finance.

In the process, Daniel had grown to be hated and symbolized in the popular press by a cartoon character with Semitic features and snarling face, clawlike hands grasping at whatever region or resource had taken his fancy. He was linked with J. Pierpont Morgan as a symbol of the evil capitalist. Once a cartoonist drew a beast threatening the world and called it "the Guggenmorgan."

Daniel died on September 28, 1930, when he was seventy-four years old, in the great old Gould castle, Hempstead House. His funeral was held at Temple Emanu-el, of which he was a trustee and to which he had contributed handsomely over the years. The honorary pallbearers were friends and business associates, including such diverse characters as Bernard Baruch, John Hays Hammond, Charles A. Lindbergh, Adolph Ochs, and Elihu Root, Jr.

Hundreds of people crowded into Temple Emanu-el for the service, and more than a thousand who could not get in stood outside. A rabbi read from the Bible, a choir sang a selection from

Mendelssohn, and Mayor James J. Walker of New York City paid the respects of the people of New York to the Guggenheims, living and dead.

Daniel was buried in Salem Fields, beside Meyer and Barbara Guggenheim, in the mausoleum of the family, and even as the plain brown casket was lowered, Daniel and the Guggenheims were praised on radio and in the press of the land.

In a few years after 1920, Daniel had managed to change the portrait of Guggenheim from one that was hated to the picture of a soft, smiling roundfaced old man in a neat overcoat and velvet collar, wearing a homburg hat and looking benignly out upon the world that had given him his wealth. Somewhere between the two pictures was the real Daniel Guggenheim, who ought to be remembered for his accomplishments in the development of the metals industries as well as for his benefactions. The myth of the Robber Barons had the Guggenheims and the other developers of great American fortunes clustering around the corpse of America, clawing at her like vultures, when actually these fortune hunters represented the story of American opportunity. Daniel Guggenheim's place in the American dream is that of the dutiful son who took his father's guidance and his capital and with those benefits and his own brains doubled and redoubled the fortune put into his hands, and who finally turned much of his fortune to public service.

33]

AMONG THOSE who praised Daniel Guggenheim loudly was Ambassador Davila of Chile, and he had good reasons for his encomiums. Through their exploitation of copper and later of nitrates the Guggenheims had given Chile's government the basis for hope that some day their country could emerge from the poverty in which it was born and had always lived.

In 1930 President Carlos Ibáñez of Chile had also been concerned about the fluctuations of the price of nitrate, for nitrate was vital to his nation's economy. He took the Cosach plan before Chile's Congress. Meanwhile the Guggenheims had been securing the agreement of some forty companies, composed of individuals from many countries. They were dealing with bankers in the United States, in London (Morgan, Grenfell), and in South America, where the Banco Anglo Sud Americana was to be involved to the extent of £12,000,000. In the negotiations with other companies and banks the Guggenheims had the assistance of Pablo Ramirez, Chile's finance minister, which did not hurt their position at all.

Although President Ibáñez was dictator of Chile, the Cosach plan—Law No. 4863 of July 21, 1930—was hotly debated in the Chilean Congress, and a young man named Osvaldo de Castro earned much local fame by opposing it and denouncing the Guggenheims. Eventually he was banished from the country for his opposition, and the merger went on.

Meanwhile, the New York Stock Market had collapsed in the fall of 1929 and Murry Guggenheim came into his own in the business world with that crash. He was then seventy-one years old, and was senior of the brothers-partners (Daniel had by then retired from active business affairs because of his bad heart).

When the crash came, J. P. Morgan, Jr., organized a quarter-billion-dollar banking pool. Morgan called on Murry to represent the Guggenheims. Murry did his part of the job and the stock market was saved. Guggenheim Brothers was the only nonbanking institution so invited, a sure proof of the wealth and importance of the Guggenheims to the American economy, if proof were needed. Murry then turned his attention to Chilean nitrate. For several years he muddled with the problems without apparent success.

And who was this Murry, the new leader of the Brothers Guggenheim after 1929? He was a many-sided person. For nearly a score of years Murry had sat with his brothers on various boards of directors: American Smelting and Refining, Nevada Consolidated Copper, and half a dozen other companies. He seldom spoke to the press, and the reason for his silence, he said, was that his brothers talked entirely too much. He had great affection for them and their families, and in spite of his brusqueness, he would do anything for a member of the family.

For example, young Harold Loeb, Rose's son, annoyed Murry once during the public troubles with Yukon gold and Alaskan development. He had asked Harold what he intended to do with his life now that he had finished school, and the youth answered smartly in the words of a popular song that he was going out West to look for "The girl on the banks of the Saskatchewan." Uncle Murry was offended. But later when Loeb's interests turned out to be intellectual and not business-directed, and he was having difficulty in finding money to support his experimental magazine, *Broom*, Uncle Murry helped him by releasing a trust fund for Harold.

In the year 1917 when Guggenheim profits had never been higher, Murry Guggenheim established multi-million-dollar trusts for his son Edmond and his daughter Lucille, then began looking around for a way in which to repay to the public some of the debt he felt because of the immense wealth the Guggenheims had accumulated.

In his search for a benefaction, Murry discovered a pressing need in New York City to which no rich person or government unit was devoting attention, a charity which would not have appealed to many wealthy persons, because in most foundations there is at least the wish of the founder to become immortal through his giving. Most builders of foundations have created with a grand and lavish hand; the Rockefeller medical foundation, for example, was created to change the shape of world health; the Ford and Carnegie foundations were no less grandiose in design.

It was typical of Murry Guggenheim that his foundation was much less grand. He learned from some of his friends in the field of public health that many New York children did not receive any dental care in their formative years and that society's failure to provide such elementary health service was costing individuals millions of dollars or countless hours of pain in later years.

In the spring of 1929, after a careful survey of the field, Murry announced the formation of a foundation dedicated to providing free dental care to school children who could not otherwise afford it. Half a dozen old tenements on East 72nd Street near the East River were purchased and torn down and a six-story building was erected to house the Murry and Leonie Guggenheim Dental Clinic. Dentists and technicians and oral surgeons cleaned teeth, filled cavities, and treated more serious conditions, without charge. A school for dental technicians was established and ran for a number of years until New York indicated that the state would fulfill this educational need. (The state proved very slow in so doing.) The foundation also supported various research projects, mobile dental units that moved about the city, and the Murry and Leonie Guggenheim Foundation Institute for Dental Research of New York University.

In its first thirty years the foundation cared for the dental needs of three-quarters of a million children. In the beginning it served only two districts of the city, but it grew until the foundation served all the city and in the middle of the 1960's it was serving 53 percent of all New York children who did not go to private dentists. The staff consisted of about two hundred persons, including a large number of "intern dentists" and "externs" who held fellowships at the foundation.

(In the 1960's the clinic consisted of seventy-eight dental chairs and a number of other facilities. Murry Guggenheim's unassuming gift was recognition of his debt to the society that had built the American dream. The foundation supported the program until 1967, when state assumption of responsibility made it no longer essential to public health. His foundation was much like the one established by nephew Harry Guggenheim years later.)

And who was Harry Guggenheim now? Very late in the 1920's Harry Guggenheim decided that he wanted to contribute to the family and the American dream in a manner other than simply presiding over the expenditure of his father's money.

During the early 1920's, Harry had become friends with Herbert Hoover, because they shared an interest in mining and in transportation. In 1928 Harry was one of Hoover's prime backers for the presidency, and one of the earliest. The campaign began in February, many months before the Republican National Convention, at a delicate time in a candidate's career, when a real backer is worth a half-dozen of the bandwagon riders.

During 1928 and 1929 the activities—the intensive promotion—of the Daniel Guggenheim Fund had slowed down. Harry was still making speeches, still attending international conferences and still keeping himself the best-informed of men about aviation. Yet he had discovered that he liked work and he liked the public eye. To combine the two, in the autumn of 1929 he received appointment as United States Ambassador to Cuba, having turned down an appointment as Assistant Secretary of Commerce for Air because he did not wish to devote his life to aviation.

There has been much criticism in America of the policy followed until the end of World War II by American government in giving embassies to various millionaires as recompense for political support. Obviously this was a big factor in Harry Guggenheim's appointment. The opposition to such appointments in the United States often stemmed from the performance of the ambassadors. Sending an ambassador to a nation where he knew nothing of the language, the customs, or the people was all too common a practice. Or, sending an ambassador to represent the government in a land where the man had business connections was common and dangerous. None of this applied to Ambassador Harry F. Guggenheim. He knew Spanish, and had since 1907 when he made his first trip through Havana on his way to South America and the Guggenheim workings there. He had no business interests in Cuba and none in any of Latin America because he had severed his connections with Guggenheim Brothers six years earlier. He did not know much about Cuba or Cuban affairs, but this deficit he set out to remedy by employing a large personal staff of experts to instruct and assist him. It is doubtful if the American Embassy in Havana ever employed so many experts as in the days of Harry Guggenheim's representation there. In addition to the State Department personnel assigned to the Havana post, Harry employed Dr. Philip C. Jessup as personal legal advisor, to help him with treaty matters; Edgar Turlington, another legal expert, who assisted with studies of Cuban laws; and Grosvenor Jones, his personal economics advisor.

Harry's appointment was confirmed in October, 1929, by the United States Senate. In November he stopped in Washington to dine with President and Mrs. Hoover, and then was off to Havana with his family.

Within a short time, Harry had acquired an understanding of Cuba and Cuban affairs, not only on the government level but on the popular level. He said then that unless the United States made drastic concessions, on the part of government and business, there would be serious trouble ahead for the United States in Cuba. It was a quarter of a century after his service that the trouble developed, but it came for almost exactly the reasons he outlined.

Harry Guggenheim discovered that at the end of the Spanish-American War, Cuba was destitute. She needed everything from banks to seeds and livestock. At that time $50,000,000 of American capital was invested in Cuba. By 1912, the investment was $220,-000,000. The foreign economic investment seemed fine, but soon Cubans began to complain that the foreign banks and companies had no interest in Cuban social conditions. Harry had some strong words for such operators:

There have been instances where American businessmen, like Cuban businessmen, have resorted to the vicious practice of attempting to influence the Cuban government by campaign contributions or by the bribery of public officials; there have been similar instances in the history of our own country. This practice has, of course, been one of the

cankerous sores on the body politic of democracy and capitalism everywhere. Those Americans who have engaged in it in Cuba have cast
discredit upon their honorable compatriots; but they have neither deserved nor received the support of their own government. Culpable
investors will argue that the only way that they can get justice and
maintain their rights is by bribery. This is a lame excuse, to which the
obvious retort is that under such circumstances they better go elsewhere
with their capital.

Those words were written by Harry Guggenheim in 1933, just
twenty years after his Uncle Simon retired from a seat in the
United States Senate which he had purchased openly by buying
the votes of Colorado legislators. Times *did* change, and with them
so did the Guggenheims.

Harry was soon aware of the American control of the Cuban
economy, and it worried him.

"The common carrier railroads," he wrote,

. . . are almost wholly divided between two companies, one American
and the other English-owned. Practically all of the ships trading with
the island are under foreign flags. These are principally American and
English, but include the ships of Spain and other European nations
and Japan. The air transportation both on and from the island is
wholly American. The cables and wireless are American and English,
although the local telegraph service is owned by the Cuban government. The street railway system is American. The electric light, power
and gas works are American. The principal mines are American-owned.
The sugar industry is roughly 70 percent American, 10 percent Canadian and English, and 20 percent Cuban. In addition, many of the
sugar companies are heavily mortgaged to the foreign banks in Cuba.

This was a picture few Americans saw even in the 1950's. The
banks were American, the life insurance companies were Canadian,
the oil industry was American and British, the packing business
was American, even 70 percent of the great Central Highway was
built by an American contracting firm, and the two leading hotels
were American. Harry Guggenheim said he believed that by 1934
the Cuban economy had benefited greatly from this incursion of
American capital but that the time had come "where it would seem

most desirable both for Cuba and for the United States, if Cubans would increase their participation in the island's business." The depression years during which he was ambassador seemed, to Harry Guggenheim, to be ideal years for this change, since values were so deflated. He suggested basic changes, including social and agrarian reforms, and the development and education of a middle class, to be stimulated by change in the archaic Cuban tax policy.

The Cuba in which Harry Guggenheim served as ambassador was ready for revolution. Unfortunately the rebellion was not led by representatives of the peasants, but became a question of one general against another, and in a year or so Harry found himself principal mediator between the government of President Machado and the revolution of former president Menocal. The revolution began in 1930. Harry, at the request of both sides, tried to mediate, but was not successful. The fighting began in August, the Machado government put down the revolution, and civil liberties of Cubans were sharply suppressed.

During the negotiations, during all his stay in Cuba, Harry Guggenheim was hampered in his efforts to represent his country by the pressures brought on him directly and indirectly by Americans who had interests in Cuba, as one anecdote indicates:

"In April, 1930," Harry wrote,

the *Union Nacionalista*—at that time the only active political group opposed to President Machado—was organizing a great political rally, to meet in Havana. In an attempt to stamp out this political opposition, the president issued a decree prohibiting any meetings during the *zafra*, the sugar harvest. The Supreme Court declared the decree unconstitutional, and President Machado, who at that time was endeavoring to rule the country within constitutional limits, revoked his decree. The meeting was then fixed for a date late in April, and it was anticipated that some ten to twenty thousand people would be present.

During this period I received a telegram from the Department of State informing me that two warships would pay a courtesy call at Havana Harbor between certain dates at the end of April, but with the usual appended phrase "if you perceive no objection to this visit." I did not think it wise to have American warships in Havana Harbor during the mass meeting for two reasons: first, I feared there might be rioting and bloodshed resulting from the meeting, since both Government and

Oppositionist nerves were on edge, and it did not seem wise to run the risk of having American naval officers and sailors in Havana where they might be drawn into a minor or major incident which could lead to serious consequences for the United States. And second, the visit of American warships would mean an exchange of courtesies with Cuban government officials which I feared might be abused by President Machado to indicate the support of the Cuban government by the government of the United States.

At this time President Machado's American supporter, to whom I have referred, informed me that he knew of the intended visit of the American warships, he was happy that they were being sent as they would create a good will between the two countries, and with the exchange of dinners between the commanding officer and President Machado (an unusual courtesy) would indeed cement existing friendships. Much to the American's surprise and great displeasure, I advised him that the warships' orders would be cancelled as the time for their visit was inopportune. I realized then that this proposed visit was not merely an innocent movement of ships. On the following day I called on President Machado to inform myself further regarding his part in this incident and to counteract any difficulties that the Americans, by this incursion into diplomacy, might make for me with the President.

As anticipated, President Machado knew all about the proposed visit of the ships, and he did everything in his power to persuade me to let them come. I told him that it would be contrary to the best interests of the United States to have warships in Havana Harbor during the proposed political demonstration, and that the visit would be unwise. The ships did not come. The Americans had suggested the visit through minor officials in Washington, and the ships had been ordered to Havana quite innocently by those in authority in the Navy Department. The proposal attracted little official notice because our warships are frequently cruising about these waters and stopping for courtesy visits at Havana. In my last two years in Havana I prevented the entry of American warships into Havana Harbor, much to the disgust of some of my old comrades in the navy whose visits I personally would have enjoyed as much as they.

There was the ambassador at work, besieged by his own countrymen whose interests might not always be those of the nation, a rich man trying to be a statesman, trying to protect his concept of the American dream.

It was hard, sometimes. In the winter of 1931, after Harry Guggenheim had first backed one government loan to Cuba and had then suggested that the Cubans undertake no more international public finance, it was reported in the American newspapers that Harry advocated a $300,000,000 loan by the United States government to Cuba. The report was the result of a trial rumor sent up by the government, and Harry and his staff knew the plan for what it was. *The New York Times* picked up the planted story. Questions were raised in the House of Representatives, one member charging that the United States had in Cuba an ambassador who represented several international financial houses and was at that time negotiating a $300,000,000 loan—on government time.

Ambassador Harry Guggenheim must be accounted a good observer in spite of such judgments as that of biographer Harvey O'Connor, who said:

Such hopefuls were doomed to disappointment. For all his intelligence and energy, Guggenheim was bounded by the business-like prejudices he had soaked up in his earlier relations in Mexico and South America. He had no sympathy with rebels who threatened law and order. He was all for postponing consideration of social and political evils until the business skies had cleared. To Cuban insurgents that was too long to wait and suffer.

But the fact was that Harry said he was not "all for postponing economic and social changes." He believed that the depression years were exactly the ones in which the changes should be made because they *could* be made. Harry saw reform as the solution, but no one in Washington heeded him, at least no one in the right places at the right times, and a quarter of a century later revolutionaries were in charge—probably, however, not exactly the revolutionaries that the biographer had envisaged. A thorough reading of Harry Guggenheim's *The United States and Cuba*, published by the Macmillan Company in 1934, would still give an American a quarter of a century later a very thorough understanding of the reasons for the success of the Castro revolution in Cuba, and a sense of wonderment as to how all those reports that reached the files of the State Department could have gone unheeded.

So, not all the Guggenheims of the fourth generation in America were economic royalists. Peggy was an out and out social rebel. Harold Loeb was a literary rebel, and an economic rebel, whose "Technocracy" was certainly not economic royalism. Edmond was a quiet, self-contained businessman who gave carefully to charities after he retired from Guggenheim Brothers, and who spent much of his time *managing* the Murry and Leonie Guggenheim Foundation. Harry was a man of great wealth and great energy who sought to promote the best interests of the United States. In Cuba, Harry entertained often at the embassy in Vedado, a fashionable part of Havana. He charmed the Cubans as he was to charm thousands of others in his career. Yet he was not primarily a charmer, but a man concerned with ideas and action. Not all ambassadors feel it incumbent on them at the end of their embassy to sort out the problems and show in print the recommendations and predictions for the future that might indicate work undone on their own parts. Harry did. His preoccupation was less with self-justification and more with problems that should be solved, and certainly no one could find fault with him for that.

34]

WHILE HER uncles and one cousin set out in their own ways to atone for the Guggenheim guilt in having become rich, Peggy Guggenheim, daughter of Benjamin, sought her own course—obviously already a very different one from all the rest of the family.

Late in the 1920's Peggy bought a divorce ($10,000 for her lawyer and $2000 for her husband's) and then went to live with her lover. This decision was relatively simple because she discovered that her lover had neglected to legalize his other union. With scarcely a tremor Peggy acquired a second-hand common-law husband. For several years she lived with him and her daughter in a house in Paris that Georges Braque, the painter, had built for himself. She made frequent visits to her son Sindbad, but she had given him up to his father as part of the price of the divorce.

Here, from her book *Out of This Century*, is an indication of their manner of life in the 1930's in Paris:

John got up late as he slept so badly. He read most of the day and we went out every night to night-clubs in Montmartre or to cafes in Montparnasse or to friends' houses, or we had people at home. John always liked society after six in the evening, so when Deirdre went down to have her supper and go to bed, we usually went out in search of people. Sometimes we brought home for dinner lots of unexpected guests for whom there always seemed to be enough food. We had a marvelous cook. If John stayed out very late, which he often did, I got so bored I went home without him. I hardly ever drank in those days and I could not keep up with him. Sometimes he spent the whole day in bed with a hangover and got up only for the evening. This used to make me extremely angry because I felt cheated of his company. He never wanted me to leave him, and was just as unhappy without me as I was without him. He was extremely dependent on me and never wanted me out of his sight.

For a time Peggy and John lived in Devonshire in a large rented country house. In 1933 they moved to London, to Woburn Square. Peggy was tired of her lover after several years and had fallen in love again. The problem was solved—in a horrible way that Peggy had never considered—when John went to a hospital for a minor operation on his wrist and his heart gave out under the anesthetic.

There were other affairs. There was one with a publisher whom she referred to in her autobiography as Sherman (this was not his name). Peggy lived with him for several years. With him she joined the Communist party (largely because he wanted her to join). Peggy never was attracted much by communism and was a very bad member of the party. In 1937 their relationship broke, on the rocks of communism and mutual irritation, and Peggy returned to Paris.

At the international exposition in Paris in 1937, Peggy became attracted to modern art. She was ready for a new adventure, something that would fulfill her more than physically, for she had gone through the act of love so many times with so many men that her senses were dulled. Someone had given her a piece of advice: become a book publisher or open an art gallery. She went to Paris from England, remembering the advice but paying little attention to it. In Paris there was another brief, grimy affair with a surrealist painter, but she tired of it much sooner than she expected.

Peggy moved again into the Hôtel Crillon and her children came up from the south. She began to cultivate modern artists, Brancusi, Marcel Duchamp, Jean Cocteau, and a dozen abstractionists and surrealists and sculptors.

Soon, she opened a modern art gallery in London, assisted by Marcel Duchamp. The first show was that of Cocteau, who sent over from Paris some thirty original drawings used in his play *Les Chevaliers de la Table Ronde*. The opening, Peggy said, was a great success, with only one marring note: Among the drawings was one which showed pubic hair. The English customs agents were outraged and would allow it into the country only if she would promise it was not to be exhibited to the general public.

Peggy came to know Kandinsky, the painter once favored by her collector Uncle Solomon, and she gave Kandinsky a show in London. She also wrote her uncle asking him if he wanted to buy a certain painting of Kandinsky's that he had long ago said he wanted. She received in reply an infuriating and patronizing letter from her uncle's curator who was at the time keeping the Guggenheim collection at what critic Aline Saarinen called "ankle-level."

Peggy became a faithful servant of art. She began to assemble a show of modern sculpture not too long after she had gone into the gallery business. Until this time the *sine qua non* of English sculpture was the Tate Gallery, and its director, a Mr. J. B. Manson, was called upon from time to time by the self-conscious authorities to rule on the merits of certain objects that were shipped for entry into England as works of art.

Peggy Guggenheim asked her artist friends all over Europe to ship their works for the show, and when pieces of bronze and marble and wood and granite began arriving at customs, the doughty customs officers scratched their heads, looked at the circles and stones and stick-togethers from all angles, and called loudly for Mr. Manson of the Tate. Mr. Manson came and examined with the air of a dowager lady entering an alley in Wormwood Scrubs, and when he had looked long and hard and the corners of his mouth were firmly turned down, he announced his edict. None of this accumulation was art, said he. Therefore the various big boxes, weighing thousands of pounds, consigned to Miss Peggy Guggenheim in London, were to be subject to the British tariff established to protect English stonecutters from cheap foreign competition. Peggy would have to pay duty on the rocks and other objects on the basis of weight.

When the newspapers of London learned of this decision they sensed a story. Under consideration were the works of Brancusi, Henry Moore, Henri Laurens, Epstein, Arp, Duchamp-Villon, Pevsner, and Alexander Calder.

The newspapers were told by the supercilious director of the Tate that the artists were no better than so many stonemasons. The art critics and the artists became furious.

Peggy was not yet experienced enough to have engineered such a *coup de publicité*, and possibly she could not have done this well had she tried. Critic Tom Driberg printed a picture of Brancusi's *Sculpture for the Blind* in his column in the *Daily Express*; other columnists leaped into the argument. Soon a question was raised in the House of Commons, and as a result the old-fashioned Mr. Manson lost his control of works of art and the Tate's position was lowered a notch or two. (Much, much later Peggy and the Tate were reconciled.) Peggy's position in England was so enhanced that Harry Pollitt, secretary of the English Communist party, decided that she was more valuable than he had believed, and wrote asking her to return to the Communist cause. Peggy had had all that. She ignored the letter.

Wading from one love affair to another, Peggy marched forward in the world of art. Usually the advancements came together, as in her affair with a character she called Mittens:

"Mittens was a Surrealist poet and the director of the Surrealist gallery, my neighbor in Cork Street. We had a united front and we were very careful not to interfere with each other's exhibitions. I bought paintings from Mittens. He was a gay little Flamand, quite vulgar, but really very nice and warm. He now wanted me for his mistress, so we were to have dinner together . . ." They had dinner and she went off to Paris with him and became his mistress. All quite casual, but that was Peggy Guggenheim.

Some of her affairs touched her deeply and involved her more, as with Irish playwright Samuel Beckett whom she chased over most of Europe, unable to secure the reaction she wanted from him.

She exhibited Yves Tanguy's paintings in 1938, and was so impressed with his work that she bought several paintings for her own collection. One might say that Peggy Guggenheim's collection stems from that exhibition. Peggy also had an affair with Tanguy, during which she encountered Madame Tanguy one day in a Paris restaurant. Madame Tanguy greeted her by throwing three pieces of fish at her, to the dismay of the management. It was all very gay.

The London gallery was called Guggenheim Jeune—the Young Miss Guggenheim's—and it very definitely was a force in the field of modern art. Peggy Guggenheim exhibited the moderns and they reciprocated by borrowing money from her and asking her for advice. Mondrian, for example, came to her for advice about night clubs in London where he might go to dance. Tanguy and other artists gave her presents, orchids and candy and sometimes paintings, although seldom their own paintings.

Peggy was among the first gallery owners to give a show of collages. Most of the work was from Paris but some was found in London. There were Picassos, Arps, Massons, and Braques in the show. Max Ernst sent several paintings. Peggy's former husband, Lawrence Vail, sent some obscene collages, which Peggy had to hide from the authorities.

Peggy's part-time affair with Tanguy lapsed (she called herself Madame Tanguy de Londres to differentiate between herself and the legal Madame Tanguy de Paris) and she had affairs with others.

She adopted the habit of buying at least one painting for herself from each artist she exhibited. Sometimes the exhibitions were unsuccessful, and in that case Peggy bought the paintings for herself under an assumed name—to give the artist hope and not pity.

Peggy's unrestrained sexual and emotional enthusiasms kept her in trouble. Early in her career in Europe she had gone to an abortionist when she became pregnant by John Holms. The abortionist was a Russian doctor named Popoff, who worked in a Swiss convent run by nursing sisters. It was his practice to admit a suffering lady to the convent for a curettage, a perfectly legal operation, and then suddenly, while in the midst of this curettage, to discover with shock that the patient was pregnant. In England in 1939 Peggy became pregnant again after a casual encounter with an English sculptor named Llewellyn, who was really more friend than lover, and she secured another abortion, but only after excruciating difficulties with the stuffiness of the English medicos. (It was finally done by a German refugee doctor who said she was too old to have a child and did away with it.)

In the spring of 1939, Peggy decided that she really preferred to be a patron of the arts rather than a businesswoman. She was losing about $2500 a year (£600). Actually, by her exposure to artists and by buying paintings she was losing nothing at all, but did not know that at the time, and she was tired of the venture, so she looked about for another manner in which to continue her patronage without commercialism. She secured the services of the distinguished Herbert Read (later knighted) who was editor of the *Bur-*

lington Magazine, and a constant promoter of the cause of modern art in England. She created a museum, gave Read a five-year contract as director, and set out to establish herself anew. She gave up her expensive car, and her expensive habits. "In fact," she said, "I had decided to live a monastic life in order to be able to produce the necessary funds." She did not really mean that statement, of course. She meant she had decided to cut down her expenses. Monasticism did not enter into it, even in the sense of self-denial, because Peggy Guggenheim had grown up so rich for so long that physical possessions meant nothing to her.

The museum idea became something of an obsession: in her own way Peggy had worked during the 1930's to give something to society for the vast fortune her family had achieved.

35]

MOST INTERESTING to those who believed that all economic development stopped with the crash of 1929, should be the realization that the Cosach nitrate project in Chile was undertaken by western capital *after* the stock market crash.

At one point in 1930 the Guggenheims considered abandonment of the entire nitrate program, and might have done so except that Daniel never lost faith in nitrate, even when the bottom began to drop out of the market with the creation of synthetic nitrate by the Germans. Daniel was forever telling the press that the natural nitrate industry would revive and surpass the synthetic because of the improvement of production methods. He was certain that the natural product was superior to the cheap synthetic. (The facts did not bear him out.)

As the depression continued the Cosach plan was about halved in scope—but it did continue. The Guggenheims put up $10,000,-000 of the money themselves, and in 1931 the monopoly was formed, taking in all but 2 percent of the nitrate production of Chile. On the board of directors were four government officials, five bankers, a representative of the German nitrate interests, a representative of the Chilean producers, and Cappelen Smith, the representative of Guggenheim Brothers. Cappelen Smith was elected chairman. The Chileans had floated a $40,000,000 bond issue, and the Guggenheims put up $10,000,000, while all the banks put up only $9,000,000.

The worst problem for the Guggenheims came in the depression. They had poured many millions of dollars into the Anglo-Chilean and Lautaro nitrate companies. In the year ending in

1929, the future prospects had looked bright. More than three million tons of nitrates were produced in Chile at a cost of $23 per ton and 2,500,000 tons were sold at a price of $40 per ton. The year ending in 1930 did not look so bad. Some 3,000,000 tons were produced at a slightly reduced cost and sold still at over $37. But this apparent prosperity represented the quiet before the storm. The 1931 production was half of that in 1930—and the price dropped six dollars a ton. In 1932, production was down again, to a million tons, and the price was down another six dollars to $25.50. In the year ending in 1933, production dropped to less than half a million tons—one-sixth of that of 1929—and the price dropped to $20, half that of 1929. Costs, of course, did not drop in the same proportions.

In 1933, the Guggenheims sat down in the big board room over the offices of American Smelting and Refining, and totaled up their investment in Chilean nitrates. They had $48,000,000 invested directly in loans, bonds, and personal credits. They had another $98,000,000 invested indirectly, through various corporations in which they held controlling interests, such as Anglo-Chilean and Lautaro. It was not an investment to be abandoned, and they did not abandon it.

In the 1930's, Murry led the brothers, and all nitrate producers, in the establishment of the nitrate trust of Chile as the one way that the nitrate business invesments of the Guggenheims could be saved. Directly and indirectly, the Guggenheims estimated their investment at around $150,000,000. If it were lost totally, and for a time that prospect seemed more than possible, the Guggenheim personal fortunes might remain to help the children over the hump, but the overall Guggenheim influence in the business world would be lost. They were so heavily committed to nitrates at this point, having withdrawn from other mining interests, that if they did not save the nitrate business they would no longer have substantial control of any mineral industry.

Cosach, the Compañía de Salitre de Chile—the nitrate trust—was Murry's creation and his major contribution to the financial history of the Guggenheims. Cosach was the greatest financial corporation in South America and the biggest gamble the Guggenheims had ever made; it would be capitalized at $375,000,000 and would issue $200,000,000 in mortgage bonds. In all, 30,000,000 shares of stock were issued. The Guggenheims took some 8,000,000 shares for their stock in Anglo-Chilean and Lautaro, and another 2,500,000 shares for the valuable Guggenheim process for treating nitrate ore. Cappelen Smith, the Guggenheim man who had developed the process, became president of Cosach.

The Guggenheims were roundly criticized for "stealing" Cosach from the Chilean government, the Chilean investors, and the British investors. Murry sat at his desk at 120 Broadway and worried over the future, reading daily in the newspapers about the "malefactors of great wealth" of whom he was said to be king. As he read, Murry also authorized huge loans to the nitrate company out of Guggenheim *personal* resources, because even with the resources of the Chilean government guaranteeing Cosach, bankers would not buy or handle the Cosach bonds.

When times continued difficult and the British and American bankers continued to cause trouble, Murry secured the services of Medley Gordon Brittain Whelpley, thirty-eight, president of the American Express Bank and Trust Company, and one of the brightest financiers in America. The Guggenheims did not have much more financial rope to pay out in order to save Cosach, but Whelpley could maneuver with relatively little extra expenditure; they wouldn't need to spend more. Otherwise the entire structure might topple, carrying the Guggenheims down with it from the thirty-fifth floor of 120 Broadway.

The depression in Chile and the virtual closing down of the industry on which the nation had pinned her economic hopes brought about a series of revolutions. One day Cosach was dissolved. The next day it was given back its charter. The next day it was dissolved again. In such a market the securities of the nitrate trust became worthless and all that stood between the abandonment of the Chilean fields and complete destruction of the investment on the one hand and government seizure on the other was the Guggenheim name. The Guggenheims were cursed and dishonored in Antofagasta, in London, in New York, but somehow their pledges were believed. Cosach was dissolved, but the principle of a monopoly was retained in the creation of a single sales corporation to handle all Chilean nitrates. The Guggenheims were co-owners of this company.

The Guggenheims remained the most important force in the Chilean nitrate business. Until World War II they were unable to retrieve much of their investment. But had it not been for Murry's quick grasp of the financial tiller of Guggenheim Brothers, the entire Chilean nitrate venture might have gone down in 1930.

36]

QUITE OUT of the nitrate business, out of all Guggenheim enterprises, was the one male member of the forth generation of Guggenheims in America who had shown any aptitude for mundane affairs.

When Franklin Delano Roosevelt's Democratic administration was elected to office in the autumn of 1932, Harry Guggenheim knew that the days of his service in Havana were coming to an end, and in April of the following year he came back to the United States.

For a time he decided to dedicate himself to pleasure. (Some said the entire period of his Havana stay had been so dedicated.) He went to his plantation, twenty miles north of Charleston, South Carolina, and began to buy horses and establish a racing stable. The plantation was called Cain Hoy (a local Gullah corruption of the words *cane hay*, which refers to a native rattan plant). Compared to other millionaires Harry's first purchase was infantile and minuscule. He paid four hundred dollars for a thoroughbred yearling named Nebraska City. (Leland Stanford paid $20,000 once for an untried stallion and $12,000 for another.) Nebraska City turned out to be worth just about what he had cost, but he helped Harry learn racing without too much investment. Soon, Harry was serious, and he began spending money on horses and winning races. He had the old family knack of turning a profit even in the risky sport of horse racing where few millionaire breeders expect to earn money. In 1959 Cain Hoy led the racing stables in purses won and the next year it was second. The purses amounted to around three-quarters of a million dollars in both years. (As for fame, Harry won the Kentucky Derby in 1953 with *Dark Star*.)

Cain Hoy was built up acre by acre as a working farm, not simply a gentleman's plaything. Since it was acquired in the Deep South during depression years, Harry managed to purchase 7500 acres for around $90,000. He built a lodge on the land, comfortable and luxurious, and began to establish a timber enterprise and a cattle ranch. He added land until he owned 15,000 acres, including a 4000 acre island. The purpose was to increase the fortune for his children and his grandchildren. Harry said he believed that agriculture was the most noble of all pursuits of mankind. Later he was to enlarge this view to include the adventure of his grandfather, mining.

In the 1930's, besides playing gentleman farmer, Harry continued his interests in aviation and rocket research. He visited Dr. Robert Goddard several times at his New Mexico proving grounds.

Daniel and Florence Guggenheim had, in 1930, become interested in the work of Robert H. Goddard, the pioneer rocket enthusiast, who had been working with much disappointment and very little assistance, except for that of the Smithsonian Institution, since 1910. It was not widely known then, but the Guggenheim interest in Goddard's experiments was triggered by Charles A. Lindbergh, the first man to fly the Atlantic Ocean non-stop. Lindbergh's friendship with Harry prompted Guggenheim support of Goddard's experiments. In the spring of 1930, according to the account given by Milton Lomask in *Seed Money*, the story of the Guggenheim foundations, Daniel gave Goddard $25,000 a year for four years, which enabled Goddard to go to New Mexico and experiment with his rockets.

At least that was Daniel's plan. It did not work out quite that way, for after two years during which the Guggenheims supported the experiments, there was no more money available from Guggenheim personal funds. Daniel had died, and only when Harry had put the Daniel and Florence Guggenheim Foundation's affairs in order in 1934 was Goddard again supported by the Guggenheims in his work. For nine years more after 1934 Goddard was supported mostly by the Guggenheim money in the basic work of rocketry.

In the middle 1930's, Harry Guggenheim was not much in the

news. Other Guggenheims made the front pages of the newspapers
in this period with family arguments and family scandals. Isaac's
daughters sued their father's estate in 1935 because they did not
believe they were being treated properly in the administration of
their trust funds. Robert's wife left for Reno in 1937. William held
forth on foreign policy, Sol bought paintings and gave them away.
Harry was out of the press but Harry's mother attended the opera
and other festivities and got her picture in the paper.

Florence Shloss Guggenheim lived a busy life in New York City
and in the big house on Long Island. She rode horseback, she gar-
dened, she played golf. She immersed herself in her associations
and in the synagogue. From time to time she emerged in the public eye to accept an award for her husband's successes or for her
own. She gave to her city and her charities, such gifts as money to
the hospitals and a set of sixteenth-century tapestries to the Metropolitan Museum of Art.

Son Harry's major activity, or at least his public one, called for a
certain quiet and reserve. He was working as president of the Citizens Committee on the Control of Crime in New York, a hopeless
task, as it appeared a third of a century later, but one to which
Harry and others gave much time and energy. This committee was
established to help Special Prosecutor Thomas E. Dewey fight the
racketeers, and it brought about a certain amount of reform after a
careful study of the underworld.

Harry and his second wife parted during the late 1930's and he
married Alicia Patterson, also twice divorced, the daughter of Captain Joseph Patterson of the New York *Daily News*, and descend-
ant of the Patterson newspaper family and McCormick Reaper
family of Chicago. Farming and horse racing were occupations that
did not take too much of a man's time unless he undertook to
manage the operations personally. Harry had the energy for such
management but not the patience to be tied down, and besides he
had many interests that required his presence in and around New
York City. He might not belong to Guggenheim Brothers, but he
kept an office at 120 Broadway on the same floor as theirs, and he
shared many investments with his relatives.

In 1939 and 1940 the exodus of New Yorkers from their unin-
habitable city was already beginning. Alexander Turney Stewart,

merchant king, had foreseen the day when men would live in luxury in the country and work in the city. This day was coming to pass, and his mansard houses in Garden City stood as beacons for the builders of Long Island. The start was small, but the Island was beginning to be a place of activity, rather than a haven for the rich to build their estates, even out among the eastern potato farms.

Here Harry Guggenheim and Alicia Patterson began to accomplish one of the "impossible" tasks of the twentieth century: to start a newspaper and make it pay.

The newspaper, *Newsday*, became a countryman's New York *Daily News*. It was founded on the premise that the newspaper should be bright and readable and dedicated to the interests of the commuter, as well as the potato farmer. This stretched a narrow tightrope for Editor Alicia but she had a disciplined and inquiring mind. With all the brilliance in the world, *Newsday* would never have succeeded had not the Guggenheims been as lucky as usual. They chose the time. They chose the place. The people of the city chose to come out to Long Island by the millions, which no one could have anticipated in 1940. The Guggenheims lost money for several years, seeing the potential and trying to live up to it. Harry invested three-quarters of a million dollars before *Newsday* began to earn profits, but long before the seven lean years was ended, it had become apparent that the Guggenheims had struck another gold mine. Twenty-five years after *Newsday* began publication its circulation was 400,000 copies daily. It served all of Long Island and that almost exclusively. (Its two competitors, aside from the New York newspapers which could not compete on the local level, were the standard-size *Long Island Press*, and a new newspaper begun by the Cowles interests.)

Harry and Alicia ran *Newsday*. Alicia supervised the editorial department. Harry ran the business department. He owned 51 percent of the stock and she owned 49 percent of it. Sometimes they disagreed, usually during Presidential election campaigns, and then each stated his case in signed editorials on the editorial page and the page opposite the editorial page. Harry was a Republican, tried and true. Alicia was a Democrat of equally loyal stripe. Thus the arguments.

When World War II began, no one would have expected Harry

Guggenheim, Lieutenant Commander in the Navy in World War I, to volunteer for service, for he was fifty-one years old and hardly a candidate for the draft.

He was engaged in various forms of community services and had been for many years. He was involved in much patriotic and even visionary work—as in the continued support of Robert H. Goddard's work with rockets, when the military would pay no attention to Goddard.

In 1940 Goddard met with Air Force, Army, and Navy officials, who said they saw little future in the rocket, and thus the leadership in the rocket field passed to the Germans, whose experts such as Wernher von Braun had studied the results of Goddard's work carefully—indeed, has been led into the field by Goddard's work. One cannot blame the Guggenheims. They tried to maintain American leadership in the field. Harry Guggenheim arranged for many meetings with the military, where the case for rocketry was continued, but all to no avail. The military men saw no more value in the rockets in 1940 in America than earlier naval officers had seen in the submarine, or than army staff officers had seen in the rapid-firing field gun, or in the airplane.

In spite of Guggenheim protest and support, during World War II Robert Goddard was reduced to employment of his talents building devices to assist in take-off of propellor-driven airplanes. Even after Goddard died in 1945 and the Germans had proved with their V-1 and V-2 rockets that the rocket was a new force in warfare, the military men were still slow to take up rocketry. For seven years, from 1945 to 1952, much of the work done in this field in the United States was commissioned and supported by the Daniel and Florence Guggenheim Foundation as a public gesture. (Two jet-propulsion centers were established, one at Princeton University and the other at California Institute of Technology.)

As to military service, Harry Guggenheim was also just beginning the *Newsday* venture—perhaps that was one reason for the quickness with which he volunteered: *Newsday* was not that important in 1941 and adventure in the service beckoned. Nor was Harry's patriotism to be questioned. Still, he was over age for his reserve grade and if he did manage to get into the service he might very well be pigeonholed on an island outpost along the Atlantic coast, watching for submarines or counting seagulls. Not so. He served first as assistant executive officer at Floyd Bennett Field, later as commander of Mercer Field, New Jersey. After all, Harry had been an ambassador and an ambassador is an executive.

While Harry was in the service his mother died. She had been failing; the big house at Sands Point had proved too much for her to manage and after using it as a reception center for British refugee children who came to America to escape the blitz, in 1942 Florence Shloss Guggenheim offered the house to the government as an aeronautical research center.

So, in June, she moved out of the forty-room house and the contents were auctioned because the children all had their own houses and furnishings. (Gladys lived with her husband Roger Straus in a big house on 93rd Street in New York and on the Straus estate at Purchase, in Westchester County. Harry lived next door to his mother—if it was possible to live "next door" to a 162-acre estate. Robert lived in Washington.)

Gladys bought a few of the family possessions at the sale, a picture or two and a large oriental rug that she particularly liked. Her father had collected Van Dykes, Rubens, and Rembrandts, but she took only the Rembrandt "Portrait of an Old Woman," and a Homer Martin landscape that appealed to her.

Daniel's widow moved into the Carlton House on 47th Street, where she lived until she died in the spring of 1944.

The highlight of Harry's war career and one of those of his life came in the spring of 1945 when he was detached for service aboard the U.S.S. Nehenta Bay, one of the new small carriers built for service in the last days of the war. He went as observer and machine gunner on raids against the Japanese. At the end of the war he was demobilized with the rank of captain. It was not a bad record for an over-age lieutenant commander; even better for the great-grandchild of Simon Guggenheim, Jew of the Lengnau ghetto. Brains and courage got a man a long way in the Navy in World War II, and anyone who thinks money had anything to do with it ought to contemplate the cases of Sergeant Peter O. Lawson-Johnston, one of Harry's nephews who served in the Mediterranean theater during the last months of military activity; Lt. (J.G.) Oscar Straus II, of the Coast Guard, another nephew; or

Dana Draper, one of Harry's grandchildren, who entered the Army in 1959 as a volunteer for the draft and spent two years and ten months at Fort Bragg, North Carolina, as an enlisted man.

When the Pacific War ended and Harry came back to Long Island he discovered that thousands, hundreds of thousands, and millions of New Yorkers were joining him, and that new industries were seeking the sprawling fields of the Island in preference to the vertical geography of New York. For ten years his work was cut out for him on *Newsday*, and then there were other matters, family matters, that required his attention.

It was all very well for the various Guggenheim brothers to establish foundations and die, hoping these foundations would do what they wished them to do. But times change, styles change, and an idea that seemed absolutely functional in one decade seems puerile in the next. In 1944 Harry's mother had died. In 1949, Solomon Guggenheim died. These two deaths heaped new responsibilities on Harry Guggenheim, probably because he was willing to undertake them, alone among Guggenheims.

In 1947 the Daniel and Florence Guggenheim Foundation, of which Harry was head, again continued support of rocket research although the United States Government's interest was still lukewarm. A number of grants was made, in the hundreds of thousands of dollars, and a hopefully perpetual program was established. New aviation research centers were established at Cornell, Columbia, and Harvard Universities, all the results of many hours of meeting and consideration, presided over by President Harry Guggenheim of the Foundation.

37]

WHEN HARRY GUGGENHEIM was approaching his seventieth year, he suddenly began to awaken at night with the chilly feelings of a man who senses his own mortality, and he began to consider what would happen to the Guggenheims when he was gone.

Harry's brother was dead, leaving him as oldest of the clan of Guggenheim and one of the very few Guggenheims left in the world.

In 1928 Robert was divorced by his second wife and was remarried shortly afterward to Elizabeth Eaton of Babylon, Long Island, this time in a Lutheran church. Elizabeth became mistress of the hounds in the local hunt and amused herself, at least one day, by seeing how many fences she could jump.

In the years between the wars, Robert moved back and forth between Long Island and Washington. He played at soldier, and he played at entertaining diplomats and the other officials of Washington.

Robert's last wife was Rebecca De Loatch Pollrad VanLennep, a Norfolk, Virginia, lady who was already married when Robert began pursuing her after his third divorce in 1938. Eventually, after many adventures, she divorced her husband, married Robert, and they went to live a life of romance at various Guggenheim houses and aboard his 170-foot yacht (one of five he owned at various times) called the *Firenze*, in honor of Mother Guggenheim.

In 1953 he became United States Ambassador to Portugal. He played at diplomacy, then. He was ejected from Portugal as *persona non grata*. He said the reason involved the matter of a piece of cutlery dropping inside the décolletage of a lady at a dinner party—and his attempts to recover it.

Robert and his wife lived in Washington, on the edge of Rock Creek Park; on the yacht; and in the winter on a 1,400-acre plantation below Charleston on the Ashepoo River. He continued to play with spoons, and occasionally got his name in the newspapers in connection with extra-marital affairs. Robert died in November, 1959, collapsing in a taxicab after a dinner in Georgetown, and he was buried in Arlington National Cemetery because he had been a soldier of the Republic. Then, and forever after, just as much as any scandalous Vanderbilt, M. Robert Guggenheim would stand as a representative of the oppressing classes in communist and socialist literature. He was the *beau idéal* of playboys: handsome, debonair, amoral, charming, and utterly useless to society. If that judgment seems harsh, perhaps it could be modified. Perhaps he was not utterly useless. Somebody had to be, as he titled himself, "the best damned general's aide in the U.S. Army," somebody had to be Ambassador to Portugal in lieu of policy, and America had not indicated any intention of changing the system that allowed for one or more "gentlemen of leisure" in wealthy families. Mr. Robert performed all those functions rather well.

Robert's son, Robert, Jr., married three times, and from his first marriage came two children, Grace Anne and Daniel Morton. Grace Anne had been married twice by 1966. Daniel Morton, born in 1938, was by midcentury the youngest male member of the family to carry the name Guggenheim.

Daniel alone among the Guggenheims fathered a line that could carry on the family dreams of old Meyer, if any of those dreams still existed in the young in the middle of the twentieth century. Such hopes were bound up in Harry F. Guggenheim, whose life and affairs kept the Guggenheims in the mainstream of American Society and society. Harry once gave many indications of going the way of other Guggenheims of the third generation, into a cocoon of luxury. He, too, married three times, twice unhappily and once happily. Of the unhappy marriages he had the grace to say the fault was entirely his own, probably a more accurate appraisal than a polite one. Harry Guggenheim began to pull himself together and realize that in the exploits of his family there was the material of legend and of history, and that responsibility did not end with the making of the money or the establishment of foundations. He had received control of Daniel's residuary estate and had become the senior of the Guggenheims, keeping the old offices at 120 Broadway and the Guggenheim mining partnership.

What would he do with the family estates? It remained to be seen. Edmond was still alive, but Edmond had retired from business and mining, at least as far as the family was concerned.

William Guggenheim II was still alive, but few of the other Guggenheims had ever set eyes on him.

After the breach with the family and his ventures into wartime public life, William I never did much with his life. In the 1920's he played the stock market, but not very wisely.

Finally he left the Fifth Avenue house to his wife and moved to an apartment on Riverside Drive, where he established a publishing house. Here he produced tracts and the autobiography which he wrote under the name of Gatenby Williams, masking it as biography. Will called his company The Lone Voice Publishing Company—an indication of his feelings about his place in family and national affairs. Seeing his brothers so prominent in the American scene must have been painful for William in his later years, for it was apparent that had he kept working in the family business he, too, could have been prominent, instead of on the outside looking in.

Occasionally, as in 1935, William would be called on to make a speech, usually at a meeting of some organization to which he had contributed. (At a reunion of the University of Pennsylvania, Class of 1889, Will spoke on the need for economic reforms in America.)More often he was reduced to writing letters to the editor of The New York Times to air his views.

William Guggenheim died in the spring of 1941, at the age of seventy-three, a tired, frustrated, unhappy man.

He was one of the famous seven Guggenheim brothers, and yet in a way he was a member of another generation and another society than his brothers. As youngest, pampered by sisters and his mother, he never came to grips with the real world. By the time that William came along the family was too wealthy for Will to receive the hard knocks or live the simple life as the older brothers had all done. Simon escaped the dangers of preciosity because he went to Europe for two years and in Spain in the nineteenth century a Guggenheim, no matter how rich, was just another wealthy Jew. He suffered hard knocks, and he suffered harder knocks when he entered the rough and tumble of Colorado politics. Ben had escaped, although not altogether, by choosing Europe and spending his later life mostly there.

Will, through no real fault of his own, was the victim of the American dream of his family, and of the ancient truth that wealth spent without restraint tends to corrupt the minds and morals of young men and render them fit for very little. Wealthy families in Europe and Asia had learned this truth many generations earlier and those families which retained their wealth set the sons to productive tasks at an early age. There was no ancient wealth in America, but there were fortunes that went back five generations in Will's day. Meyer Guggenheim was too busy establishing the fortune in Will's formative years to examine the possible ill effects of it on one of his children, so Meyer could not be blamed too heavily for this.

In Will's case, the tragedy must be laid to a combination of small physical size, a weakness of character, strong feelings of inferiority when faced with his four oldest brothers, and too much money and power handed to him at too early an age. If Ben Guggenheim did nothing else he died a hero's death and thus preserved himself a place in the saga of the world. Poor Will, he was simply snuffed out like a guttering candle that has burned itself down, lighting an obscure corner that no one really wanted to see.

Following the Guggenheim split in 1900 the family was far less homogeneous than the outside world was ever allowed to know, and given the natural aggressiveness that was so much a reason for the building of the fortune, Guggenheims quarreled with Guggenheims very frequently in the years of the twentieth century.

Although the Guggenheims had nothing like the position they occupied around World War I, they were still an important force in the metals industry, if only for the amount of stock they owned in copper and other metals.

38]

AS TIME went on, Anglo-Chilean nitrate and Lautaro Nitrate recovered from the debts that had piled up in the 1930's, even though synthetic nitrates overtook the natural product, and instead of representing 30 percent of the world's production, as Chilean nitrates did in the 1920's, in the 1960's Chilean nitrate accounted for less than 1 percent.

By 1948 the companies began paying dividends again.

Until his death in 1939 Murry had been active in the salvation of nitrates—Murry, the "no-man," the others sometimes called him. He did not live to see the emergence of the nitrates from their deep depression, but Sol Guggenheim did.

If in his later years it could be said that Daniel Guggenheim had the placid smile of a contented cat, one must say that among all the brothers Solomon aged the most handsomely. A picture taken near the end of his life shows him clean-shaven, with relatively few of the wrinkles one expects in age, an almost translucent skin, and a smile of great tolerance peeping out from beneath a prominent nose and reflected in bright eyes beneath grayed, beetling brows. Sol was always a dandy, by far the most stylish of the brothers. In his tailored shirts and double-breasted pinstripe suits he was the epitome of the retired business mogul, well turned out, well fed, well satisfied, who knew exactly where he had been, and was optimistic about where he was going.

Solomon died in 1949. If his was not the wisdom of his biblical namesake, let it at least be said that he was endowed with the ability to make one stroke of judgment which would carry his name through history and make him in one way the most notable of all the Guggenheims. He would decide at a time of life when other men had quit taking on new responsibilities, that he would collect art, and abstract art at that. With the sure-mindedness of a Philadelphia matron he would pursue his aim when others snarled that he was wasting on trash, money that should go to "real" art. The final monument to Sol's judgment would be the creation of a great museum, itself the object of as much controversy as the collection had been a generation earlier.

Sol was among the most fortunate of the Guggenheims in one respect: The woman he married came from an eminent and highly cultured Jewish family of New York. Irene Rothschild was a beauty and all the attributes of her character conformed to beauty. She was serene. She was patient. She was slow to smile and slow to frown and slow to criticize. Irene introduced Solomon to the old masters that she adored and collected. The transfer of his affections to nonobjective painting was something else again, but Sol's original appreciation of art was fostered by his wife, and in her lifetime she collected masterworks, nearly a third of a million dollars worth of them, as they were valued at auction when they were sold at midcentury. Irene was collector and patron of artists and sculptors, and she brought Solomon into a world as far removed from mining and business as any could be.

The Solomon Guggenheims began their collection of paintings early in the twentieth century. Irene liked Watteaus and the safe paintings of the Renaissance and Reformation, the paintings of the French Academy that nobles and rich merchants throughout Europe hung in their Victorian drawing rooms; the paintings with which she had grown up as a girl.

One might suspect that Solomon Guggenheim's interest in fine art was merely an attempt to please his wife, until the year 1926. Sol was sixty-five that year. He and his brothers had left the management of American Smelting and Refining, and even Guggenheim Brothers was largely managed by outsiders who came in following the resignations of Harry and Edmond after the dispute over selling the Chuquicamata holdings.

Sol was ripe for a new activity when he met the Baroness Hilla Rebay von Ehrenweisen, who came to visit New York in 1926 bearing a letter from Irene Guggenheim's sister in Paris. The Baroness was an artist. She had begun as a conventional academician, had changed to become an impressionist in the style of Cezanne and Van Gogh, then an expressionist, one who used common stereotypes nonobjectively to express a point of view. Finally the Baroness had turned to cubism. In 1926 she was dedicated to art that was totally "nonobjective," using only form and color to achieve effect, without regard for nature.

Solomon Guggenheim listened to the Baroness' expositions on the functions of art, and then asked her to paint his portrait. He did not mean a nonobjective, regardless-of-nature, portrait. She said she did not want to paint a portrait, he said she was unable to paint it, and the matter ended with her painting it, and becoming a close friend. Eventually this friendship led to her appointment as curator of the Guggenheim collection.

Soon Solomon Guggenheim became known in the world of art. The work of the Russian-born Vasily Kandinsky became the mainstay of Solomon's collection, but soon he had Klees, Chagalls, Picassos, as well as samplings (and later much more) of the works of Fernand Léger and Ladislas Moholy-Nagy.

Although the Baroness insisted that the only art was totally nonobjective, Sol had the faculty of listening to her and going his own way. He bought Impressionists and Cubists and others without regard for her opinion. Through the Baroness, Solomon bought many paintings of a Polish-born nonobjective painter named Rudolf Bauer, which later experts said were not great or even fine art. In spite of such involvements the Guggenheim collection of modern paintings became one of the most notable in the world.

In 1937, when Sol had established a collection of several hundred paintings, he set up the Solomon R. Guggenheim Foundation to establish and maintain a museum of modern art, and to serve and encourage art education. The Baroness became director of the museum, which was housed at first in rented quarters. Later Sol decided to build a permanent museum. He commissioned the controversial Frank Lloyd Wright to draw the plans.

As a museum director, the fiery little Baroness with her red hair and blue eyes was not popular with critics. They complained that she exhibited many of her own paintings and those of Bauer, confining Cezanne's and other fine paintings to the basement because they contained recognizable objects.

After 1949 when Sol died, the directrice was for a time without much restraint, and the critics noted it. Aline Saarinen of *The New York Times* suggested quite seriously in 1951 that the Guggenheim Museum of Non-Objective Painting had so confused its affairs that it had best turn over its collection and its funds to one of the established museums. Some paintings were being tampered with by people at the museum. One artist charged that part of his painting was *actually repainted* after he left it there for display. One may edit writers but one does not repaint artists.

In 1952 the directrice, Baroness Rebay, decided that her health was such that it was wise for her to retire to her house in Greens Farms, Connecticut, where she kept a number of paintings that were not housed in the museum. Harry was running the Foundation at this time, and he may have had something to do with the fact that the Baroness was so suddenly taken sick. Little time was lost in appointing a professional, James Johnson Sweeney, as director of the museum. Sweeney swept away the third-rate nonobjectives with a sure hand. He began buying Picassos, Cezannes, and other valuable paintings. He was to acquire some 250 new works, without particular reference to the schools of philosophy behind them.

All this time, since 1943, architect Frank Lloyd Wright had been considering the problems of the museum. The Baroness, who entered herself into the consideration, was quite impossible and he paid no attention to her. Robert Moses entered this picture as New York City's Park Commissioner. Moses, of course, was determined to have his own way, to have a new park with a museum attached. First Moses argued with Sol. Then, after Sol's death, he argued with Harry, who took charge of the Foundation. All this while Moses also argued with Wright. Moses wanted the Guggenheims to endow a park on the Spuyten Duyvil, on the west edge of the Bronx overlooking the Hudson River—a totally inaccessible place for the majority of New York museum-goers. Moses did not much care what happened to the museum—he was willing to give it a place in his new park. Frank Lloyd Wright, who hated the verticality of New York anyhow, was not displeased with this idea since the site gave him eighty acres to work with, but Sol did not like it and bought the land at Fifth Avenue and 89th Street, where the museum would eventually be erected.

After Sol's death in 1949, for the next seven years there were quarrels. Frank Lloyd Wright, who was to receive $75,000 to draw the plans and handle construction, eventually received nearly a quarter of a million dollars. The foundation could afford the cost. Sol had left it $13,000,000 in all, five million of that for the building. Problems arose about the building permit (Wright's original design violated the New York City building code in thirty-two different ways). Wright warred with the city and for four years nothing happened. Construction actually began in 1956, with Wright trying to make changes in his design down to the last moment, and Harry intervening to keep order.

Wright and Director Sweeney began quarreling the moment they met, and Harry stepped in from time to time to keep their arguments under control. Sweeney, administrator, wanted the building built for the administrator's convenience; he wanted an efficient museum. Wright wanted a building that would be a monument to Wright and to Sol Guggenheim, a public monument. The administrator and the architect argued about office space, storage space, and the color of the walls. Wright wanted the paintings to become decorations for his building. All this temperament was difficult to subdue, and Harry said he felt as though engaged in the labors of Hercules as he struggled. Sweeney resigned on June 15, 1958. He reconsidered a week later. The argument between director and architect was resolved by Wright's death in the spring of 1959, before the building was completed. Sweeney had his way in part, enough to cause Wright's widow to remark that her husband would have stayed away from the opening rather than have the ugliness of the Sweeney touch inflicted on him. The public was invited to come on October 21, and thousands of people came, more than could get in that day. They saw a handsome beehive building, with the paintings arranged around a circular walkway that ascended above a central lobby, or atrium. Most people liked the structure, some did not. Sol Guggenheim might have shrugged at the latter—some of them had not liked his collection of paintings either, or for that matter, his way of doing business.

The next summer Sweeney resigned as director of the museum for good, proving that it was not usually wise for the director to confront the board of directors with too many *faits accomplis.* In 1960, Sweeney's resignation was anticlimactic. Harry had been through the wars, World War I, World War II, and, he said, the War of 89th Street. By then, in 1959, Harry Guggenheim's mind was already turned in a new direction. He had made the most important decision of his career.

39]

IN 1939 the other "arty" Guggenheim, Peggy, was still pursuing her own plan to establish an art museum. Peggy was willing to make many sacrifices. Although she had been rebuffed and ignored by her Uncle Solomon, she now went to Irene and asked if Solomon would not give her a painting or two for the museum. Irene assessed the situation with her customary shrewdness: Sol would do nothing but consult his Baroness, and then Peggy would get, if anything, a painting by Rudolf Bauer. Since Peggy considered Bauer to be a third-rate Kandinsky when she was in a jolly mood, she did not pursue the matter.

Peggy was now calling herself Mrs. Guggenheim. She was not Mrs. Vail because she had been the unofficial Mrs. Holms and had held half a dozen other unofficial titles since. She continued to support Vail with a regular allowance, and she gave allowances to other artists she knew. In all, in 1939, she said, she was committed to about $10,000 a year in support money for old friends. Her commitment to art in 1939 was complete. When the museum project was disturbed by the coming of World War II in the summer of 1939, Peggy was in France, not giving up the idea, but seeking a holiday and waiting to observe political developments. She was also lining up paintings for the new museum.

When war came Peggy was living in Grasse, traveling from time to time to Cannes to send wires and conduct her business, for the museum was very much in her thoughts. Yet she could only get a visa if she proposed to take her children and live in England during the rest of the war, and she did not wish to tie herself down so.

The museum project was abandoned, and Peggy remained in France.

She continued to buy works of art, not quite sure of their eventual destination, but sure of her purpose as a patron of modern art. She negotiated endlessly with Brancusi, the Rumanian-born sculptor. She bought several Brancusis in time. She bought Dalis. In Paris Peggy met Max Ernst, the painter and sculptor, but did not buy any Ernst work because she was looking for other types.

She found a suitable building for her museum but then the war became very real with the end of the "phony" period and it became apparent that as a Jew she would be in danger if she remained in the path of the Nazis. She fled to the south of France, took a house on the Lac d'Annecy, and brought her children Sindbad and Deirdre (later to be called Pegeen) to live with her.

As the war progressed, Peggy was asked to sponsor the voyages of a number of artists to America. She sponsored the trip of Max Ernst, of the family of André Breton, and she gave a considerable sum to the Emergency Rescue Committee which was trying to get notables out of occupied and unoccupied Europe before it was too late.

Peggy began an affair with Max Ernst in Marseilles where he had come to sail for America. They came to America together and Peggy took Ernst to see Uncle Solomon's museum, operated by the Baroness Rebay.

". . . It really was a joke," she wrote later.

There were about a hundred paintings by Bauer in enormous silver frames which overshadowed the twenty Kandinskys. There was one marvelous Léger of 1919, a Juan Gris, a lot of Domelas, a John Ferren. a Calder, a Delaunay and a few other less interesting painters, whose names I can't remember. From the walls boomed forth music by Bach —a rather weird contrast. The museum is a beautiful little building completely wasted in this atrocious manner. Max called it the Bauer house . . .

They went to see a much finer collection of Uncle Sol's paintings, one kept at the Plaza Hotel where he and Irene lived during the war. Here there were the Picassos, Seurats, Braques, Klees, Kandinskys, Gleizes, Delaunays, and Chagalls—which interested

Sol himself, and which proved that although he might have a weakness for Baroness Rebay, he was not blinded to the real values in modern art as much as his museum would suggest.

Yet the Baroness had sold Sol on Bauer, there was no question about it. In her forthright way, Peggy suggested to Aunt Irene that she persuade Uncle Sol to burn the Bauers and move the paintings at the Plaza to the museum as a nucleus. "Shush," said Aunt Irene, "don't let your uncle hear that. He has invested a fortune in Bauer."

Just after the Japanese attacked the Americans at Pearl Harbor and the United States declared war on the Axis powers Peggy and Max Ernst were married, Peggy had no objections to living with Max without legal complications, but she did object to living in sin with an enemy alien, she said. They opened a gallery on West 57th Street, just off Fifth Avenue, a surrealist display called Art of This Century. It was an overwhelming publicity success.

Business always sapped Peggy, for she was so intense a person that she must devote her total effort to what she was doing at the moment, whether it be a gallery or a man. Her romance with Max Ernst sagged. He went to New Orleans where a show had been arranged for him, and while he was gone Peggy was unfaithful with an old friend. But that was symptom, not cause, for Peggy was growing away from Max. She was too busy with her work. She quarreled with her designer, whose costs had gotten entirely too high for her liking. She had many troubles about money and while culturally the gallery was all that she could have hoped, financially it threatened her resources.

Peggy gave an exhibition for thirty-one woman painters—an idea Marcel Duchamp had given her in Paris some years earlier. There was one young painter in particular, a girl from the Midwest, who was after Max Ernst, and it was unmistakable. She had imitated his style and she treated him in the manner he liked best—as grand master of the arts. The marriage soon became a contest of mutual infidelity: Peggy sleeping with her paramour and talking about it and Max sleeping with his new inamorata and bragging equally. It was a conjunction of hatreds now more than a marriage at all. Soon it collapsed.

Peggy Guggenheim had much to do with the acceptance of nonobjective art by Americans. She worked endlessly at the task. Gypsy Rose Lee became a friend, patron, and artist who exhibited in her gallery. Mondrian came to New York and he showed his paintings. Mrs. Eleanor Roosevelt came to the gallery, but apparently did not like what she saw since she pleaded ignorance of modern art. Peggy tried to instruct her, without success.

In America Peggy fostered a number of young painters during these war years, including Clifford Still, Robert Motherwell, Mark Rothko, Adolph Gottlieb, and one other, Jackson Pollock.

She met Pollock when he was working as a carpenter at Uncle Sol's museum. She saw his paintings and sensed his talent and added him to the list of her monthly beneficiaries. She gave him $150 a month to support his wife and baby and commissioned a twenty-foot-long mural from him. She bought several Pollocks and talked to her friends about doing the same thing.

Looking back she said later, "I suppose it was the best thing I have done. In the days when he was little known I gave twenty of his pictures away. Fortunately I still have eleven left."

Peggy continued her stormy life in America during the war, living among old loves, old loves turned sour, and new ones. In 1946, when the world had settled to an uneasy peace, she assessed her situation and found that as much as she liked America, she loved Europe, and her heart was there. Specifically, she found Venice often in her thoughts, the Venice of the *vaporettos* and the canals and the quiet of city squares that remained squares.

She moved to Venice and found herself a palazzo. She took with her twelve Lhasa Apsos terriers, small, intensely loyal, intelligent dogs that originated in Tibet but were soon appreciated in China and India and in the twentieth century found their way to the New World.

She continued to collect art. She bought the works of Tancredi Parmeggiani and Edmondo Bacci, and she sponsored the artists in her way. She had her museum at last. In a way, by 1949 Peggy was more successful as an art collector than her Uncle Sol.

Peggy had called herself the Poor Guggenheim. She began with the fortune of around a half million dollars, and then, in 1939, after her mother's death, she inherited another fortune, but in all, her wealth as inherited was never much more than a million dollars (some put it at less), nor did she have it all at one time. Peggy proved, by her tastes and habits, to be as shrewd in the field of art selection as her grandfather and father and uncles had been in choosing business enterprises. In the 1960's her collection of modern art was valued at more than $5,000,000.

Peggy was very much the modern woman of the twentieth century. She called herself one of the "lost" generation of Hemingway and Fitzgerald and her cousin, Harold Loeb. Yet she felt that she was *committed*, and that word perhaps sums up her career better than any other. She became one of the prototypes of the free American woman of the twentieth century, a bohemian, of course, her actions distasteful to many conservatives and prudes, her sexual freedom called license by friends and family, and her antics shocking the genteel Jewish community of New York. Yet, Peggy spent all her adult life in serious study of the values of modern painting and late in life she became one of the foremost critics of modern art, an expert whose judgments had been backed by her personal purchases and by *success*.

Peggy's investment in Jackson Pollock had been successful in the sense that she had backed an artist whose works became extremely popular after his death. In 1961 Peggy sued Pollock's widow for $122,000 because she had not received some fifteen works that she expected to come to her—paintings done by Pollock during those years 1946–1948 when she supported him and he had agreed to give her his artistic productions. The matter was eventually settled. Peggy also came to some terms with herself and with other members of the Guggenheim family, and in 1967 she planned to send her collection from its Venice museum for a showing at the Guggenheim Museum in New York. Tentatively, the showing was set for the summer of 1968.

After many years and serious, straightforward dedication to art and artists, Peggy Guggenheim ceased to be slurred as a bohemian and became fashionable. She, too, added a notable portion to the American dream of the Guggenheims, just as had Sol, in an unusual field.

40]

AFTER Sol's death the Guggenheim nitrate business continued to improve, and as far as active Guggenheim business enterprise was concerned, this was the major concern. The Guggenheims were heavily invested in other mining and metals businesses, but for the most part in this they were simple capitalists, not entrepreneurs.

In 1951 the nitrate companies merged to become Anglo-Lautaro Nitrate, with 4,391,002 shares of Class A stock and 2,200,000 shares of Class B stock. Some 800 stockholders were listed in the stock records, but the Guggenheims were by far the most important of these.

The nitrate investment was saved, and although the nitrate itself was less important than before, a new byproduct—iodine—became very important to the Guggenheims. By 1967 Anglo-Lautaro was producing nearly half of the western world's iodine.

As to profits, Anglo-Lautaro had not failed to pay a dividend since 1948 except for 1957 when a strike affected operations adversely. In 1965 the company paid nearly four and a quarter million dollars in dividends, and the Guggenheim interests received a large share of this sum. In later years Anglo-Lautaro was expanding too. It owned 90 percent of a Chilean publishing company which, in turn, owned newspapers in Antofagasta and Tocopilla. In 1964 a subsidiary company was formed in the Bahamas to explore nitrate and iodine possibilities. The nitrate investment was still paying off, but slowly but surely the Guggenheim direct influence in the mining and metals business declined. When Daniel resigned as president of ASARCO and Simon took over, there was no diminution of interest by the Guggenheims but there was lessening of their economic power over the company. When Simon died in 1941, the presidency fell to Roger W. Straus, Gladys Guggenheim's husband and Daniel's son-in-law, who had joined the company in 1915. Except for this connection, the Guggenheims in 1941 were out of the management of American Smelting and Refining.

As the brothers died, one by one, the Guggenheims' investments in the metals business became smaller and by the 1930's their major interest was nitrates, although they were large stockholders in a number of copper companies and other metal companies (tin, for example). Yet the eruption of temperament which had caused the resignations of Harry Frank Guggenheim and Edmond Guggenheim from Guggenheim Brothers in 1923 had struck a blow to the Guggenheims that seemed mortal. After that breakup and with the depression in the world of the 1930's to threaten the nitrate business, the Guggenheim name faded from the public eye. The Guggenheims were rich. Their sons-in-law were rich. But the Guggenheims of the male line were dying off, and of these none except old Sol were engaged in the metals industry after the 1940's. Guggenheim Brothers became virtually moribund, a company holding assets; no longer a functioning business which was producing or exploring.

All this was on Harry Guggenheim's mind in the 1950's.

Harry Guggenheim in 1959 gave some serious thought to the life and history of his family. The Guggenheims were growing away from one another. This was true in his own family, the Daniel Guggenheim line. Daniel was dead. Florence was dead. Robert was dead. Robert had married four times, but the son of his first marriage had died in 1925; Robert, Jr., the second son, had no interest in Guggenheim affairs. This second Robert Guggenheim had married three times, but children had been born only of the first union. There were five great-grandnephews to Harry in the line of Robert.

After Harry's sister, Gladys Guggenheim, had married Roger W. Straus in 1914, Straus had worked his way up through American Smelting and Refining to become head of the company. They had three children. For thirty years the Strauses had lived at Purchase in the summers and on weekends. They had tried various city residences, from the Sherry Netherland Hotel to a house on 79th

Street, before finally settling down in the house at 6 East 93rd Street. They also kept a fishing preserve in the Catskills that included three miles of the bank of the Neversink River, and Roger and Gladys were both enthusiastic trout fishermen.

Florence Straus, their third child, grew up to marry Max Hart, son of the Hart of Hart, Schaffner and Marx, and to go to Chicago to live. She had two children, Pamela and Daniel. Of Gladys Guggenheim's sons, Harry's nephews, first was Oscar Straus II, who was born in 1914. Oscar had gone to grammar school in New York City, then to St. Paul's in New Hampshire, to Princeton, and to the University of Dijon.

Oscar had learned business the hard way, as a teller in a bank in Kansas City. From there he had gone to the Mexico City office of American Smelting and Refining. Undecided as to his next step in life, in 1939 Oscar had applied simultaneously for admission to Harvard Business School and the foreign service of the United States. He passed his foreign service examinations and went to Montreal as a vice-consul. In 1914 he married Marion Miller, a Canadian citizen, and they had a son, Oscar Straus III. (Oscar Straus III married Geraldine Coors of the Colorado brewery family, and in 1962 William Miller Straus was born.) Oscar Straus II rose quite satisfactorily in the State Department. When war was declared he became an ensign in the United States Coast Guard intelligence division, then went back to the State Department in 1944. After the war ended Oscar went to work for American Smelting and Refining Company as assistant to the treasurer, and trained in every department of the company. It was apparent that he was being groomed to be president and chief executive of American Smelting and Refining at some time. In April, 1959, when Harry was thinking things through, Oscar Straus II was chairman of the company finance committee and third ranking officer of the company but he was extremely unhappy because it seemed that unfriendly officers in the company would block his ambition to become president of ASARCO. Gladys Guggenheim Straus and Harry exerted all their influence in his behalf, but it was mark of the fall of Guggenheim influence in the company the Guggenheims once controlled that they were unsuccessful in bettering Oscar's position.

Second of the Straus children was Roger, Jr., born in 1917. He had never shown any interest in the mining business. After attending Hamilton College and the University of Missouri, he had worked as a newspaper reporter and writer, later going into the publishing field and founding Farrar, Straus and Company in 1945. Later the company would become Farrar, Straus and Giroux, with Roger as president. Roger was close to the Guggenheims, he would serve on several Guggenheim committees and foundations, but he had nothing to do with the Guggenheim mining that had made the fortune.

In the spring of 1959, Harry Guggenheim considered the family tree and Oscar Straus's serious problems at ASARCO. He decided to revitalize Guggenheim Brothers, the mining exploration and investment firm.

Guggenheim Brothers was still deeply involved in the nitrate business, but by 1959 no active mining business was being conducted by the firm. It was an investment company for the most part. Its members were Albert E. Thiele, financial secretary for many years to Solomon Guggenheim, who represented the interests of that branch of the family; James F. Doetsch, head of Chilean Nitrate Sales Corporation (the government-controlled nitrate monopoly), Albert C. Van de Maele, husband of Joan Guggenheim and son-in-law of Harry (Van de Maele was also vice president of Anglo-Lautaro Nitrate); and John A. Peeples, chairman of the board of Anglo-Lautaro Nitrate Company. Then there was Harry, who had rejoined the firm.

Harry decided to try to bring members of the family into the business. He was particularly interested in providing for his own children, grandchildren, and their descendants. He was equally interested in perpetuating the family name, difficult as this seemed to be, since no Guggenheims save himself had any apparent interest in the Guggenheim tradition.

He persuaded Oscar Straus to give up his unpromising career with American Smelting and Refining and become the senior operating officer of Guggenheim Brothers. (Harry was to retain the senior partnership, which would give him veto power, but Oscar was to be chief executive of the various companies that would shoot off from Guggenheim Brothers.)

Harry also wrote to his daughter, Nancy, second child of the marriage with Helen Rosenberg. Nancy had married George T. Draper, a San Francisco newspaperman, and they had two children before they were divorced: Dana Draper, born in 1940, and George T. Draper, Jr., born in 1942.

"I have reached the time of life," Harry said,

when it is wise that I prepare for the future, either with or without the help of my children. I have always hoped that my children and grand-children would carry on the best traditions of the family to the best of their abilities. Briefly, the best traditions have been developing some of the great natural resources of the world, i.e. creating wealth for the use of mankind and, as a reward in our free enterprise system, amassing fortunes which have been bequeathed in very large part to imaginative foundations for the future benefit of mankind.

I am the sole Guggenheim member of the firm which I hope to revitalize. Albert (Van de Maele) is a member of the firm, and to add to family continuity I am about to invite Oscar Straus to join the firm and take an active part in future explorations.

I have been the head of three Guggenheim foundations, which have contributed, and will continue to contribute, to the benefit and prog-ress of mankind.

I wonder if you and your boys know, except vaguely, about the fam-ily enterprise, the foundations, their accomplishments and their contri-butions to this country and to civilization. These endeavors should be and will be perpetuated. . . .

Harry offered his grandsons the opportunity to come into the family enterprises. As far as the future was concerned, he said, he had left small trust funds for all the family so that no Guggenheim, even under another name, need ever go in want. But, he said, "their greatest heritage is opportunity to carry on the family tradi-tion" and if they did not take it, the opportunity in business would be given to others, and the family tradition would be lost.

Harry said he planned to use his fortune and the trusts he con-trolled to conserve the family enterprises and to establish a new foundation which would be imaginative and meet a new need, "in the family tradition, for the benefit of mankind."

Harry noted that he had developed new fortunes in the Cain Hoy plantation, his racing and breeding farm, and his interest in

Newsday. He had added perhaps another $50,000,000 to the family fortune in one way or another.

In response to his letter, Dana Draper, Harry's grandson, chose to join the family enterprises. Dana had gone to Menlo Park Junior College, then into the army for nearly three years, and then to Columbia University's School of General Studies. In the summers, he had worked on the Cain Hoy cattle ranch as a cowhand until the summer of 1956 when he went to Chile to work in the nitrate mines. In the summer of 1965 he had worked at the Solomon Guggenheim Museum. Dana was not very much interested in the metals business. His interest seemed to lie in *Newsday*. Or at least he thought so in 1965 and 1966. But after working for several months at the newspaper, Dana Draper decided that the newspaper life was not for him and he returned to New York City. Then Harry Guggenheim employed an outside publisher for the newspaper, Bill Moyers, until that time Press Secretary to President Lyndon Johnson. Harry Guggenheim had been functioning as editor and publisher of *Newsday* since Alicia Patterson Guggenheim's death in 1963.

Oscar Straus came to the Guggenheim Brothers in 1959 and so did Peter Lawson-Johnston, grandson of Solomon, and Harry's second cousin, although nearly forty years separated them. Peter had attended the Lawrenceville School, then entered the army at the end of World War II, and then had graduated with honors from the University of Virginia in 1951. He had worked as a reporter on the Baltimore *Sun* and for the Maryland Civil Defense Agency. In 1956 he went to work for Feldspar Corporation, a subsidiary of Pacific Tin Consolidated Corporation, a Guggenheim enterprise.

There certainly was opportunity for members of the Guggenheim family, and Peter Lawson-Johnston's affiliations in 1966 indicated just how great that opportunity had become. That year he was partner in Guggenheim Brothers; director and vice president, The Feldspar Corporation; director, Pacific Tin Consolidated Corporation; director, Kennecott Copper Corporation; director, Braden Copper Company; director, Minerec Corporation; director of the advisory board of Anglo-Lautaro Corporation; vice-president, Elgerbar Corporation. He was also trustee of three foundations.

Harry Guggenheim's plans for rejuvenation of the family tradition succeeded in part, but not wholly. No stir could be heard from the Guggenheims who bore the family name, the Guggenheims of the West Coast. This became a private tragedy for Harry, because as fine as the men of the family around him might be, they were not Guggenheims, and nothing in the world could make Guggenheims of them. Isaac had tried the technique of getting names changed, without success.

Still, Harry had done the best that he could with the weapons at hand. After 1959 Guggenheim Brothers began investigating mining opportunities in the United States, Canada, Central America, and South America. Joint ventures were organized with Cerro Corporation, Homestake Mining Company, American Smelting and Refining, American Metal Climax, and Reynolds Mining Company. Guggenheim Brothers was not Guggenex, the old swaggering firm headed by Daniel with John Hays Hammond in charge, but it was becoming known again as a shrewd and progressive firm that could be approached on a sound mining property, with the knowledge that if the opportunity was there, the money for "exploration" and "development" could be found. These were new words for new times. The old word had been "exploitation," a perfectly sound capitalistic word, but it had become tarnished by the Ballinger-Pinchot affair, by the struggles in Chile over nationalization of nitrate, by the rising tide of social reform and socialization. The old capitalist had made "exploitation" a dirty word, and although that kind of capitalism was long gone, the Guggenheims and their associates stirred a little uneasily when the word was mentioned. They did not use it in the 1960's.

As time went on, the Guggenheim Brothers firm expanded. In the Philippines the company began drilling on a potential porphyry copper mine. In Haiti the Guggenheims searched for copper. In Spain, they found copper. In Cornwall, England, their engineers in 1966 discovered a small virgin tin mine in the heart of the district that had been producing tin for the Romans at the turn of the Christian era.

A most exciting prospect for Guggenheim Brothers was a venture in diamonds. In Brazil, Guggenheim Brothers placed a dredge on the Jequitinhonha River near Diamantina, the center of the old

Brazilian mining district. In the clay mud of the river, years before, naked Indian slaves had grubbed for diamonds. It was a wasteful and difficult way of mining, but until the Guggenheims came to Brazil there was no other. In the century that began in 1900 the Brazilian diamond mines lost much of their importance because the South African companies maintained a virtual monopoly of jewel stones, and the market for the yellowish South American stones virtually disappeared.

Old Meyer would have welcomed such new opportunities if they had come to him.

So now did Harry Guggenheim, son of Daniel, grandson of Meyer, and preceptor of the clan. The great-grandson of old Simon, who had brought the family to the New World, was now seeing a new facet of the Guggenheim participation in the American dream.

In the middle of the 1960's, after the death of Roger Straus, Gladys Guggenheim Straus sold the house on 93rd Street and moved into an apartment at 1040 Fifth Avenue. She took with her the Rembrandt and the Homer Martin and a Corot she had acquired. She had no pretensions about maintaining an art gallery, she simply kept a few paintings that she liked, among the antiques and treasures of her home.

In her later years Gladys Guggenheim Straus was giving nearly all her time to her various charities, and chief among these was the Mt. Sinai Hospital, to which she contributed heavily in money and time. In the best tradition of New York City's well-to-do families she was repaying a part of the debt of the Guggenheims to the country that had made them rich.

41]

OLD SIMON GUGGENHEIM, born in 1792 in the ghetto of Lengnau, had a dream of the future and he followed it to the promised land where he never ceased to marvel that the dream came true. At the end of his life he was prone to shake his head and remark to Meyer that it was almost impossible to believe that they had come to America just twenty years before without a penny. Old Simon died in 1869, as contented as a man can be who has taken a giant step into the unknown and has discovered that he was right. He had lived to see his family become not just safe and prosperous, but wealthy in a new world. What more could an old man ask?

Simon's son, Meyer, asked for much more. He foresaw the results of attrition on the family fortune, and he had seven sons and three daughters. He wanted not just one fortune, but seven fortunes, plus smaller sums for the girls. Meyer dreamed of giving the boys the chance to make as much as a million dollars apiece. He never thought of more. Few men thought in terms of a million dollars in the middle of the nineteenth century.

Daniel had no time for dreaming until he was an old man, for Daniel was a doer, a man of action, a man of finance, a man of ideas. Daniel looked beyond the horizon when he backed aeronautics, but in the matter of family, Daniel never saw beyond the horizon. He did not have the capacity of Simon or old Meyer to plan for the family future; otherwise, Daniel would never have allowed the family breakup of 1923 when Harry and Edmond deserted the business and nearly put an end to the Guggenheim tradition.

As a young man, Harry Guggenheim gave little promise of seeking immortality. He was a wild young fellow who left his grandfather's funeral cortege outside Temple Emanu-el and sneaked off with cousin Edmond for a beer. He married wilfully and unhappily, not once but twice. He went to South America, but never distinguished himself there. Harry's personal opportunity came in a different way. He discovered aviation in its infant days, and through aviation he discoverd the pleasures and thrills of accomplishment. His father might have harangued him for years without surcease and Harry might have continued to be the dilettante he began to be, but aviation taught Harry much about wealth and work. Later he tried to pass this knowledge on to his daughter:

"I believe," he wrote her, "that there is a responsibility to use inherited wealth for the progress of man and not for mere self-gratification, which I am sure does not lead to a happy life."

Almost too late, among the Guggenheims, Harry learned that "very few in their youth feel this need and less have the will as well as the wish to sacrifice everything for success.

"I feel that children must be encouraged, inspired and directed, or they will take what seems a rosy path of least resistance."

Daniel had never taken the time to sit and philosophize, to come to so basic a conclusion. Harry took the time, even though by 1959 the male line of Guggenheim had few name-bearers. The properties would be preserved. The foundations would carry the proud name of Guggenheim for many, many years and perhaps forever, as long as western civilization should last; yet even in the foundations the way was clear by 1966. The John Simon Guggenheim Foundations's roster of trustees did not contain the name of a single Guggenheim.

The fortunes, the enterprises, the instruments of wealth, would all too soon pass from Guggenheim hands into the hands of others. Guggenheim Brothers would ostensibly continue, under Oscar Straus II, for many years after Harry Guggenheim's death; but Oscar was a Straus, the bearer of a name as distinguished in Jewish and American society as the other, and a few years older than Guggenheim, as far as that was concerned. The problem was the age-old problem of genes and genius; the lines of many hundreds of exalted families have died out for the lack of sons. Yet even if the Guggenheim strain died in a generation or two and the name disappeared from the business world, the Guggenheims, down to the fourth generation, had proved to America that the American dream existed, was real, and was renewable.

THE AUTHOR is deeply indebted to the Guggenheim family and to a number of people connected with it for assistance in the research on this book, although it is in no way an official or authorized history of the Guggenheim family and not all its members will approve of this view. A debt is owed particularly to Harry Guggenheim, who made it possible to meet a number of other members of the family and provided much information on request. George Fountaine, secretary to Harry Guggenheim, was also helpful in many ways. So were Mrs. Roger W. Straus, Roger W. Straus, Jr., Oscar S. Straus II, Robert Guggenheim, Jr., Peter O. Lawson-Johnston, Albert C. Van de Maele, Dana Draper, Peggy Guggenheim, John J. and Julia Lipsey, and Mrs. Fred Smith of Leadville, Colorado. Harry Guggenheim read the manuscript in draft and was most helpful in clearing up several points where the author had fallen into error.

Sources of research for the book include the New York Public Library, Yale University's Sterling Library, Healy House Museum (Leadville, Colorado), the Denver Public Library, the Colorado Historical Society, the Colorado College Library in Colorado Springs, and the Leadville Chamber of Commerce. Newspapers and magazines consulted at length include the *New York Times, Wall Street Journal,* Leadville *Herald-Democrat,* Rocky Mountain *News, Denver Post,* Denver *Express,* Denver *Times,* Pueblo *Chieftain,* Colorado Springs *Gazette,* Aspen *Times, Colorado Magazine, Hampton's, Time, Newsweek, Engineering and Mining Journal, The Arena, Life, Munsey's, Cosmopolitan,* and *Illustrated Weekly.*

The general bibliography includes Isaac F. Marcosson, *Metal Magic,* the story of the American Smelting and Refining Company (New York: Farrar Straus and Co., 1949); Milton Lomask, *Seed Money* (New York: Farrar Straus and Giroux, 1964); Harvey O' Connor, *The Guggenheims* (Covici Friede, 1937); *Who's Who In America* 1910–1966; Wilbur Fisk Stone, *History of Colorado,* (Chicago, 1918); *Sketches of Colorado* (Western Press Bureau, 1911); B. C. Keeler and E. L. Ayer, *Leadville and Its Silver Mines* (Chicago, 1879); Henry R. Wagner, *Bullion to Books* (Los Angeles: The Zamorano Club, 1942); Thos. Fulton Dawson, *The Life and Character of Edward Oliver Wolcott* (Knickerbocker Press, 1911); *The Leadville City Directory* 1890–

1904; Willis Sweet, *Leadville and 10 Mile* (Kansas City, 1899; privately published); *History of Denver* (Denver: *The Times*, 1901); George B. Dresher, *A Description of Colorado*, Leadville and the Sovereign Consolidated Silver Mines (Philadelphia: Arms Co., 1881); Oscar Wilde, *Impressions of America* (Sunderland: Keystone Press, 1906); Harold Loeb, *The Way It Was* (New York: Criterion, 1959); Gatenby Williams, *William Guggenheim* (New York: The Lone Star Press, 1934; William Guggenheim's third-person autobiography); *The Autobiography of John Hogs Hammond.*

Many sources for comments and statements of fact are given in the text, but not all are so listed. In the following chapter notes are given sources for other material.

I

For the study of the plight of the Jews in Europe in the last few hundred years, the author turned to *A Historian's History of the World*, and to his own *A Brief History of Science* (2 vols; New York: John Day, 1965, 1966), which contains a thorough bibliography on the subject. Milton Lomask's *Seed Money* contains excellent information about the Guggenheims in Europe, since Mr. Lomask made a trip to Lengnau, the Guggenheim seat in Europe, and examined the cantonal records. Much of the information about the Guggenheims in Switzerland comes from *Seed Money*. Some comes from Harvey O'Connor's *The Guggenheims*, and some comes from Guggenheim family papers, one of which hangs on the wall in the office at 120 Broadway.

II, III, IV

The study of the Guggenheims and Philadelphia in the nineteenth century comes from various works on the Guggenheims, and from *History of the United States* by Charles and May Beard. The story of Meyer's early years in America comes from a large number of sources, listed in the bibliography, most of which seem to have depended on tales he and the boys told at various times. Most of the sources agree on general facts, although some details are different in various magazine, newspaper, and book accounts. Harvey O'Connor provided the basic information about the Guggenheims' movements about Philadelphia by checking the records, and according to the family his account is accurate in most respects. Some of the story comes from the recollections of William Guggenheim in later years, in his autobiography. The tale of Meyer and the source of his wealth comes from Lomask. The description of Barbara on page 27 is from William Guggenheim's book.

V

The basic sources for the Leadville tales are mentioned in the general notes on bibliography. The story of smelting in Colorado comes from an article by Eugene P. Lyle, Jr., in the February, 1910, issue of *Hampton's* magazine. The accounts of the Guggenheims' activities comes from such sources as the Denver and Leadville city directories, and a number of collected clippings about Colorado mining on file in the Western History Room of the Denver Public Library.

VI

The story of the miners' strike comes from the pages of the Leadville *Herald* in the spring of 1880. The quotation of Meyer comes from a widely printed, contemporary newspaper report, which was also carried by O'Connor in *The Guggenheims*. The figures on the production of the A.Y. and the Minnie are from the Leadville *Herald*. The tale of Oscar Wilde's trip to Leadville comes from his own writings, as noted in the bibliography. Benjamin's activities were reported in many sources, but especially the Leadville sources and William's book.

VII

The story of the Guggenheim smelters comes from the Pyle article in *Hampton's* (February, 1910), as does the direct quotation of Meyer's conversation with Edward Holden. The story of the establishment of the Philadelphia Smelter comes from the Denver and Colorado Springs and Pueblo newspapers of 1888. The mining engineers' comments on the Guggenheims and the building of the smelter is from the Pyle article. The story of William's affairs in the West comes from his own book and from O'Connor. William's description of his father is from his book.

VIII

William Guggenheim's and Harvey O'Connor's books are the basic sources for the early Mexican ventures. *Metal Magic*, the story of ASARCO, has some of the facts and some statistical material not found elsewhere. *Seed Money* has less. For the details on the McKinley tariff, the author consulted his own *Grover Cleveland* (Reilly and Lee,

1962), and *William McKinley* (Reilly and Lee, 1967). Much of the Edgar Newhouse story came from *Metal Magic*.

IX

Much of this part of the story of the Mexican venture comes from William Guggenheim's autobiography, but some is from Denver and New York City newspaper files, and some from the Pyle articles in *Munsey's*.

The source for much of this material in the latter part of chapter IX is Harold Loeb's *The Way It Was*, and unpublished portions of this manuscript and other writings lent to the author by Mr. Loeb. Part of it also came from Mr. Loeb's recollections of conversations and his early life as a Guggenheim grandchild. Tales told by Harry Guggenheim to Milton Lomask were also used, and Mr. Guggenheim repeated some of them to the author.

X

The material for this chapter comes from the files of the Denver newspapers as noted, also those of Leadville and Pueblo, and from various books that deal with the Guggenheims. Henry Wagner told the story of the Glove Smelter's winning an ore bid over Ben Guggenheim. The discussion of the Sherman Silver Act comes from the author's *Jumbos and Jackasses* (New York: Doubleday, 1960). The Lyle article in *Hampton's* gave an excellent brief account of smelting and refining.

XI

This chapter relied heavily on Wagner, William Guggenheim's autobiography, and O'Connor. The entire Urioste story is from Wagner.

XII

The story of the Guggenheim relationship with the smelters' trust comes from Denver newspaper files and from O'Connor. The story of the formation of the metals trust is told in every account of the Guggenheims; it has been pieced together by the author from the many sources, especially the New York newspapers of 1899 and 1900. While O'Connor's account of the trust is most interesting, its figures are not entirely reliable.

XIII

The running story of the family as summed up in these pages comes from nearly every source earlier cited, with particular emphasis on Lomask and William Guggenheim's autobiography. The newspapers of New York (and Denver, for that matter) were filled with the story of the William Guggenheim marriage, not in 1900 and 1901, but when the matter finally reached the courts nearly a decade later.

XIV

The details in this chapter come from O'Connor, Marcosson, Lomask, the author's personal observations, and materials lent the author from the Guggenheim Brothers' file. George Fountaine, secretary to Harry Guggenheim, was most helpful in reconstructing the scenes and in providing materials with some of the figures. The material dealing with the association of John Hays Hammond and the Guggenheims comes from Hammond's autobiography and papers (at the Yale University Library).

XV

The story of the Guggenheims and the acquisition of the Puget Sound smelter comes from Marcosson and O'Connor, with materials from the New York newspapers of 1905 and 1906, and the newspaper clipping files of the Denver Public Library's Western History Room. The story of Guggenex and American Smelters Securities is from newspaper files, Marcosson, and O'Connor. The material about Meyer's personal life in this period comes from Harold Loeb and his book, and from the files of the *New York Times* for March, 1905. The Baruch story comes from Bernard Baruch's memoirs and from Marcosson.

XVI

Hammond and *Metal Magic* are the primary sources for the story of the Guggenheims and Leopold; these and O'Connor are primary sources (along with the New York newspapers of 1906) for the Nipissing Bubble story. The Utah Copper story comes from *Metal Magic*, O'Connor, and various materials, pamphlets, and clippings, collected by the author in Colorado Springs between 1951 and 1955, and in the clipping file of the Denver Library Western History Room. The story of the expensive Chihuahua smelter is from Wagner.

XVII

The story of F. Augustus Heinze and his speculations in copper was taken almost intact from the author's *House of Morgan* (New York: Dodd, Mead, 1966), and from O'Connor. The examination of Daniel Guggenheim's character and habits comes from many sources: Harry Guggenheim, Gladys Guggenheim Straus, the *New York Times* files, Harold Loeb, and all the books that deal with the Guggenheim family and their industrial enterprises. The study of the Guggenheims and American anti-Guggenheim sentiment comes largely from study of the various Denver and Colorado newspapers of the period 1906–1910. The quotation from the *Juneau Daily Dispatch* was found in O'Connor.

XVIII

The story of Simon Guggenheim comes from the files of the Denver newspapers, *Colorado* magazine, (Vols. XVI and XXII), *The Colorado Portrait and Biography Index*, the T. F. Dawson scrapbooks in the Colorado Historical Society files (Vol. XXII), and the files of the Denver *Post, Republican,* and *Rocky Mountain News* for the period 1900–1913. The anonymous letter (one of a series) appeared in the Denver *Post.* The tale of the Guggenheim's refusal to close their smelters comes from Dawson scrapbook clippings (undated), as does the quotation from the *Rocky Mountain News,* specifically from an article by Charles Edward Russell which originally appeared in *Cosmopolitan* (undated).

XIX

The description of the Guggenheim house in Denver comes from a number of newspaper clippings in the files of the Denver Public Library Western History Room, and that and other materials from an article in the Denver *Republican* of June 9, 1901. The article in the Arena is from the Dawson collection in the Colorado State Historical Society, as are the quotations on page 185 from Simon and William Jennings Bryan.

XX, XXI

The discussion of the Guggenheims leaving Denver on page 187 is from the Denver *Post* and *Republican* of January 25–27, 1907. The story of Yukon gold comes from O'Connor, Marcosson, and the William Guggenheim autobiography. The story of the Alaska promotion comes from O'Connor and from the author's research for the *House of Morgan.* The quotation about the building of the Alaska railroad is from O'Connor. The narrative dealing with the Ballinger–Pinchot controversy comes from materials collected by the author in preparation of his *Teddy Roosevelt in Africa* (New York: Duell Sloan and Pearce, 1966). The remark of the Denver *Post's* editorial writer about the Guggenheims having Alaska in "their grasp" appeared on September 27, 1908.

XXII

The Guy La Coste story appeared in the Denver *Post* on September 14, 1908; for the next three months the *Post* conducted an unremitting campaign against the Senator.

XXIII

The story of the great Guggenheim divorce scandal appeared in various newspapers across the nation between 1908 and 1913; for this, the files of the Denver *Post* and the *New York Times* were used, and an account in O'Connor was most helpful. The assessment of Senator Guggenheim's career appeared in the Denver *Republican* on February 9, 1913.

XXIV

Much of the material about Benjamin Guggenheim's life comes from Peggy Guggenheim's autobiography *Out of This Century,* some from O'Connor, and some from various newspaper accounts. The story of Ben and the sinking of the Titanic comes from the Denver *Post* of issues of April 15–30, 1912.

XXV

The story of the Gladys Guggenheim–Roger Straus marriage was told to the author by Mrs. Straus, except for that portion that appeared in the *New York Times* of January 11, 1914. The discussion of labor in the Guggenheim industries comes from O'Connor. The material on Mexico and Chuquicamata Copper comes from Marcosson and Wagner. The information about William Guggenheim's activities comes from his autobiography and from the newspaper accounts of the Guggenheim partnership trial.

XXVI

The material about Daniel Guggenheim comes from Lomask and O'Connor, and from his testimony in 1915 before the Industrial Relations Commission, as reported in the newspapers. The quotation on page 236 is from the *New York Times* of January 22, 1915.

XXVII

The material about Daniel Guggenheim comes in part from the *New York Times* obituary (September 29, 1930), from O'Connor, and from a file of newspaper clippings about Florence Shloss Guggenheim lent the author by Harry Guggenheim's office. Much of the story of Harry Guggenheim comes from Lomask. O'Connor is used as cited. The material about William comes for the most part from his autobiography, buttressed by various contemporary articles in the *New York Times*.

XXVIII

Marcosson is used heavily here, as well as the *New York Times* for 1919–1921. The story of the fight for control of ASARCO comes from Marcosson, O'Connor, and files of the New York newspapers for 1920–1922. The tale of the beginnings of the Guggenheim interest in nitrates comes from George Fountaine and from reports and materials supplied the author by Albert C. Van de Maele of Guggenheim Brothers. Information about Isaac comes from O'Connor, Lomask, and the files of the *New York Times*, particularly Isaac's obituary in the issue of October 11, 1922, and in the following weeks.

XXIX

The basic sources for the materials about the family are Lomask, Loeb, William Guggenheim, O'Connor, and materials supplied by Harry Guggenheim's office.

XXX

Nearly all material here comes from Peggy Guggenheim's *Out of This Century*, with some assistance from Mrs. Guggenheim in correspondence.

XXXI

The struggle with Red Mike Hylan was gleefully reported in the New York newspapers in the summer of 1924. Details about Daniel and the others come from materials supplied by Harry Guggenheim, from Lomask, from Harold Loeb in conversation, and from a report given the author by Albert C. Van de Maele.

XXXII

Most of the information about the foundations comes from Lomask, which was written to explain the operations of the various Guggenheim charities. The materials about the Guggenheims and aviation also come from the 1920's files of the *New York Times*, especially 1926 and 1927, when the names of Daniel and Harry were constantly in the press in this connection.

XXXIII

Harold Loeb told the story of annoying his uncles. The material about Murry's foundation comes from Lomask, with new material from the *New York Times* of 1966 and 1967. Harry Guggenheim's period as Ambassador to Cuba is discussed largely from within the framework of his book on the subject; it is true that he employed many experts to help him in his work, but the book could not have contained its sentiments or the expositions of the Cuban situation had Harry Guggenheim not agreed with the position taken.

XXXIV

Peggy Guggenheim's career is recounted from her autobiography and from the pages of the *New York Times* for the period covered.

XXXV, XXXVI, XXXVII

The discussion of the nitrate business comes from materials supplied by the Guggenheim offices and from O'Connor, whose book ends with the mid-1930s. Material about Harry Guggenheim came from Lomask, from conversations with Harry Guggenheim, from the files of the *New York Times* and *Time*. The information about other family members came from O'Connor, newspaper clippings, and works cited in the text.

XXXVIII, XXXIX

Lomask has a definitive and amusing discussion of the Baroness Rebay's relationship to the Guggenheims, particularly of the difficulties Harry had with her after Solomon's death. Peggy's story is told in her autobiography and in materials supplied the author by various Guggenheims.

XL

Much of this material comes from Guggenheim family members, including the letter written by Harry Guggenheim to his daughter in San Francisco, a copy of which was supplied the author. The estimate of Harry's contribution to the family fortune is the author's own, and is based largely on estimates of the going prices of successful newspapers in 1967.

XLI

The quotation is from Harry Guggenheim's letter to his daughter in the spring of 1959.

INDEX]

[365]